LAWYER, KNOW THYSELF

The LAW AND PUBLIC POLICY: PSYCHOLOGY AND THE SOCIAL SCIENCES series includes books in three domains:

Legal Studies—writings by legal scholars about issues of relevance to psychology and the other social sciences, or that employ social science information to advance the legal analysis;

Social Science Studies—writings by scientists from psychology and the other social sciences about issues of relevance to law and public policy; and

Forensic Studies—writings by psychologists and other mental health scientists and professionals about issues relevant to forensic mental health science and practice.

The series is guided by its editor, Bruce D. Sales, PhD, JD, ScD, University of Arizona; and coeditors, Bruce J. Winick, JD, University of Miami; Norman J. Finkel, PhD, Georgetown University; and Valerie P. Hans, PhD, University of Delaware.

* * *

The Right to Refuse Mental Health Treatment
    Bruce J. Winick
Violent Offenders: Appraising and Managing Risk
    Vernon L. Quinsey, Grant T. Harris, Marnie E. Rice, and
    Catherine A. Cormier
Recollection, Testimony, and Lying in Early Childhood
    Clara Stern and William Stern; James T. Lamiell (translator)
Genetics and Criminality: The Potential Misuse of Scientific Information in Court
    Edited by Jeffrey R. Botkin, William M. McMahon, and
    Leslie Pickering Francis
The Hidden Prejudice: Mental Disability on Trial
    Michael L. Perlin
Adolescents, Sex, and the Law: Preparing Adolescents for Responsible Citizenship
    Roger J. R. Levesque
Legal Blame: How Jurors Think and Talk About Accidents
    Neal Feigenson
Justice and the Prosecution of Old Crimes: Balancing Legal, Psychological, and Moral Concerns
    Daniel W. Shuman and Alexander McCall Smith

LAWYER, KNOW THYSELF

A PSYCHOLOGICAL ANALYSIS OF PERSONALITY STRENGTHS AND WEAKNESSES

SUSAN SWAIM DAICOFF

AMERICAN PSYCHOLOGICAL ASSOCIATION • Washington, DC

Published by
American Psychological Association
750 First Street, NE
Washington, DC 20002
www.apa.org

To order
APA Order Department
P.O. Box 92984
Washington, DC 20090-2984
Tel: (800) 374-2721
Direct: (202) 336-5510
Fax: (202) 336-5502
TDD/TTY: (202) 336-6123
Online: www.apa.org/books/
E-mail: order@apa.org

In the U.K., Europe, Africa, and the Middle East, copies may be ordered from
American Psychological Association
3 Henrietta Street
Covent Garden, London
WC2E 8LU England

Typeset in Goudy by World Composition Services, Inc., Sterling, VA

Printer: Edwards Brothers, Ann Arbor, MI
Cover Designer: Naylor Design, Washington, DC
Project Manager: Debbie Hardin, Carlsbad, CA

The opinions and statements published are the responsibility of the author, and such opinions and statements do not necessarily represent the policies of the American Psychological Association.

Library of Congress Cataloging-in-Publication Data

Daicoff, Susan Swaim.
    Lawyer, know thyself : a psychological analysis of personality strengths and weaknesses / by Susan Swaim Daicoff.—1st ed.
        p. cm.—(Law and public policy)
    Includes bibliographical references and indexes.
    ISBN 1-59147-096-X (alk. paper)
    1. Practice of law—United States—Psychological aspects. 2. Lawyers—Job satisfaction. 3. Professional ethics. 4. Substance abuse. I. Title. II. Series.

    KF300.Z9D35 2004
    347.73'504'019—dc22   2003017399

British Library Cataloguing-in-Publication Data
A CIP record is available from the British Library.

Printed in the United States of America
First Edition

CONTENTS

PREFACE

Like many attorneys, John Souder[1] went to law school for questionable reasons. They were probably the same reasons that many others chose law school, but they were still questionable. They included the fact that he could not get into medical school (he could not hack the science classes); he wanted to make money and have social status and prestige approximately equivalent to that of his father (who was a professional); he did not want to feel underprivileged, poor, undesirable, unwanted, or vulnerable in society; he was afraid he would not find a job if he merely got a doctoral degree in music or political science (his two interests in college); and he thought a law degree might be practical. Last, but not least, he was accepted into a reasonably high-ranking law school (i.e., he was smart enough, verbal enough, and talented enough to get in and to do the work). So there he was, a relatively directionless, confused young person with uncertain values and absolutely no experience in the real world, with no clear plans about what to do with a law degree.

At the time John entered law school, he embodied the law student–lawyer stereotype. He was competitive, achievement-oriented, scholastically inclined, enjoyed a higher than average socioeconomic status and background, and wanted to make money and garner status and prestige. His career goals were undefined. He enjoyed competing with others and, although today he might admit that he was then a little insecure, for the most part he came

---

[1]"John Souder" is a fictional character. His story is in part pure fiction and in part based on an amalgam of countless stories of attorneys and law students around the country whom I have known through my work as a therapist, lawyer, law professor, commentator on the legal profession, and national lecturer. Any similarity of John (or his story) to any particular individual is unintentional and completely serendipitous.

off as a dominant, confident, socially ascendant, and strong individual. He was a first-born child in a highly educated family that emphasized reading and scholastic achievement. He excelled in school. He believed that feelings and emotions had only brought him pain, and so he had focused on school and intellectual pursuits instead.

Unlike many law students, however, John had always had an altruistic bent. He wanted to do something to make the world a better place, so in law school he initially focused on constitutional and public interest law. Despite his intention to do good works, after making it on to the law review of his university and into the top 10% of his class, he found himself being courted by a large, private, commercial firm for a summer clerkship. The salary and setting were staggering. His classmates were insanely jealous of this summer clerkship opportunity, so he figured it must be a good thing. Thus began his slide into materialism and ethical uncertainty.

John says today that he hated the clerkship but could not admit it to himself or anyone else at the time. He got through the summer but found himself increasingly in morally questionable situations, both personally and professionally, and he began wondering about his own behavior. Deciding that he was just experiencing growing pains, he returned to law school, where he pursued corporate law, because the senior partners at his clerkship firm told him he could "write his own ticket" if he went into corporate work. He had indeed become interested in writing his own ticket. He enrolled in two advanced corporate law classes. Surely he was in the right place, doing the right thing, he thought. His achievement needs were met by his academic successes; he earned the Order of the Coif (a prestigious award), graduated, and accepted a job with the large private firm where he had clerked the summer before. Right before graduation, his first-year constitutional law professor tapped him for a rare but low-paying job opportunity in the constitutional law field. Dazzled by the large firm's offer, John instead took the private firm job. He negotiated and received the highest salary then being paid for any new associate in his million-population town. His boss was a Harvard Law School graduate who promised John the most challenging and stimulating work in the city. He received yet another staggering signing bonus just to join the firm, and he went to work. Surely he must be happy, he thought; look at all he had achieved.

But it did not work. John was vaguely miserable the first three years of private practice, with no real understanding of why. He only knew he worked too hard and too much and was not enjoying it. The 15-minute drive to work was the best part of his day; it went downhill from there. All too often, he wound up at the local downtown bar in the evening, grousing about work with other young attorneys in town. His lifestyle was fast-paced, glamorous, and (he thought) enviable. To deal with the stress of his work, however, he found himself drinking more and more. Friends turned him on to expensive restaurants, exclusive clubs, and designer drugs. The money flowed and he set about to acquire "stuff." Eventually, however, the pleasures of materialism wore off and he sought to make a change. He thought perhaps he was just working too hard in the glamorous but demanding area of corporate takeovers, and he set about to find a different kind of work.

At first, he quit the large firm to join one of his clients in starting a new investment banking firm. It sounded like a dream: unlimited income potential, interesting work, and all the autonomy he could want. This venture quickly failed, however. His former client moved on to find more steady employment, and John went back out to find a job with a law firm. He eventually settled in a medium-sized firm with a diversified client base and did transactional work with a greater variety of clients and legal issues. At first he enjoyed the challenge of the new position, but eventually this "cure" did not work either.

It took several more years for John to experience the ethical conflicts that would eventually drive him out of the practice of law. In the end, he was slammed with three cases in rapid succession in which he strongly disagreed with the clients' positions. He felt that what he was being asked to argue for and represent was immoral, unethical, or wrong. Working on the cases was difficult, and he had to force himself not to be half-hearted in his efforts. Discussing his quandary with the other lawyers in his firm was futile; they did not understand his discomfort and told him to do what the client wanted, regardless of the client's best interests. The profession's answer was, "It's none of your business."

John quit. He saved face, in his mind, by garnering a full-time position as a business consultant with a small investment company where he would use his law degree but not actually practice law. He sailed out of the practice of law saying, "I'm going on to better and brighter things; clearly I was meant to be in business all along and was simply misplaced in a private firm." For a while his self-deception worked; a few years later, however, the conflict once again reappeared in full force.

John recalled his aspirations as a law student to "make a difference." He recognized the conflict between what he was doing and what he had intended to do as a young adult. He felt caught between his inherent competitiveness, desire for achievement, and need to succeed and his desire to do something meaningful with his work. He had been left empty by his successes in the legal profession. However, he felt like a failure deep inside because he had left the practice of law. His new job was not quite as intellectually challenging or stimulating as law, and when he socialized with his attorney friends, he felt vaguely inferior as he listened to them brag about their cases, their clients, and their new partnerships. His new job felt somehow not as good as the private practice of law. He was worried that maybe his lawyer buddies thought so, too.

As a lawyer, John had struggled when he had to work on cases and take positions he did not believe in. He had struggled to work for clients whose values and goals he did not respect. He had never resolved the conflict between how he wanted to behave as a lawyer and how he had actually behaved. He had never resolved the conflict between who he wanted to be and who he had been professionally. He had simply run away, and he knew it.

What was the answer? John felt like Michael Douglas's character in the film *Full Disclosure*, who, obsessing over defending a sexual harassment claim from his female superior, keeps receiving e-mails saying, "Solve the Problem." Solve the Problem. It was not law school, or law practice, or what he did with his law degree. It was not a matter of finding the right place or right practice area in which to exercise his talents. The problem was that his values, which had never adequately developed, disappeared once he took the lucrative private firm summer clerkship in law school years before. Years and years of wrong values, wrong reasons, and wrong actions is a long time. Solve the Problem.

John began to wonder if he could ever practice law again. Toying with the idea of going back to work as a lawyer, he did some reading about the professional role of the lawyer and decided that maybe he just needed to learn how to be a "hired gun." This concept holds that lawyers should offer work for hire and that there is honor in that; our professionalism lies in how well we serve our clients' ends, regardless of the morality of those ends. Maybe that was the solution. A lawyer friend told him that this was the true definition of humility and that his old law school idealism had really been arrogance. John began to wonder if he had had the wrong approach to being a lawyer. Maybe *this* approach to lawyering was the answer.

Then he happened on the movie version of Ayn Rand's *The Fountainhead* one day when his head was swimming with the Problem and the question of whether he should return to law practice. He had loved the book in college but, predictably (his values being uncertain at that time), could not really remember the moral of the story. The movie appealed to him because he understood it to be about integrity. John had recently been reevaluating his life. He had been changing. He was becoming more and more down-to-earth compared with his early days as a young-buck attorney. His drinking and partying had slowed considerably. He had begun to act with integrity in his personal life, and he liked it.

After the movie was over, he dug the book out of a dusty box in his garage, just to re-enjoy the architect, Howard Roark's, closing argument in court. Roark is being tried for dynamiting a building he designed because it had been altered by others in the construction process so that it no longer resembled his design. Roark is found not guilty, and his argument (delivered by Gary Cooper) is wonderful. John thought this movie had nothing to do with his Problem, though, until he read Roark's monologue:

In all proper relationships there is no sacrifice of anyone to anyone. An architect needs clients, but he does not subordinate his work to their wishes. They need him, but they do not order a house just to give him a commission. Men exchange their work by free, mutual consent to mutual advantage when their personal interests agree and they both desire the exchange. If they do not desire it, they are not forced to deal with each other. They seek further. This is the only possible form of relationship between equals. Anything else is a relation of slave to master, or victim to executioner.[2]

Slowly, John began to conceive of practicing law like this. As a lawyer, he had wanted to be a creator and an architect of people's legal affairs and contractual relationships. And he wanted, like Roark, to be able to stand back from his work and feel proud of what he had helped to create. It was one of the reasons he had enjoyed corporate law, because his work had helped businesses prosper and flourish. To be involved in creating something—be it a building or a legal relationship between people or entities—that he could be proud of sounded appealing. To be involved in creating something he felt was wrong was anathema to him, like it was to Roark. As Roark would put it, it made John a slave to his clients. For someone motivated by dominance and ascendancy, slavery was not attractive.

Here, finally, were those values that had been missing since early in law school and that had been unwittingly causing him grief. *The Fountainhead* helped John identify his true values, which had been submerged once his academic and material successes mounted and drew him into a type of law practice that did not allow him to stand fast to those values. Once surfaced, named, and identified, his values refused to resubmerge.

I do not know if John is a typical lawyer, nor do I know how many of his colleagues and fellow lawyers need what John needs, but I believe attorneys like John need an answer to the Problem that allows them to stay in the legal profession and do something they feel right about. Aristotle argued that one's character comes from one's actions. John had not been proud of his actions as a lawyer in the past, and his character (e.g., self-esteem) had suffered.

In John's life, lawyer distress manifested as job dissatisfaction, alcohol and drug abuse, and mild depression. I believe these were caused by all three of the possible causes that I explore in chapter 6 of this book. John's typical traits of competitiveness, materialism, and achievement orientation kept him in competition with his peers and ever striving for more successes. Law school's encouragement of his focus on extrinsic rewards, combined with his already competitive and achievement-oriented nature, resulted in

---

[2] Ayn Rand, The Fountainhead (Plume, 2002).

his striving to acquire what other people thought was desirable (regardless of what he really wanted): law review, Order of the Coif, a lucrative private practice clerkship and associate position, and a high salary. Constitutional law or public interest work, two areas in which he had expressed an interest, were simply not prestigious or financially rewarding enough for someone with his high law school grades. His surprisingly high law school grades maximized his options, to his delight, but then he exercised his options in pursuit of external, extrinsic rewards rather than asking what kind of legal work might be intrinsically satisfying to him. Finally, he had quickly realized that his atypical traits of feeling and altruistic, humanitarian impulses were rare in law school; unless he learned to submerge or conceal them, he would be isolated, outcast, and ridiculed in law school and law practice. As a result of concealing those traits, however, an inner conflict emerged between his true, internal values and the work he did, causing discomfort, uncertainty, and distress. Knowing that his own values were not generally approved of in the profession, he attempted to adopt the values of others around him, and as a result became morally uncertain and confused.

John was looking for a way to be a "real" lawyer, even in a possibly less lucrative way, in which he could respect what he did, who he was, and what he helped create. He wanted to be a lawyer to satisfy his typical lawyer materialism and his desires for dominance, social ascendancy, achievement, and ambition. But being *this* kind of lawyer would also satisfy his atypical traits of feeling, an ethic of care, humanitarianism, and altruism. It would return him to the intrinsic values he had begun to identify before law school but that were squelched early in his legal education, thus giving him a better chance for mental well-being and satisfaction. Finally, it would be consistent with John's growing desire to be true to himself instead of basing his self-worth on money, prestige, degrees, or Martindale–Hubbell ratings.

John is not alone. The breadth and rapidity with which the comprehensive law movement—discussed in chapter 7—has spread are evidence that other lawyers have experienced stories similar to his and are seeking more fulfilling ways to be a lawyer. The wild success of Steven Keeva's book, *Transforming Practices*,[3] and its multiple, spin-off seminars is additional evidence of a longing within the profession for meaningful work. I have met countless attorneys, mostly well-seasoned, successful attorneys in their 40s and 50s, who have told me stories similar to John's. Some say they are ready to leave the profession unless they can find a way to practice law that allows them to have integrity, allows them to be true to their own internal values, and allows them to feel good about who they are and what they do. Not

---

[3] STEVEN KEEVA, TRANSFORMING PRACTICES: FINDING JOY AND SATISFACTION IN THE LEGAL LIFE (Contemporary Books, 1999).

every lawyer needs this kind of approach to lawyering, but for those like John whose values require it, I believe it is crucial.

Eventually, someone will coin the catchy phrase by which we will come to know this new approach to lawyering; until then, my working title for it is the cumbersome and nondescript *comprehensive law movement*. It could also be called meaningful work, value-laden lawyering, humanistic law, or even Roarkian law. Maybe we will think of it simply as "the architect's way."

Lawyer, Know Thyself is an exploration of lawyer personality that discusses how, despite professional success, lawyers sometimes feel dissatisfied, empty, or even miserable. It investigates what it is that makes lawyers different from other people; why there is, arguably, a crisis of professionalism in the field; and why there is a relatively high level of dissatisfaction and depression among lawyers. The book is not necessarily designed to be read from start to finish. Instead, it is more akin to a reference volume. You may want to read it cover to cover, or alternatively, to dip into it at random.

I chose to include much of what I have discovered about the psychology of lawyers during my 20 years in the profession to avoid leaving out anything of importance. I hope you will find much that is thought-provoking and helpful.

For example, read chapters 2 and 3 if you want to explore lawyer personality in detail and are particularly interested in the volume of empirical research documenting how we differ from other people.

Read chapters 1 and 4 if you are concerned with the apparent lack of professionalism and respect in our profession and want to explore how the profession got into the shape it is in.

Read chapters 5 and 6 if you are particularly interested in what has come to be known as "lawyer distress," referring to the amount of depression, anxiety, substance abuse, dissatisfaction, and general psychological malaise suffered by lawyers.

Finally, read chapter 7 if you are interested in hope for the future of the profession, as it changes and evolves to include more humanistic approaches to law and lawyering.

Each chapter tackles a question I have encountered in my quest to understand lawyers and the legal profession. Each question is related to the others and, connected together, they cohere for me into two basic inquiries: How did we get here as a profession? And where are we headed? The future of the profession looks exciting, albeit not at all what I expected when I entered law school in 1980. I invite you to explore it with me.

ACKNOWLEDGMENTS

This book represents more than seven years of research, thought, and writing. At the same time I began this project, my first child was born, my son Arizona, followed by the arrival of my daughter Graylin. I dedicate this book to them—two precious souls who, during their earliest years, shared me with this work and who I hope someday will be proud of me for writing it. Besides becoming a parent, the other life changes I underwent during these seven years were nothing less than breathtaking. I came to know God. I survived cancer.

I acknowledge the unfailing support of my wonderful academic parents, Mary Jane Swaim Daicoff and George Ronald Daicoff Sr., their spouses Bob and Mary, my sister and brothers, and my dear friends, sponsors, and mentors during this time. I especially appreciate the constant encouragement of Susan Rose Laudenslager Thomas. I acknowledge the assistance and support of my children's father, Robert Neal Baskin Jr. I am grateful for the unflagging and firm guidance of Donald A. Hughes Jr. of Capital University School of Law and the support of the dean and my colleagues there. I thank David B. Wexler and Bruce J. Winick for continually encouraging and supporting me. I am grateful for the contribution to the manuscript of John McShane and for his enthusiasm and support. I appreciate the support of all of my dear friends in the humanizing legal education movement and in the comprehensive law movement, who are too numerous to mention. I thank the administration, faculty, and staff of Florida Coastal School of Law for their support and encouragement of this project. I am grateful for the research assistance of my former students Lisa Edwards, Dennie Rose, Brandon Tomasello, and many others at Capital and Florida Coastal. And finally, I thank my children for loving me even when I was too tired to play because I had stayed up all night working on "the book."

I also dedicate this book to the memory of Kim Erin McConnell, who always encouraged me to do amazing things and would have loved seeing it in print.

LAWYER, KNOW THYSELF

1

THREE KINDS OF DISSATISFACTION WITH THE LAW: PERSONAL, PROFESSIONAL, AND PUBLIC

Few people, whether lawyers or nonlawyers, appear to be satisfied with the law, the legal profession, or the American legal system. Complaints such as those heard in the wake of the O. J. Simpson trial in the mid-1990s have become normal. Antilawyer jokes abound, even among lawyers. The attitude toward lawyers within Western society has become deplorably poor.

Within the profession, by the late 1980s, many commentators had identified three emerging problems. This tripartite crisis facing the legal profession consisted of (a) a lack of "professionalism," evidenced by frequent complaints of incivility, discourtesy, "Rambo-style" litigation, near-unethical behavior, and general poor conduct of judges and lawyers; (b) low public opinion of lawyers and the legal profession, according to recent polls; and (c) low levels of job satisfaction and mental well-being among lawyers, as revealed by surveys of attorney job dissatisfaction and distress. In 1995, Seth Rosner, chair of the American Bar Association's (ABA) Standing Committee on Professionalism, said,

> a continuation of the explosion in the number of lawyers at the same time that the demand for lawyers has shrunk dramatically; a startling growth in legal malpractice litigation . . . an equally shocking incidence of fraud, theft and abuse of the fiduciary relationship with clients by

lawyers . . . a growing awareness that . . . lawyering has become a nasty business . . . in that of the nastiness of behavior of other lawyers, occasionally of judges and court personnel; which has led to many, many lawyers leaving the practice, seeking alternative careers, saying "it is no longer fun to practice law."[1]

By the end of the 1980s, many commentators had discussed these three phenomena in the same breath, but no one had explicitly noted their separate but interdependent natures. For example, as professionalism declines and lawyers become increasingly competitive, crass, commercial, discourteous, and rude, public opinion of lawyers is likely to deteriorate. As public opinion deteriorates, lawyer satisfaction, morale, and pride in the profession decline. Dissatisfaction among lawyers is likely to result in mental distress such as depression, anxiety, and hostility. When lawyers cope with such stress by abusing substances, isolating themselves, and working harder, the stress in turn can lead to more unethical or overly aggressive behavior or even malpractice, thus further eroding professionalism.

Therefore, one of the fundamental assumptions of this book is that these problems are interrelated. Another is that these problems are worth investigating, because they affect society as a whole. Because lawyers constitute the vast majority of our legislators,[2] judiciary, and other influential U.S. government workers, problems in the legal profession have consequences reaching far beyond the profession itself. They inevitably affect public policy and the public's confidence in all branches of the government.

This book explores the empirical evidence for these three problems in the profession: deprofessionalism, low public opinion of lawyers, and lawyer dissatisfaction and distress, before turning to potential causes, correlates, and cures.[3] In contrast to the vast majority of material written on these problems, however, the book explores causes and correlates of these problems that are internal or psychological in nature. The bulk of this exploration is devoted to empirically studying and identifying what it is about lawyers that contributes to these problems within the profession. The final chapter investigates emerging "cures" for these issues facing the legal profession.

DEPROFESSIONALISM

Evidence of the decline in professionalism is said to include frequency of disciplinary actions against lawyers and ethics code violations by attorneys;[4] frequency of malpractice suits against lawyers;[5] uncivil, discourteous, and aggressive behavior by attorneys toward other attorneys and nonlawyers;[6] "Rambo"-style litigation tactics;[7] a win-at-all-costs mentality;[8] the commercialization of the legal profession;[9] and blatant and offensive advertising by attorneys,[10] which are all frequently cited as evidence of a decline in professionalism. There is no dearth of disciplinary actions against attorneys[11] nor of malpractice claims. Attorneys generally are aware of, and acknowledge, this decline in professionalism in the bar.[12] However, hard empirical evidence of "deprofessionalism" is hard to find. Actually, nationwide data on malpractice suits and disciplinary actions revealed that the per capita, per lawyer rate of these problems had not substantially changed from 1986 to 1996.[13] The existence of the unprofessional, discourteous, Rambo-type behavior so often complained of by practicing lawyers and judges is thus largely anecdotal. However, one source claimed in 1986 that intentional malfeasance such as dishonesty, intentional wrongs, and frauds were responsible for 11% of claims and disciplinary actions against lawyers.[14]

To the extent that it exists, unprofessional attorney behavior can cause poor public opinion of lawyers. A 1985 study indicated that public opinion of attorneys is affected by ethical or unethical attorney behavior.[15] People who heard a story about a lawyer misbehaving were more likely to view that lawyer less favorably than were those who were told stories about a lawyer behaving appropriately.

LOW PUBLIC OPINION

Negative attitudes toward lawyers have been expressed since the 16th century (remember Shakespeare's "the first thing we do, let's kill all the lawyers")[16] into the 21st century (recently the Eagles sang, "The more I think about it, old Billy was right, let's kill all the lawyers, kill 'em tonight").[17] However, negative attitudes toward attorneys appear to have dramatically increased in recent years. Movie audiences in the 1993 film *Jurassic Park*[18] cheered when a dinosaur ate a lawyer. A BMW advertising campaign in the 1990s listed "hang up on a lawyer" as one of the "Twenty Things You Should Do in This Lifetime," until a complaint from the president of the American Bar Association forced the German auto manufacturer to retract the newspaper and magazine ads.[19] A Reebok advertisement touted "Planet Reebok"—a utopia devoid of lawyers.[20]

Public opinion polls and surveys indicate that lawyers are poorly viewed by the public and that lawyers' public image has been worsening in the past decade or so.[21] It has been said that attorneys "have become symbols of everything crass and dishonorable in American public life."[22] This low public opinion is evident in the results of an extensive poll reported by the American Bar Association in 1993:

> The majority view is that, compared to lawyers in the past, today's attorney is less caring and compassionate. This is based on the percentage replying that today's lawyer is no longer a leader in the community

(fifty-six percent), a defender of the underdog (fifty-five percent), and a seeker of justice (sixty-four percent). Fewer than one in five felt the phrase "caring and compassionate" describes lawyers, as contrasted to nearly half (forty-six percent) who said the phrase does not apply. Only thirty-six percent said most lawyers are "a constructive part of the community." . . . [B]arely one in five (twenty-two percent) said the phrase "honest and ethical" describes lawyers. Nearly twice as many (forty percent) said this description does not apply. Almost half (forty-eight percent) of those surveyed said that as many as three in 10 lawyers lack the ethical standards necessary to serve the public, which matches exactly the proportion who say the same thing about auto mechanics. . . . Three-fifths of respondents (sixty-three percent) said lawyers make too much money, fifty-nine percent said lawyers are greedy, and fifty-five percent said it is fair to say that most lawyers "charge excessive fees."[23]

This poll also debunked the idea that people hate lawyers in general but like their own, as is often said about doctors[24] and representatives of Congress.[25] Only two thirds of Americans who had used the services of a lawyer were satisfied with their representation.[26] Also, people who had been exposed to the legal system, such as jurors, litigants, frequent users of legal services, and those who knew a lot about the legal system were more cynical and critical of lawyers, according to the company who performed the poll.[27] A *U.S. News & World Report* poll found that the percentage of respondents viewing athletes as civil was greater than the percentage so viewing attorneys in this fashion.[28] Declining public opinion of lawyers and the legal profession may also be reflected in part in the consistent decline in the number of applications to the nation's law schools in the 1990s.[29] This decline has slowed or reversed a bit in 2000 and 2001, but law school applications today are still lower than they were in 1995 and well below the 1990 levels.[30]

LAWYER DISSATISFACTION

Lawyer satisfaction data are grim. For example, a 1995 author asserted that "California attorneys were 'profoundly pessimistic' about the law, with only half saying that they would choose again to be a lawyer"[31] and "seven in 10 lawyers responding to a 1992 *California Lawyer* magazine poll said they would change careers if the opportunity arose."[32] American Bar Foundation researchers claimed in 1998 that three out of five lawyers who responded to a poll by the *Michigan Lawyers Weekly* said they would not choose to become lawyers again if they had the chance to start their careers over.[33] The American Bar Association reported in 1991 that 48% of lawyers in private practice who stay with their firm "but are not happy ... would change jobs if they had a reasonable alternative."[34] A 1995 study found that only 51% of lawyers were satisfied with their lives, compared to 78% of federal judges.[35]

The American Bar Association's Young Lawyers Division (ABA/YLD) conducted three surveys of lawyer job satisfaction, in 1984,[36] 1990,[37] and 1995,[38] and found an alarming rate of dissatisfaction, approximating 20% of the lawyer population. In 1984, 19% of lawyers surveyed were dissatisfied or very dissatisfied (15%) or neutral (4%).[39] In 1990, 24% were dissatisfied or very dissatisfied (19%) or neutral (5%).[40] In 1995, 27.5% reported being dissatisfied or very dissatisfied, and the neutral category was dropped.[41] Dissatisfaction in these surveys thus increased from 1984 to 1995. The number of very satisfied attorneys decreased from 41% to 33% from 1984 to 1990.[42]

Similarly, a 1992 survey found that 27% were dissatisfied or very dissatisfied (23%) or neutral (4%). This study extensively reviewed the existing studies of lawyer satisfaction and concluded that "convincing evidence exists regarding the increasing levels of job dissatisfaction of the legal profession."[43] It asserted that "there is considerable consensus" among studies from 1984 to 1991 that "approximately 20% of all lawyers are quite dissatisfied with their jobs" and that this dissatisfaction had increased over time.[44]

A somewhat more positive outcome was reported by researchers at the American Bar Foundation (ABF) in a study reported in 1998.[45] Their survey of satisfaction among Chicago lawyers in 1994 and 1995 found that only 16.6% were dissatisfied or very dissatisfied (6.6%) or neutral (10%), whereas 84% were satisfied or very satisfied.[46] However, importantly, this study conducted in-person interviews with the lawyers surveyed instead of relying on anonymous questionnaires used in other studies.[47] Although it is possible that Chicago lawyers are happier than most, it is more likely that the lawyers surveyed did not want to admit to as much dissatisfaction face to face as they would have if they had been filling out anonymous, pen-and-paper, mailed-in questionnaires.

Another study also concluded that almost no comprehensive data on satisfaction among the entire legal profession existed before 1984.[48] It reported that professionals in general (including lawyers) usually report higher job satisfaction than do other groups,[49] suggesting that these findings for lawyers are particularly distressing. The ABF study also noted that previous general research has found that most employed people are satisfied with their careers.[50]

In summary, about one in five lawyers is somewhat or very dissatisfied with his or her job. Lawyer dissatisfaction appeared to increase from 1985 to 1995. Given the prevalence of this problem, the time is ripe for research that explores why such high levels of lawyer dissatisfaction exist.[51]

LAWYER DISTRESS

Lawyer distress data is even more depressing than the job satisfaction research. Lawyers experience depression, anxiety, alcoholism, and other psychological problems at a rate that is often twice the rate found in the general population.[52] Attorneys are in the top three occupations for depression, along with secretaries and "other" teachers and counselors (a miscellaneous category including prekindergarten, special education, and educational and vocational counselors).[53] Approximately one in five lawyers, or 20%, is suffering from a clinically significant psychological problem severe enough to warrant intervention. In addition, this distress appears to develop in law school, not before, and never returns to prelaw school levels after graduation.

Whenever these statistics are presented to a lawyer audience, invariably someone says, "Yes, but isn't this true for all professionals, like doctors, dentists, engineers, etc.?" The only appropriate response that comes to mind is, "Does it matter?" Psychological distress may be prevalent in other professions, but to me, this level of distress is intolerable within my own profession. It is also intolerable to society and to our clients.[54] (Incidentally, the true answer to the question appears to be "no," as explained next.)

DEPRESSION

Depression occurs among attorneys at least twice as frequently as it occurs in the general adult population. About 18% of attorneys are depressed, according to consistent research. This statistic is based on studies from 1986 to 1996, of attorneys of all ages, in various practice settings, in different states in the United States. In contrast, depression occurs in about 3 to 9% of adults in Western countries.[55]

How severe is this depression? Psychologists in 1996 found that 23.4% of attorneys in Washington state reported depression levels that exceeded two standard deviations above the mean, on standard measures of depression. Statistically, only 2.27% should score this high. Ten years earlier these researchers also found that 20% of young lawyers in Arizona "developed depression levels that exceeded two standard deviations above the normal population mean."[56] And in 1990 they found that 19% of Washington and Arizona attorneys were clinically depressed.[57] Of this 19%, most were thinking about suicide.[58] A final, chilling statistic is that 11% of North Carolina attorneys polled in 1991 "admitted they consider taking their lives once a month."[59] Clearly, this is not simply "the blues," "feeling down in the dumps," or dysthymia; many attorneys are reporting severe depression.

Is this not true for other professionals, such as doctors and dentists? Is this not just endemic to the stress of such high-pressured jobs? Apparently not. Although other professionals may be more inclined to commit suicide than lawyers (one 1983 study found that medical students and graduate students committed suicide more frequently than did age-matched law students), other professionals do not necessarily report as much depression as do attorneys. A 1991 Johns Hopkins University study found that the incidence of depression among lawyers was up to four times that found in other professionals.[60] One 1990 study of almost 100 occupations found that 10% of the lawyers they studied met standard psychiatric[61] criteria for major depressive disorder. In contrast, such clinically diagnosable depression is typically found in 3 to 5% of the general population.[62] In fact, only three occupations (typists, attorneys, and "other teachers and counselors"—meaning prekindergarten and special education teachers and education and vocational counselors[63]) had these levels of depression. These researchers then corrected the data by adjusting for demographics, race, gender, and other variables to eliminate the possibility that depressed people were simply attracted to these three professions. After adjustment, three professions still emerged as disproportionately depressed: lawyers, secretaries, and "other teachers," *not* physicians or other professional people. Physicians had almost a zero depression rate.[64] Depression does not seem to simply go hand-in-hand with professional work. This problem seems to be specific to lawyers.[65]

However, the inordinate levels of depression found in lawyers are not present in law students before entering law school.[66] The lawyer depression experts found that depression levels among prelaw students were nearly average—only about 10% were significantly depressed—compared with the usual 3 to 9% of adults in Western nations who are depressed.[67] By late spring of the first year of law school, 32% of law students reported significantly elevated depression levels. This number rocketed to a stunning 40% by late spring of the third and final year of law school and did not return to prelaw school levels, ever. Two years after graduation, 17% of the same research participants were still reporting that they were depressed. Later studies of practicing lawyers confirm that, no matter how long they have been practicing law, a consistent 17 to 18% of lawyers still suffer from clinically significant depression.[68]

OTHER PSYCHOLOGICAL DISTRESS

Perhaps spurred on by the depression studies, the lawyer depression experts in 1996 studied a wide array of psychological distress symptoms among lawyers. Their findings on depression were consistent with their previous studies: It was present in about 20% of lawyers. However, their findings in other areas were shocking. Not only did large numbers of lawyers report clinically significant depression, they also reported higher than normal levels of global psychological distress and specific symptoms such as anxiety, obsessive–compulsiveness, social alienation and isolation, insecurity, self-consciousness, paranoia, hostility, stress, anger, and marital dissatisfaction. In addition, the researchers adjusted the data to account for the fact that men tend to underreport problems and women tend to overreport them; after adjustment, more of the male lawyers were distressed than the women lawyers (for every symptom except hostility).

For example, 18% of male lawyers and 10% of female lawyers reported a severity of global psychological distress that was more than two standard deviations above the mean.[69] From 15% to more than 30% of lawyers scored more than two standard deviations above the mean on measures of obsessive–compulsiveness, interpersonal anxiety and discomfort, depression, general anxiety, and social alienation and isolation. Only about 2.27% of the general population would be expected to have such severe symptoms of distress.[70] Stated another way, lawyers' scores were significantly higher than normal scores for the general population on 9 of the 10 symptoms studied (excluding somatization, which refers to turning emotional problems into physical complaints).[71]

How many nonlawyers score this high? Comparable data is not available, but the base rate for some of these conditions is known and can be roughly compared to these results. For example, in a general population, 8.5% of males and 14.1% of females are depressed, compared to 16% of female lawyers and 20.8% of male lawyers scoring more than two standard deviations above the mean in this study. Between 1.4 and 2% of adults have obsessive–compulsiveness, compared to 15.0% of female lawyers and 20.3% of male lawyers scoring this high in the study. Four percent of adults have generalized anxiety disorder, compared to 19.8% of female lawyers and 27.8% of male lawyers in this study complaining of anxiety.[72]

This study also found that lawyers reported feeling more stress and anger than the general population and were more dissatisfied with their primary (marital) relationships than the general population. In addition, although both male and female lawyers were angrier than most people, male lawyers tended to feel more stressed and female lawyers tended to be unhappier in their primary relationships.[73]

A 1991 study confirmed these findings for anxiety among law students, finding that both male and female law students at Loyola University School of Law in New Orleans had higher stress-related anxiety than undergraduates.[74]

ALCOHOLISM AND OTHER SUBSTANCE ABUSE

As with depression, alcoholism also occurs about twice as frequently among lawyers as it does in the general adult population. Consistent research findings show that alcoholism as measured by standard clinical instruments occurs in about 18% of U.S. attorneys. This was true for attorneys in Washington, Arizona, and other states.[75] Informal estimates of alcoholism among attorneys range from 3 to 30 times the incidence in the general population.[76]

About 10 to 13% of the adult population in the United States are diagnosed with alcoholism.[77] A 1987 source estimated that 15% of all lawyers were diagnosed with alcoholism,[78] meaning that about 50,000[79] to 95,000[80] lawyers in the United States are diagnosed with alcoholism. Another source estimated that "nationwide there are 50,000 lawyers and judges who are alcoholic."[81] Thirteen percent of attorneys surveyed in 1990 reported that they "drink six or more alcoholic beverages a day."[82] Thirteen percent of newly practicing male attorneys and 10% of newly practicing female attorneys in one state scored above a clinical cutoff on the Michigan Alcoholism Screening Test–Revised[83] for current alcohol-related problems.[84] A 1996 study confirmed that alcoholism among Arizona lawyers and Washington state lawyers was about the same—more than 20% of the male Washington state lawyers scored "above the cutoff for alcohol-related problems for the current year." And an astounding 70% of Washington state lawyers were likely to develop alcohol problems sometime during their lives, compared to an estimated base rate of 13.7% for the general population of lifetime alcohol abuse or dependence problems.[85]

The problem with alcohol is also likely to stay hidden. One senior partner in a Midwestern state died in his early 50s of a mysterious kidney failure. When one of his partners was asked about his death, he said, "Well, you know he was an alcoholic. No one knew, though. He actually died of alcoholism, but no one is talking about it." Apparently, the toothbrush kit he carried to the bathroom every day after lunch contained alcohol, but "no one knew." Even after the death of this well-respected senior partner and local and state bar leader, the truth was being denied.

At another medium-sized urban firm, a senior associate was well-known for his alcoholism. About once or twice a year, he would disappear on a drinking binge for three days or so. Familiar with his problem, the other lawyers would quickly allocate his files among themselves "to cover" and make sure no balls got dropped. The files would be returned when he came back and very little would be said. Repeated attempts at mandated "rehabs" or treatment had been unsuccessful with him, and he was an excellent lawyer otherwise. Feeling helpless to change his alcohol use and desperate for his services, the firm had learned to work around his problem. Again, the problem stayed hidden.

Lawyers tend to use alcohol to deal with the inordinate amount of stress they feel. Thirty-three percent of Wisconsin lawyers reported using alcohol regularly as a way to reduce stress; 46.5% reported using it sometimes for this purpose.[86] The stereotype of the lawyer hitting the local bar every day after work is well-known. I recall standing in the special "lawyer line" at the courthouse one day to get my client's file before appearing in court. My client was there to straighten out his driver's license troubles, caused by several convictions for driving under the influence of alcohol. Behind me in line were two other lawyers who were obviously acquainted. As they began talking, I overheard the louder one say he was actually there to get his own file, not a client's. He was representing himself on a driving under the influence charge, his third DUI. Despite the obviously recurrent and significant nature of his problem, he boasted loudly about how he would handle his court appearance and sounded completely sure that he did not have either a legal or an alcohol problem. For this lawyer, it was just another day in the lawyer line at the courthouse. I have often wondered what happened to him.

Information on other forms of attorney substance abuse is sparser. Some estimate that "the incidence of chemical dependency in legal professionals might be as much as 50 percent higher than for the general population."[87] About 3% of the adult population in the United States have abused cocaine, whereas fewer than 1% of attorneys have abused cocaine. However, more attorneys than the general population have used cocaine at some point in their lives (26% versus 12%).[88] This is disturbing because cocaine use is illegal and attorneys are sworn to uphold the law, unlike nonlawyers.

Finally, alcoholism is a progressive illness, meaning it worsens as the individual's drinking career goes on. This progression is evident in statistics showing that older attorneys have the highest frequency of alcoholism. In 1990, "approximately 18 percent of the lawyers who practiced 2 to 20 years had developed problem drinking."[89] However, 25% "of those lawyers who practiced 20 years or more were problem drinkers."[90]

After hearing these statistics on attorney substance abuse, some people wonder if the stress of law practice is responsible. Yet, there are studies suggesting that substance abuse problems may start as early as law school.[91]

CONSEQUENCES OF LAWYER DISTRESS

Lawyer distress also tends to be linked with other problems, such as lawyer malfeasance and attorney job dissatisfaction. For example, substance abuse and depression have been linked to malpractice suits and disciplinary actions against attorneys. One source claimed, "Neglect cases tend to arise among lawyers who are procrastinating because they are clinically depressed. Finally, [impaired] lawyers who go untreated often become defendants in malpractice suits." This source also estimated that 60% of malpractice cases involved an attorney who was abusing substances.[92]

Estimates of the involvement of drug and alcohol abuse in lawyer disciplinary cases range from 27% nationally to almost 100% in some states. One source stated,

> Alcohol and drug abuse have had a profound impact on our disciplinary system. Unfortunately, in many instances the disciplinary agencies do not look behind the violation to determine the core cause. But when they do investigate, they find that the culprit in more than 50 percent of the cases turns out to be alcohol and drug abuse. For example, the figure reported by one disciplinary agency in New York was 65 percent. And, an in-house survey of major cases in a New England state revealed that each and every one of them was drug or alcohol related.[93]

However, the ABA's national estimate was considerably lower—in 1988, it claimed that only 27% of the discipline cases in the United States involved alcohol abuse.[94]

Alcohol dependence and depression are related to disciplinary actions in England as well. One British study made the additional point that the number of cases involving substance abuse is probably underestimated because of denial, saying, "There are probably many other cases where the fact that the solicitor is addicted is concealed. One of the features of alcohol dependence is the inability of the drinker to face up to the real cause of his problems even, sometimes, where the source of his livelihood is at stake."[95]

Obviously, substance abuse and depression, alone or in combination, can lead to neglect of cases or clients, which is one of the most common reasons for disciplinary and malpractice actions against attorneys. A more covert relationship exists, however. Other studies suggest that as lawyers feel more stress and tension, their ways of coping can lead to unprofessional behavior. For example, law students have been shown to cope with psychological discomfort and tension by abusing alcohol and drugs, isolating socially, and becoming more ambitious and aggressive.[96] Lawyers may cope with mental distress through substance abuse, social isolation, and working harder. Unfortunately, these poor coping skills themselves can result in unethical behavior. Alcohol and drug use releases anger and aggression[97] and has been linked to ethical violations.[98] Social isolation can foster unprincipled behavior[99] as a result of the lack of peer review of the attorney's actions. Unchecked ambition and aggression can blossom into uncivil, discourteous, competitive, or aggressive actions, if not outright ethical violations.

Empirical evidence supports the existence of three problems in the legal profession—deprofessionalism, low public opinion, and lawyer distress (and dissatisfaction)—to different degrees. Lawyer distress, or lawyers' psychological and mental well-being, is the most well-researched (although perhaps the least well-understood). The other two parts of the tripartite crisis in the legal profession, the crisis in public opinion of lawyers and the professionalism crisis, are much less well-developed. Empirical evidence of the existence of low public opinion is scarce. Evidence of deprofessionalism is virtually nonexistent.

Perhaps Burnele Powell, dean of the University of Missouri–Kansas City Law School and past chair of the American Bar Association's Standing Committee on Professional Discipline, was correct in characterizing the "professionalism crisis" as simply an artifact of the profession's obsession with self-introspection. Perhaps public opinion of lawyers has always been low. As the joke suggests, it may have existed since Shakespearean times.

However, the fact that clinically significant levels of lawyer distress clearly exist, and that they are about double the levels found in the general population, remains. Whether or not individuals in other professional occupations exhibit such alarmingly low psychiatric well-being is irrelevant. What is important is that such levels of distress in my own profession is intolerable to lawyers, to the profession, and to the clients we serve. Fully one fifth of us, one in five lawyers, is "walking wounded," meaning working, functioning, and representing clients while being psychologically impaired enough that intervention is indicated.

This book asks whether, despite the enormous pressures of law school and current legal practice, there are internal personality characteristics of lawyers that predispose us to develop these shocking levels of distress. The following two chapters examines 40 years' worth of empirical data on the personality of the typical lawyer and law student before concluding on a set of traits that exemplify the typical lawyer. Chapters 4 and 5 explore the relationship between the empirically derived "lawyer personality" and professionalism and low public opinion before turning to the complex topic of lawyer distress.

Lawyers by nature tend not to be introspective. They are action-oriented and achievement-oriented. Yet to survive and thrive as attorneys in the 21st century, it is imperative for us to "know ourselves."

This book was written to assist lawyers in doing so. The psychological research reviewed in this volume will demonstrate that there is indeed a typical lawyer personality and that this personality explains (in part) both the success of lawyers within the profession and the barrage of complaints, jokes, and innuendoes about lawyers emanating from the cocktail party to the talk show circuit.

The research in this volume will also be of interest to lawyers with an "atypical" personality, who may have been feeling a bit alienated, isolated, or displaced within the profession. These lawyers may find that their atypical traits are better suited to some of the emerging forms of law practice described in the last chapter of the volume.

Those in law school will be interested to discover that there is a pattern to the distress they experience while in law school. They may think that they are unique in what they experience in their first, second, and third years of law school, and this sense of isolation may add to their stress. However, they are likely to find that they are simply experiencing the traditional effects of law school on law students. In addition, identifying to what extent they have the full set of "lawyer characteristics" and to what extent they are atypical will help them make career choices in law school and after graduation that could maximize their satisfaction and professional success as lawyers.

Professionalism is related to how satisfied one is with one's professional role. One's ideal professional role is in turn related to one's personality, values, and preferences. There is no single "ideal" to which all lawyers can and should conform, although the psychological homogeneity of the legal profession may make it seem as if there is a monolithic ideal. Success in law, as in other complex professions and callings, is dependent on identifying one's strengths, values, and preferences, and then pursuing the most appropriate way of practicing one's profession, based on those identified characteristics. Knowing yourself is the first step.

NOTES

1. Seth Rosner, A Decade of Professionalism, 6 PROF. LAW. 2, 2 (August, 1995).
2. Lawrence R. Richard, Psychological Type and Job Satisfaction Among Practicing Lawyers in the United States (1994), at 254 (unpublished PhD dissertation, Temple University).
3. These three problems are circular. Lawyer dissatisfaction contributes to uncivil behavior by lawyers, which contributes to the poor public image of lawyers; lawyer unhappiness causes lawyer–client problems, which contribute to the poor public image of lawyers; and the low public opinion of lawyers contributes to job dissatisfaction among lawyers. For example, empirical studies have demonstrated a relationship between lawyer distress and lawyer dissatisfaction: The most dissatisfied lawyers are the most mentally and physically distressed (in terms of stress-related problems, substance abuse, depression, and other psychiatric symptoms). Linda M. Rio, Time for an Ideality Check: If You Had Your Ideal Job, Would You Be Satisfied? 13 BARRISTER MAG. 15 (Spring 1995) (discussing ABA/YLD NATIONAL SURVEY OF CAREER SATISFACTION/DISSATISFACTION (1984 and 1990)).

4. The overall estimated number of complaints filed against attorneys and the number of formally charged attorneys increased almost steadily from 1986 to 1995. In addition, although the total number of American lawyers also increased from 1986 to 1995, the per capita/per lawyer rate of complaints during this period actually increased from 8% to 12%. The per lawyer rate of formal disciplinary charges remained relatively constant from 1986 to 1995, at three tenths of 1%. Am. B. Ass'n Center for Prof. Resp., Survey on Lawyer Discipline Systems: 1986, at 7 (1987) (complaint and charges estimated at 54,000 and 2,200, respectively, in 1986) and Am. B. Ass'n Center for Prof. Resp., Survey on Lawyer Discipline Systems: 1995, at 5 (complaints and charges estimated at 117,000 and 3,000, respectively, in 1995).

5. However, arguments that malpractice claims are becoming increasingly frequent appear to be unfounded. According to the Am. B. Ass'n Standing Committee of Lawyers' Prof. Liability, Legal Malpractice Claims in the 1990s, at 20 (Oct. 1996), "Although there are variations from company to company, most malpractice insurers have seen only a small and gradual increase in frequency and severity [of malpractice claims] over the last decade. A few companies have actually seen occasional decreases in frequency, severity, or both, especially in jurisdictions where there was a previously unexplained increase." This 1996 study compared data to a 1986 study of malpractice claims conducted by the American Bar Association, reported in Am. B. Ass'n, Standing Committee of Lawyers' Prof. Liability, Characteristics of Legal Malpractice: Report on the National Malpractice Data Center (1989).

6. Amy R. Mashburn, *Professionalism as Class Ideology: Civility Codes and Bar Hierarchy*, 28 Val. U. L. Rev. 657 (1994).

7. *Id*. *See also* Roger C. Cramton, *Delivery of Legal Services to Ordinary Americans*, 44 Case Wes. Res. L. Rev. 531, 610 (1994).

8. Edward D. Re, *The Causes of Popular Dissatisfaction With the Legal Profession*, 68 St. John's L. Rev. 85 (1994) at text accompanying nn. 22–27 (the "Sporting Theory of Justice").

9. *Id*. at text accompanying nn.35–56.

10. Warren E. Burger, *The Decline of Professionalism*, 61 Tenn. L. Rev. 1, 5 (1993).

11. Richard Greenberg noted in 1991 that the monthly publication of *The Florida Bar News* has "no shortage" of attorney discipline cases to report each month. *Attorney Discipline: Nipping Grievances in the Bud*, 65 Fla. B. J. 31, 31–34 (1991).

12. *See, e.g.*, Debra Moss & Mark Hansen, *Lawyer's Perspective*, 77 A.B.A. J. 40 (May, 1989), at 40 (noting that 62% of lawyers surveyed in 1991 did not believe that lawyers were doing an adequate job of policing lawyer misconduct); Louis P. DiLorenzo, *Civility and Professionalism*, 68 N.Y. St. B. J. 8, 25 (1992) (stating that 42% of lawyers and 45% of judges surveyed by the Committee on Civility of the Seventh Federal Judicial Circuit believed that civility and professionalism among members of the bar were significant problems); Gary Blankenship, *Members Concerned About Public's Perception of Lawyers*, Fla. B. News, July 15, 1995, at 10 (noting that when 1,707 members of the Florida

Bar were surveyed, lack of ethics and professionalism was cited by the second largest group (275) as being a serious problem for the profession, with the largest number (416) listing attorneys' poor image or poor public perception as a serious problem).

13. AM. B. ASS'N, STANDING COMMITTEE ON LAWYERS' PROFESSIONAL LIABILITY, LEGAL MALPRACTICE CLAIMS IN THE 1990S, at 20 (Oct. 1996) (this 1996 study was done on a national basis and it compared data with a 1986 study of malpractice claims also done by the ABA). *See also* note 5, *supra*.

14. Lawyer malpractice claims most often involved incompetence and neglect. William H. Gates, *Lawyers' Malpractice: Some Recent Data About a Growing Problem*, 37 MERCER L. REV. 559, 559–567 (1986); Richard A. Greenberg, *Attorney Discipline: Nipping Grievances in the Bud*, 65 FLA. B. J. 31, 31–34 (1991).

15. Jack Hartnett & Gayle Secord, *Perception of Unethical Behavior in an Attorney as a Function of Sex of Observer and Transgressor*, 61 PERCEPTUAL & MOTOR SKILLS 1159, 1159–1162 (1985).

16. WILLIAM SHAKESPEARE, THE SECOND PART OF KING HENRY SIXTH act IV, sc. 2.

17. EAGLES, *Get Over It*, on HELL FREEZES OVER (Geffen Records 1994).

18. JURASSIC PARK (Universal Pictures 1993).

19. Joseph Wharton, *BMW Changes Ad: Lawyers Say Company "Auto" Know Better Than to Slam the Profession*, 83 A.B.A. J. 41, 41 (January 1997) (the slam was replaced with "be able to recite three good toasts").

20. John A. DeVault, III, *My Lawyer's Dialing Finger Is Broken*, FLA. BAR J. July/Aug 1995, at 12.

21. *Id.*

22. Raquel A. Rodriguez, Chairperson's Column, Uncivil Litigation, BARRISTER MAG., Summer. 1996, at 2 (citing John Marks, The American Uncivil Wars: How Crude, Rude and Obnoxious Behavior Has Replaced Good Manners and Why That Hurts Our Politics and Culture, U.S. NEWS & WORLD REP., April 22, 1996, at 1).

23. Gary A. Hengstler, *Vox Populi: The Public Perception of Lawyers: ABA Poll*, A.B.A. J., Sept. 1993, at 60, 62–63 (reporting the results of a study outlined in PETER D. HART RESEARCH ASSOCS., A SURVEY OF ATTITUDES NATIONWIDE TOWARDS LAWYERS AND THE LEGAL SYSTEM 1 (1993) (hereinafter HART SURVEY). Other writers have since relied on this data, *e.g.*, John C. Buchanan, *The Demise of Legal Professionalism: Accepting Responsibility and Implementing Change*, 28 VAL. U. L. REV. 563, 566 (1994).

24. HART SURVEY, *supra* note 23, at 30 (finding that although 78% of users felt favorably toward their own doctor and 7% felt unfavorably, only 45% felt favorably toward their own lawyer and 16% felt unfavorably). *See also* Leslie E. Gerber, *Can Lawyers Be Saved? The Theological Legal Ethics of Thomas Shaffer*, 10 J. L. & RELIGION 347, 347 n.1 (reporting that only 22% of people rated lawyers as having high or very high honesty or ethical standards; citing John Benson, *Leadership in the 90's: Tracing the Public's Perception*, CHRISTIAN SC. MONITOR, Mar. 22, 1991, at 19) compared to 62% for pharmacists; 50% range scores for doctors, college teachers, clergy, dentists, and engineers; 35% for

funeral directors, bankers, and journalists; 24% for newspaper reporters; 20% for building contractors, 16% for real estate agents; 12% for advertisers; and 6% for car sales persons).

25. Gerber, *supra* note 24 (citing Benson); John Dillan, *Congress Takes on Task of Mending Its Ways*, CHRISTIAN SC. MONITOR, Feb. 9, 1993, at 1 (citing a June 1992 Gallup poll showing that lawyers earned "high approval ratings from only 18% of respondents" compared to senators and congressional representatives who were "at 11 and 11% respectively").

26. HART SURVEY, *supra* note 23, at 31.

27. *Id.* at 31–32. This contrasts with a survey of British lawyers and users finding that users liked lawyers better (77%) than did nonusers and users together (47%). Sue Farron et al., *Public Perception of the Legal Profession: Attitudinal Surveys as a Basis for Change*, 20 J. LEGAL PROF. 79, 87 (1995–1996). This study found mixed results regarding public opinion toward lawyers; negative attitudes were focused on value for money and not giving adequate information to clients. Note that the model of lawyering predominant in England differs from the zealous advocacy favored in the United States, according to Robert A. Kagan in *Do Lawyers Cause Adversarial Legalism? A Preliminary Inquiry*, 19 LAW & SOC. INQUIRY 1, 37 (1994).

28. Rodriguez, *supra* note 22, at 2 (citing Marks at 1).

29. Drops in applications of 8.4% in 1997, 9.6% in 1996, 7.2% in 1995, 2% in 1994, and 6% in 1993 have been reported. Law School Admissions Council, *Report: Counting Down for the Sixth Year in a Row*, SYLLABUS, Spring 1997, at 11. In 1994, "about 4.2% [of college freshmen] said they wanted to become lawyers, down from a peak of 5.4% in 1988 and 1989." Dirk Johnson, *More Scorn and Less Money Dim Law's Lure*, N.Y. TIMES, September 22, 1995, at A1. *See also* Jeff Barge, *Fewer Consider Law: Schools Report Applications Declining*, A.B.A. J., June 1995, at A1 (documenting drops in applications in 1993, 1994, and 1995), and Christine Riedel, *The Big Squeeze*, NAT'L JURIST, Sept. 1996, at 20 (documenting the decline in law school applications and law schools' responses).

30. With the declining economy in 2001, the number of law school aptitude test takers and law school applications rose again. Jonathan D. Glater, *Law School Calls as Economy Slows*, N.Y. TIMES, August 24, 2001, at A1, p. 5 (24,000 took the LSAT in June 2001, which was an 18.6% increase from 2000; law school applications in fall 2001 were almost 79,000, an increase of 5.6% since 2000, but still does not compare to the 84,000 who applied in 1995 and the nearly 100,000 who applied in 1991 during the last economic recession).

31. Maura Dolan, *Surveys: Many Lawyers Disillusioned*, L.A. TIMES, June 28, 1995, at E2 (citing *Fax Poll: It Becomes a Miserable Profession*, CAL. LAW., March 1992, at 3).

32. *Id.* at E2.

33. John P. Heinz, Kathleen E. Hull, & Ava A. Harter, *Researching Law: An ABF Update, "Content With Their Calling? Job Satisfaction in the Chicago Bar,"* 9 AM. B. FOUND. PUB. 1 (1998).

34. A.B.A., *The Report of at the Breaking Point: A National Conference on the Emerging Crisis in the Quality of Lawyers' Health and Lives—Its Impact on Law Firms and Client Services*, April 5–6, 1991, at 10.

35. Arian Campo-Flores, *An Ambivalent Profession*, THE AMERICAN LAWYER, April 1998, at 26, reporting results of a 1995 survey by professors Amy Black of Franklin & Marshall College and Stanley Rothman of Smith College, both professors of government, who surveyed nine "elite" groups (e.g., business executives, journalists, religious leaders, lawyers, and judges), later published in Amy E. Black & Stanley Rothman, *Shall We Kill All the Lawyers First?: Insider and Outsider Views of the Legal Profession*, 21 HARV. J. L. PUB. POL. 835 (1998).

36. A.B.A. YOUNG LAW. DIVISION, THE STATE OF THE LEGAL PROFESSION: 1984 (1984) [hereinafter ABA/YLD 1984].

37. A.B.A. YOUNG LAW. DIVISION, THE STATE OF THE LEGAL PROFESSION: 1990 (1991) [hereinafter ABA/YLD 1990].

38. A.B.A. YOUNG LAW. DIVISION, CAREER SATISFACTION: 1995 (1995) [hereinafter ABA/YLD 1995].

39. ABA/YLD 1990, *supra* note 37, at 52. The 1984 and 1990 surveys studied dissatisfaction with the current job.

40. *Id.*

41. ABA/YLD 1995, *supra* note 38, at 13. This survey studied dissatisfaction with current job and with the practice of law.

42. ABA/YLD 1990, *supra* note 37, at 52, 55 ("regardless of job setting, there has been a 20% reduction [from 41% to 33%] in the number of lawyers indicating that they are very satisfied, accompanied by an increase in dissatisfaction").

43. Richard, *supra* note 2, at 44.

44. *Id.* at 222.

45. Heinz et al., *supra* note 33.

46. *Id.*

47. Kathleen E. Hull, *The Paradox of the Contented Female Lawyer*, 33 LAW & SOC'Y REV. 687, 697–698 (1999) (acknowledging the potential social desirability bias that happens when in-person interviews are used instead of anonymous questionnaires).

48. Richard, *supra* note 2, at 26. Richard reported that before the ABA/YLD survey in 1984, the studies focused on satisfaction among various segments of the population, such as Black attorneys, female attorneys, and older attorneys.

49. *Id.* at 25, *citing* E. A. Locke, *The Nature and Causes of Job Satisfaction*, in M. D. DUNNETTE, ED., HANDBOOK OF INDUSTRIAL AND ORGANIZATIONAL PSYCHOLOGY (1976).

50. Heinz et al., *supra* note 33, at 6.

51. Specifically, additional empirical research needs to clearly establish the precise and replicative correlates of dissatisfaction among lawyers.

52. Connie J. A. Beck, Bruce D. Sales, & G. Andrew H. Benjamin, *Lawyer Distress: Alcohol Related Concerns Among a Sample of Practicing Lawyers*, 10 J. L. & HEALTH 1, 18 (1995–1996) [hereinafter Beck et al.] G. Andrew H.

Benjamin, Alfred Kazniak, Bruce Sales, & Stephen B. Shanfield, *The Role of Legal Education in Producing Psychological Distress Among Law Students*, AM. B. FOUND. RES. J. 225 (1986) [hereinafter Benjamin et al. 1986]. G. Andrew, H. Benjamin, Elaine J. Darling, & Bruce Sales, *The Prevalence of Depression, Alcohol Abuse, and Cocaine Abuse Among United States Lawyers*, 13 INT'L. J. LAW & PSYCHIATRY 233, 240 (1990) [hereinafter Benjamin et al. 1990]. Stephen B. Shanfield & G. Andrew Benjamin, *Psychiatric Distress in Law Students*, 35 J. LEGAL EDUC. 65, 68–69 (1985) [hereinafter Shanfield].

53. William W. Eaton, James C. Anthony, Wallace Mandel, & Roberta Garrison, *Occupations and the Prevalence of Major Depressive Disorder*, 32 J. OCCUPATIONAL MEDICINE 1079, 1081 (1990).

54. *E.g.*, depression and substance abuse appear to be related to professional malfeasance by attorneys, as described later.

55. *See generally* sources cited in chapter 5 and in this section of chapter 1 on depression.

56. Benjamin et al. 1990, *supra* note 52, at 240.

57. Of these individuals, most were thinking about suicide. *Id.* at 240–241.

58. *Id.*

59. Dolan, *supra* note 31.

60. Paula A. Franzese, *Back to the Future: Reclaiming Our Noble Profession*, 25 SETON HALL L. REV. 488 and n.5 (1994) (reviewing SOL LINOWITZ & MARTIN MAYER, THE BETRAYED PROFESSION: LAWYERING AT THE END OF THE TWENTIETH CENTURY (1994)), *citing Excerpts: The Betrayal of the Lawyering Profession*, NAT'L L. J., February 28, 1994, at 36, for the claim that this Johns Hopkins University study found lawyers were the most depressed group of 12,000 persons surveyed. Professor Franzese also noted that the leading researcher of this study commented that "lawyers constantly operate in 'moral ambiguity' sometimes representing clients or issues that 'they might not like or believe in.' " Franzese, at 490–491.

61. AMERICAN PSYCHIATRIC ASSOCIATION, DIAGNOSTIC AND STATISTICAL MANUAL OF MENTAL DISORDERS, 4th ed., 1994.

62. Eaton et al., *supra* note 53.

63. This was a catch-all category for prekindergarten and special education teachers and education and vocational counselors. *Id.* at 42.

64. *Id.*, though perhaps these three occupations were overly depressed because the individuals in them felt out of control of their work, because other studies showed that feeling out of control was linked to depression. So they measured the extent to which individuals in various professions felt "in control" of their work. The lawyers and secretaries felt out of control of their work, yet the disproportionately depressed "other teachers" felt in control. In addition, physicians also felt out of control of their work and had almost a zero depression rate, so they concluded that feeling out of control of one's work did not explain the depression in various occupations. *Id.* at 1026.

65. For example, in 1985, medical students overall scored lower than law students on a standard measure of psychological distress (but 10–20% of the medical

students also scored more than two standard deviations above the mean and above the cutoff on five submeasures, indicating significant distress among medical students as well). Beck et al., *supra* note 52, at 4 and nn.11 & 15, *citing* Shanfield, *supra* note 52. Evidence to contradict the statement that distress is greater among lawyers than among doctors does, however, exist. There are studies finding that medical students are not as distressed as law students, for example, but there are also other studies finding the opposite; the differences may be a result of different definitions of "distress." These studies are explored in more detail in chapter 5.

66. Benjamin et al., 1986, *supra* note 52.

67. Richard Gater, Michele Tansella, Ailsa Korten, et al., *Sex Differences in the Prevalence and Detection of Depression and Anxiety Disorders in General Health Care Settings*, 55 ARCHIVES OF GEN. PSYCHIATRY 405, 405–413 (May 1998).

68. Benjamin et al., 1986, *supra* note 52.

69. Beck et al., *supra* note 52.

70. *Id.*

71. *Id.*

72. Beck et al., *supra* note 52, at 50.

73. *Id.* at 30–31.

74. Roseanna McCleary & Evan L. Zucker, *Higher Trait- and State-Anxiety in Female Law Students Than Male Law Students*, 68 PSYCHOL. REP. 1075 (1991) (also finding higher trait- and state-anxiety among female law students than male law students and noting that women tend to score higher than men on these scales anyway).

75. Benjamin et al., 1990, *supra* note 52, at 241 (1990) ("this percentage is almost twice the approximate 10 percent alcohol abuse and/or dependency prevalence rates estimated for adults in the United States"). *Id.* at 240, *citing National Clearinghouse for Alcohol and Drug Information, The Fact Is . . . 1* (Oct. 1988). Benjamin and his colleagues also asserted, "Alcoholism among the male attorneys is likely to be occurring at the same rate in the two states," referring to Washington and Arizona; Benjamin et al., 1990, *supra* note 52, at 240.

76. Michael A. Bloom & Carol Lynn Wallinger, *Lawyers and Alcoholism: Is It Time for a New Approach?*, 61 TEMP. L. REV. 1409 (1988), *citing* Maher, *Addicted Professionals: A Growing Problem*, PA. L. J. REP., March 7, 1988, at S1. "Some studies . . . suggest the incidence of chemical dependency in legal professionals might be as much as 50 percent higher than for the general population." Andrew V. Hansen, *Alcoholism in the Lawyer's Context*, 7 LEGAL REF. SERV. Q. 231, 236 (1987).

77. *Id. See also* Benjamin et al., 1990, *supra* note 52, at 241 (1990), *citing National Clearinghouse for Alcohol and Drug Information*, *supra* note 75.

78. Hansen, *supra* note 76, at 236.

79. Laurie Bilz Dowell, *Attorneys and Alcoholism: An Alternative Approach to a Serious Problem*, 16 N. KY. L. REV. 169, 170 (1988), *citing* Haliburton Fales, *The Lawyer and His Health—Alcoholism*, 56 N.Y. ST. B. J. (1984).

80. Hansen, *supra* note 76, at 236.

81. Dowell, *supra* note 79, at 170.

82. Richard Kirkeby, *Drunk, Drugged and Stressed: Problems Pervade Lawyers' Lives Lucky Attorney Drank Her Way Through Life With Everything Lost, The Other Bar Started*, 871 PLI/CORP. 355 (1994) *citing* A.B.A. study in 1990.

83. CERARD J. CONNORS & ARTHUR R. TARBOX, *Michigan Alcoholism Screening Test*, in 3 TEST CRITIQUES 439, 444 (D. J. KEYSER & R. C. SWEETLAND, EDS.).

84. Beck et al., *supra* note 52, at 45.

85. *Id.* at 29, 51.

86. Dennis W. Kozich, *Stress Is Taking Its Toll on Wisconsin Attorneys*, WIS. LAW., April 1989, at 12.

87. Dolan, *supra* note 31, at E2.

88. Benjamin et al., 1990, *supra* note 52, at 233, 241.

89. *Id.* at 241.

90. *Id.*

91. AALS Committee Report, *Report of the AALS Special Committee on Problems of Substance Abuse in the Law Schools*, 44 J. LEG. EDUC. 35, 40 (1994).

92. Benjamin et al., 1990, *supra* note 52, at 244 *citing* C. Greene, *Half of Lawyer Malpractice and Discipline Stems From Substance Abuse–Annual Meeting of the National Conference of Bar Presidents*, August 6, 1988; D. Muchogrosso, *Profile of Legal Malpractice—A Statistical Study of Determinative Characteristics on Lawyers' Professional Liability Fund*, OR. S.B.A. (May 1986) (internal program memorandum).

93. Association of American Law Schools Committee Report, *Report of the AALS Special Committee on Problems of Substance Abuse in Law Schools*, 44 J. LEGAL EDUC. 35, 63, *citing The Guiding Principles: There Is Light at the End of the Tunnel for Substance Impaired Lawyers*, Jan./Feb. 1991, at 12.

94. R. Theis, *Center for Professional Responsibility*, A.B.A. (Jan. 1989) (personal communication), *as cited in* Benjamin et al., 1990, *supra* note 52, at 243.

95. Jonathan Goodliffe, *Alcohol and Depression in English and American Disciplinary Proceedings*, 89 ADDICTION 1237, 1243 (1994).

96. Beck et al., *supra* note 52 (alcohol and drug abuse almost twice as frequent among attorneys as the general population); Robert Stevens, *Law Schools and Law Students*, 59 VA. L. REV. 551, 678 (1973) (law students become more ambitious and aggressive the more tension they feel in law school); Michael J. Patton, *The Student, the Situation, and Performance During the First Year of Law School*, 21 J. LEGAL EDUC. 10, 43–45 (1968) (law students rely less on social support when stressed than do medical students).

97. Beck et al., *supra* note 52, at 53 (alcohol use releases anger and aggression).

98. Regarding the relationship of alcohol use to disciplinary actions, *see* Benjamin et al., 1990, *supra* note 52, at 244, *citing* C. Greene, *Half of Lawyer Malpractice and Discipline Stems From Substance Abuse–Annual Meeting of the National Conference of Bar Presidents*, Aug. 6, 1988; D. Muchogrosso, *Profile of Legal Malpractice—A Statistical Study of Determinative Characteristics on Lawyers' Professional Liability Fund*, OR. S.B.A. (May 1986) (internal program memorandum). *See also*

Jonathan Goodliffe, *Alcohol and Depression in English and American Disciplinary Proceedings*, 89 ADDICTION 1237, 1243 (1994).

99. This can occur either by failing to provide the attorney with social support when stressed or by failing to provide peer review of the attorney's actions. The resulting anonymity has been hypothesized to be responsible for unethical behavior by attorneys. William H. Rehnquist, *The State of the Legal Profession*, LEGAL ECON., March 1988, at 44.

2

THE LAWYER PERSONALITY: HOW LAWYERS DIFFER FROM "REGULAR PEOPLE"

Forty years' worth of empirical research has investigated lawyers' personalities, satisfaction, motives, and mental health. From these studies, certain characteristics, personality traits, attitudes, qualities, motivations, goals, values, ideals, and morals appear to be typical of lawyers. This chapter and the next (focused on law students) exhaustively review this research.

First, the studies separate into those about prelaw students, law students before law school, law students during law school, and lawyers roughly establishing a developmental sequence for the "making of a lawyer."[1] Some studies investigated students' motives for entering law school and data on the effects of law school. Moral development of attorneys appeared to be a distinct and rich area of inquiry. Then, from the vast amount of data—sometimes conflicting, sometimes consistent—emerged several groups of traits characteristic of the "lawyer personality." Although law school fosters and inculcates some of the "lawyer traits," many of them have their origins in early childhood, long before law school. This debunks two common myths: that lawyers are aggressive and competitive only because the practice of law demands these traits and that law school and law practice make people "act like lawyers." What do people mean when they say, "act like a lawyer?" There is evidence of a lawyer stereotype, resembling some of the stereotypes portrayed in popular lawyer jokes.

Portions of this chapter were adapted from an article by the author titled *Asking Leopards to Change Their Spots: Should Lawyers Change? A Critique of Solutions to Problems With Professionalism by Reference to Empirically-Derived Attorney Personality Attributes*, XI GEO. J. L. ETHICS 3 (1998). The author reserved the right to adapt and publish the material.

STEREOTYPE

Social science research stereotypes law as a masculine occupation. It stereotypes lawyers as self-confident, dominant, argumentative, aggressive, combative, cunning, highly intelligent, ingenious, required or permitted to use drama for effect, committed above all else to prevail for their clients and causes, involved in work, well-dressed, driven toward competence, ambitious, competitive with others in the field, and interested in social issues. It also portrays lawyers as working long hours; writing convincingly, interestingly, and creatively; not being uncomfortable lying; living in suburban, upper-middle-class neighborhoods; and driving sports cars.[2] Some (but not all) of these traits are supported by the research on lawyers.

LAWYER ATTRIBUTES

In general, there is a dearth of research on lawyers. The studies that do exist are sparse, scattered, incohesive, and widely divergent in their methodologies. Very few researchers have systematically studied the lawyer personality (with the exception of several social scientists who have examined lawyer distress). However, the existing studies do support the existence of several traits fairly consistent with the lawyer stereotype.

Competitiveness

Consistent with the stereotype, lawyers are competitive and aggressive. We like to win. One senior litigator even recharacterized his losses as wins, saying, "This is a great job. I win whether my client wins or loses—I get paid either way."

Two studies focused specifically on competitiveness. One 1992 study defined it as "the desire to win in interpersonal situations" and then found that male and female attorneys were more competitive than nurses.[3] A 1983 study found that female attorneys were more "masculine" than were female physicians, meaning more competitive and aggressive.[4]

Two other studies hint at a possible biological explanation for the competitiveness of lawyers, particularly trial lawyers. First, a 1979 study found women lawyers' testosterone levels to be higher than those of female nurses, teachers, or athletes.[5] Second, a fascinating 1998 study found that both male and female trial lawyers had elevated testosterone levels, compared to other lawyers. The researchers actually asked lawyers to provide a saliva sample, which was then analyzed, to conduct this study.[6]

How is testosterone related to competitiveness? Although testosterone is the principal male sex hormone, both sexes have it. Previous research indicates that it is associated with sexual activity, interpersonal dominance, competition, energy, persistence, higher spatial ability and lower verbal ability, antisocial behavior, alcohol and drug use, marital discord, and violent crime. It increases with the winning of fights and decreases with the losing of fights; it increases in anticipation of important athletic contests. Blue-collar workers typically have higher testosterone levels than do white-collar workers.[7]

Overall, the 1998 study found that lawyers' testosterone levels were similar to those of other professional, white-collar workers and were significantly lower than those of blue-collar workers. But trial lawyers of both sexes had higher testosterone levels than did nontrial lawyers, leading the researchers to conclude that, among lawyers, "trial lawyers are like blue-collar workers in a white-collar world."[8] Perhaps both blue-collar workers and trial lawyers are required to be active and energetic, focused on concrete details rather than abstractions, and comfortable with interpersonal confrontation.

Although these biological findings alone do not indicate that all lawyers are more competitive, dominant, or aggressive than other people, they do suggest that trial lawyers are. And trial lawyers probably have the most contact with the public, garner the most media visibility, and serve as the basis for most people's concept of the "ideal lawyer." Thus, the high-testosterone trial lawyer image may have come to represent the profession as a whole.

This competitive, aggressive trial lawyer image may be desirable in litigation. For example, a 1996 study found that people were more persuaded by aggressive attorneys than by passive ones.[9] Also, some lawyers themselves may idealize the high-testosterone trial lawyers as representative of the ideal lawyer. Some experienced attorneys are admittedly afraid of the courtroom (hence, they excel at transaction planning to avoid future conflict); these are the kinds of lawyers who might admire the trial lawyer's confidence and panache.

Achievement Orientation

Perhaps as part of our competitiveness, lawyers also like to achieve. We are psychologically motivated to achieve. Psychological research has identified three basic drives that explain most people's motivations: power, affiliation with others, and achievement.[10] The need for achievement is described as the need to compete against an internal or external standard of excellence; the need for affiliation is the desire for friendship, love, or belonging; and the need for power is the need to lead or have an impact on others. Psychologists expected lawyers to have a high need for power,[11] but a 1984 study determined that lawyers are actually more achievement-motivated, with moderate needs for power and relatively low needs for affiliation.[12] Notable exceptions were criminal lawyers, law librarians, and judges, who were more motivated by needs for power than for achievement.

This study had some interesting conclusions. First, it concluded that the more time an attorney spent in court, the more important it was to need power to be happy doing the work.[13] Second, it illuminated some important differences between lawyers and judges and suggested that, because they were so different, happy judges were probably unhappy as attorneys. Third, it recommended motivation testing by law schools, large law firms, and judicial appointments committees to place law students, new lawyers, and politically appointed judges, respectively, and ensure that they would be "good fits for the position."[14]

As students, we probably channel this need for achievement into a drive for academic success. Then, on graduation from law school, we must rechannel our need for achievement into some other area. We may then come to measure professional achievement by the quality of our work, the quality of our clients, the number of our "wins," our material success or possessions, or by the grade-like Martindale-Hubbell ratings assigned to us by our peers.

Materialism

Lawyer jokes repeatedly portray lawyers as money-grubbing and money-oriented. An extensive 1997 study indicates that lawyers are indeed more focused on the economic bottom line than are most people.[15] In this study, lawyers evaluated litigation options and settlement offers differently than did nonlawyers; lawyers were more focused on the economic bottom line and were less swayed by noneconomic, psychological factors.

In this study, practicing lawyers in the San Francisco–Palo Alto area were compared to Stanford undergraduates who were asked to pretend they were litigants.[16] Both lawyers and "litigants" were presented with hypothetical personal injury cases and asked whether they would settle for the offered amount or go to trial. All settlements offered the same net economic value—the variations were in the nonmonetary aspects. For example, in one scenario, the amount of the opponent's opening settlement offer varied. In another, the opponent behaved poorly (e.g., refused to apologize). In another, the car that hit the litigant varied (Toyota versus BMW). The lawyers tended to evaluate whether to litigate or settle a lawsuit on the basis of a traditional economic model of litigation that focused on maximizing expected financial return from the litigation, regardless of perceived treatment by others, emotional issues, or perceived justice or fairness. In contrast, the noneconomic factors affected the undergraduate litigants' decisions about whether or not to settle.[17]

It may be that lawyers are focused solely on the economics of the deal. Alternatively, lawyers' preference for cool, rational, logical analysis (plus a little materialism) allows us to cut to the chase and assess these hypotheticals "carefully and unemotionally rather than [reacting] to them viscerally."[18]

These findings are important for two reasons. First, if lawyers are focused on maximizing wealth, then we are inherently always biased toward settlement, because litigating is costly. This might in part explain why more than 90% of lawsuits settle before trial.[19] Second, there are many cases in which the litigants want something other than money. For example, in libel, discrimination, or harassment suits, the legal system's most effective use may be in vindicating psychological or emotional needs.[20] Because of our psychological makeup, lawyers may overlook the value of these nonmonetary incentives.[21]

Altruism

Altruism is a difficult concept to define or study. In studies, it has meant lawyers' interest in public interest work or social concerns. A 1973 Australian study found that altruism and idealism declined among lawyers during early practice in a way that did not occur among engineers.[22] This study found that the first three years of professional practice "reduced the proportion of lawyers expressing an altruistic motivation in the handling of clients' problems or a social concern in the orientation of their careers," whereas similar changes were less evident among engineers in their first three years of practice.[23]

A study of the University of Wisconsin Law School class of 1976 found that, by 1985, nine years postgraduation, nontraditional jobs were less popular than they were at graduation. This study viewed "nontraditional work" as synonymous with public interest work, meaning "work in legal aid, as a public defender, or in a nonprofit organization."[24] By 1985, more than half of the attorneys had switched job categories[25] and the overwhelming majority (82%) of those whose first job was nontraditional were no longer in a nontraditional job, suggesting a postgraduation move away from public interest work.[26] One might think this happened because of the graduates' need to pay back student loans. Not so. Of those who were interested in public interest work in law school, those who dropped that interest and ended up in a traditional job were more likely to have high grades than crushing amounts of student debt. Taking a nontraditional job after graduation was instead more related to how committed one was to left-liberal or radical political orientations and one's record of previous political activism than it was to the size of the student's debt.[27]

Goals

Lawyers' stated goals confirm the emphases on achievement and materialism, among other things. A 1995 survey of St. Louis lawyers revealed that their most important goals were to "do the highest quality work I can" and to "be happy with my work."[28] Their least important were to "advance to a position of power" and to "improve the public good." Other highly important goals were "make a substantial income," "serve the client," "have control over work life," "be respected," and "be intellectually challenged." These St. Louis lawyers also cited as important having "time for myself/family," perhaps reflecting the heavy stress and time pressure felt by lawyers in the 1990s.[29]

Gender Differences

Many studies of lawyers in the 1970s and 1980s focused on gender differences. The percentage of women in the legal profession, which was quite low in 1970, has dramatically increased since then.[30] The women who entered law in the 1970s were likely to be nontraditional trailblazers. Their characteristics may not depict women lawyers today, so the following results should be read with caution.

In 1979, women lawyers had higher testosterone levels than did female nurses, teachers, or athletes. In 1983, women lawyers had more achievement motivation than did women doctors, secretaries, and medical assistants. In fact, women in all levels of law, whether legal secretary or lawyer, had more desire to achieve than did women in medicine, whether medical assistant or physician.[31] Women lawyers had significantly higher "masculinity" scores than women physicians,[32] meaning competitiveness and aggressiveness. Women lawyers also reported more traditionally masculine play patterns in childhood and less parental pressure to fit a traditionally feminine stereotype.

However, both women doctors and women lawyers in 1983 were more "masculine," scored higher on intellectual ability, were more likely to have been first-born or only children, had unhappier adolescences, more often preferred sports, were more verbal and intelligent, and received stronger family support for their achievements than did women legal secretaries and medical assistants.[33] Because these characteristics were shared by doctors and lawyers, they may simply reflect what was true about women who trail-blazed into traditionally masculine occupations in the 1970s and early 1980s.[34] Although these traits differentiated women doctors and lawyers from medical and legal paraprofessionals, other traits such as achievement motivation, competitiveness, and aggression determined whether they chose law over medicine.

It is difficult to make a generalization about the legal profession from these two studies, because they excluded men and surveyed an atypical group of women. These women would have entered the law when it was still a male-dominated profession and might have had to be—or believed they had to be—more masculine to succeed. In the 1980s, women lawyers often dressed like men to "fit in," down to wearing bow ties, Brooks Brothers suits, and buttoned-down oxford shirts. However, these studies do suggest that women lawyers may be generally more achievement-oriented and "masculine" (meaning competitive and aggressive) than other women.[35]

Inconsistent results are reported on women lawyers' job satisfaction. Some studies find that their job satisfaction is lower than that of male attorneys, whereas others find no gender differences in job satisfaction.[36] In the studies finding more dissatisfaction among women attorneys, their dissatisfaction appeared to be related to two principal factors: (a) lack of autonomy, respect, or professional advancement opportunities; and (b) inadequate financial rewards. Problematic work atmosphere and lack of time for self and family were secondarily important.[37] Finally, an excellent study of lawyer distress in 1995 discovered that women lawyers were actually less psychologically distressed than men lawyers. These researchers took into account a typical gender effect: Women generally tend to overreport distress and men tend to underreport it. Once the data were adjusted to account for this phenomenon, the higher levels of stress among male attorneys emerged.[38]

Finally, a 1997 study of the conversations of Israeli lawyers with their clients revealed that women's and men's lawyering styles were not really different. For the most part, the female lawyers appeared to have adopted the male lawyers' approach to professional interactions with clients. The differences came in women's "occasional willingness to grant legitimacy to the clients' emotional concerns . . . [and their] stress on professional identity."[39] The study's findings about lawyers' bedside manners sheds light on another lawyer trait.

Decision-Making Styles

This 1997 Israeli study found that lawyers of both sexes generally ignored the emotional aspects of the clients' problems and tended to avoid, ignore, or undermine any expression of emotions by the clients in the lawyer–client interactions.[40] This tendency may explain the popular perception that lawyers are unemotional, logical, rational, "cold fish." However, there are personality-based reasons that lawyers are perceived as emotion-avoidant or even cold and uncompassionate, based on the ways that we make decisions.

A consistent finding over the past 30 years or so is that certain decision-making preferences or styles predominate in the legal profession. Since 1967, lawyers have overwhelmingly preferred a style of decision making measured by the Myers–Briggs Type Indicator (MBTI) that emphasizes logical analysis, principles, cool and impersonal reasoning, and cost–benefit analyses.[41] This mode, the "thinking" preference, tends to deemphasize harmony, personal relationships, pleasing others, and avoiding conflict and criticism. In addition, MBTI "thinkers" are more tolerant of criticism and conflict with others.[42]

The Myers–Briggs "Type" of Lawyer

The MBTI is designed to help people assess into which of 16 "psychological types" they fall. This information is used to help them interact and work together more effectively. People's scores on four continua of the MBTI categorize them into 1 of 16 possible combinations or types. The theories of the famous psychologist Carl Jung about personality form the basis for the four continua.[43] The dimensions are extraversion versus introversion; sensing versus intuiting; thinking versus feeling; and judging versus perceiving. The MBTI evaluates individuals' personal preferences with respect to these four dimensions. A person's preferences on each of these four continuua yields a four-character personality "type"; for example, a person preferring introversion, sensing, thinking, and judging would be an "ISTJ."[44] One psychologist–lawyer explained that it is "not a clinical test—that is, it does not measure whether you are mentally healthy," rather, it demonstrates ways in which individuals prefer to focus mental energy, gather data, make decisions, perform mental tasks, and deal with the external world.[45]

The test was developed in the 1940s by Katharine Cook Briggs and Isabel Briggs Myers, based on Jung's theories about personality differences, and has become widely used in corporate and professional settings as a tool to understand individual differences in work habits and approaches.[46] It has also been widely used in legal education to understand different learning styles among law students.[47] However, it is often criticized by clinical psychologists because it does not measure mental health and does not contain safeguards to ensure that its results are reliable or valid. Despite its controversial aspects, it has become extremely popular. It appears to be the only general psychological test of personality that has ever been administered to a large number of practicing attorneys.[48]

Types. Extraversion and introversion are an attitude. Extraverts focus on the outer world and feel energized by contacts with other people; introverts focus on their inner world and often feel drained if they spend too much time with other people. Introverts are likely to enjoy quiet concentration, thinking things through, reflecting, reading, and writing. Extraverts like to talk things out with others—the extreme extravert is the person who sweeps into the lunchroom, talking to himself the whole time about whether he should buy one car or another. Still talking, he makes his decision out loud, and then announces to the people around him, "Thanks so much for helping me sort this out. You've been great. I know just what to do, now."[49] Lawyers are slightly more likely to be introverts.

Sensing and intuition are two different ways of perceiving and processing incoming information. Sensors attend to concrete, real world things and enjoy working with real facts and details. Intuitors would rather think about the big picture, abstract ideas, and global themes, learn new things, and solve complex problems. Attorneys tend to be intuitors.

Thinking and feeling are two different ways of making decisions. Thinkers prefer "logical analysis, principles, cool and impersonal reasoning and cost/benefit analyses" and are "more tolerant of conflict and criticism." Feelers prefer "harmonizing, building relationships, pleasing people, making decisions on the basis of [their own] . . . personal likes and dislikes, and being attentive to the personal needs of others" and like to avoid conflict and criticism.[50] One of the foremost researchers in this area explained that the dimensions of thinking and feeling both represent

> rational, valid decision-making methods. Both involve thought, and neither process is related to emotions. . . .
>
> Those who prefer to make decisions on the basis of Thinking prefer to come to closure in a logical, orderly manner. They can readily discern inaccuracies and are often critical. They can easily hurt others' feelings without knowing it. They are excellent problem-solvers. They review the cause and effect of potential actions before deciding. Thinkers are often accused of being cold and somewhat calculating because their decisions do not reflect their own personal values. They focus on discovering truth, and they seek justice.
>
> Those who prefer to make decisions on the basis of Feeling apply their own personal values to make choices. They seek harmony and, therefore, are sensitive to the effect of their decisions on others. They need, and are adept at giving, praise. They are interested in the person behind the idea or the job. They seek to do what is right for themselves and other people and are interested in mercy.[51]

Lawyers overwhelmingly prefer thinking to feeling.

Judging and perceiving are general approaches to life. Judgers prefer structure, schedules, closure on decisions, planning, follow through, and a "cut-to-the-chase" approach. They tend to work on one task at a time and like to complete projects. Perceivers prefer a "go with the flow and see what develops" approach. They are the kind of people who have several projects spread all over their desks, all of which are in process, in flux, and being worked on. Lawyers are more likely to prefer judging.

TABLE 2.1
Types in the General Population and Among Lawyers

MBTI results:	Extro-version	Intro-version	Sens-ing	Intuit-ing	Think-ing	Feel-ing	Judg-ing	Per-ceiving
Most people	**65%**	35%	**68%**	32%	48%	**53%**	**55%**	45%
Attny. studies	41–44%	**56–59%**	31–44%	**56–69%**	**65–77%**	24–35%	**54–63%**	37–46%

Note. Bolded numbers denote the majority-preferred dimension within that group (most people or attorneys).

Lawyer type. An extensive, nationwide study of lawyers reported in 1994 that lawyers overwhelmingly prefer thinking as a style of decision making to feeling on the Myers–Briggs Type Indicator.[52] This large study joined approximately 11 previous studies finding the same thing: About 75% of lawyers and law students prefer thinking to feeling. This differs from the distribution of "thinking" and "feeling" in the general population and is highly consistent over almost 30 years—from 1967[53] to 1994[54]—despite the influx of women into the legal profession.[55]

This 1994 study also confirmed that, statistically, lawyers' type was significantly different from most other adults in the United States.[56] In three studies of lawyers' MBTI type, attorneys were more often INTJs, preferring: (a) introversion; (b) intuiting; (c) thinking; and (d) judging.[57] Yet the majority of adults as a whole in the United States are ESFs, preferring the opposite dimensions of extroversion, sensing, and feeling. Introversion and intuition are thought to be stable, life-long preferences, so lawyers are likely to have had these two characteristics before law school. Finally, most people prefer judging, but lawyers preferred it even more. In all three lawyer studies, the most frequent type among lawyers was INTJ, and ISTJ was also among the top three lawyer types.[58]

The distribution of these preferences in the general population and among lawyers is demonstrated in Table 2.1.

The thinking versus feeling dimension deserves a closer look. Even though overall a slight majority of the general population prefers feeling, more men prefer thinking and more women prefer feeling. This result can be thought of as the "men are from Mars; women are from Venus"[59] gender difference. It explains why men and women can feel so different from each other. However, both male and female lawyers overwhelmingly preferred thinking—81% of male lawyers and 66% of female lawyers were thinkers in the 1994 study. Women lawyers thus appear radically different from nonlawyer women in terms of this preference.

The 1994 study explains that the INTJ lawyer type makes sense. Most of what lawyers do involves introverted activity: quiet, concentrated work, reading, writing, researching and analyzing cases, reviewing and drafting legal documents, and thinking through fact situations and strategies.[60] Although extroversion would be useful in trials and meetings, the majority of most lawyers' days are spent in solitary, concentrated work. When lawyers solve clients' complex problems, learn new areas of case law with each new client, feel intellectually stimulated by their work, and fit the client's problem into the big picture, they are engaging in intuitive activities. Logically analyzing cases and arguments, assessing a client's situation objectively, and rendering impartial, clear-headed advice are all well-suited to thinkers. In contrast, feelers would rather create harmony between people, build relationships, please others, and fulfill their needs. Although some feeling-type activities are performed by lawyers in their daily work, it is not the bulk of what they do. Thinking-type activities are more central or crucial to the lawyer's daily success. Finally, because judgers enjoy structure and schedules, this preference probably works well for lawyers, who have to meet deadlines; track statutes of limitation; schedule and order their calendars and workdays; and keep multiple cases, files, and documents well-organized. Again, although the open-ended approach of the perceiver might be useful in some unpredictable settings, the decisive approach of judging is probably more useful in law.

However, although being different from most people may be adaptive to the practice of law and fit well with the daily tasks of lawyers, lawyers' differences may create a gap in understanding between lawyers and nonlawyers. These differences in part explain why people perceive lawyers as "different" and why they are critical of attorneys. For example, clients may be speaking from the perspective of the more popular ESFJ type while their lawyers are speaking from the typical lawyer INTJ perspective. Clients may want to talk things out with others, focus on facts and practicalities, avoid conflict, and consider the effects of decisions on others. In contrast, their lawyers may prefer to make decisions in quiet solitude, focus on the legal theory of the case and how it fits into the big picture, and arrive at conclusions through logical analysis of rights, duties, and liabilities.

The exception may be corporate clients. Although the MBTI differences between lawyers and "regular people" are dramatic, top corporate executives are surprisingly similar to lawyers in MBTI type. Like lawyers, top corporate executives overwhelmingly prefer thinking (95%) and judging (87%). In addition, the most frequent types among top corporate executives were ISTJ, ESTJ, and INTJ, whereas ISTJ and INTJ are among the top three most frequent types for lawyers. Among corporate executives, the INTJ and ISTJ types were represented in numbers way out of proportion to their usual frequency in the overall population.[61] These similarities suggest that top corporate executives may understand and relate to their lawyers better than most clients do. It also suggests that some of the qualities needed to be a lawyer or a top corporate executive are the same, centering on thinking and judging. This makes sense, because thinker–judgers are likely to be objective, rational, logical, analytical, decisive, and confident.

A 1989 study illuminated some differences in Myers–Briggs type among lawyers in private practice, judges, and lawyers working in administrative agencies. Lawyers in private practice were more likely to be introverted, intuitive, and thinking. Their most frequent types were ISTJ, ENFP, INTJ and least frequent types were ESTP, ISFP, ESFJ, and ESFP. They were more likely to have the "NT" combination of intuition and thinking, which another MBTI authority describes as the rational combination.[62] Like private practice lawyers, administrative attorneys were more likely to prefer intuition, thinking, and judging and have the rational NT combination. Their most frequent types were INTJ and ENTJ.[63] Rationals have been described as people who, "although they focus on a possibility, they approach it with impersonal analysis. Often they choose a theoretical or executive possibility and subordinate the human element."[64] Rational NTs have also been called analytical, systematic, abstract, theoretical, intellectual, complex, competent, inventive, curious, scientific, and research-oriented.[65]

Like top corporate executives, judges were more likely to prefer thinking and judging. Their most frequent types were ISTJ and ESTJ and least frequent type was ISFP. They were more likely to have the ST combination of sensing and thinking, suggesting that they were more attuned to concrete, tangible, details than were the more theoretical and abstract private practice lawyers and administrative attorneys.

Ethical decision making may be linked to one's MBTI preferences. One MBTI author contends that each MBTI type has its own unique value system or ethics. The lawyers' typical preference of INTJ suggests a moral code that is rule-based and clear. For example, thinkers see ethics as objective principles that must be enforced. If someone does not follow the rules, he or she must be dealt with. For judgers, ethics are black and white and nonnegotiable. In contrast, feelers link ethics to human interactions and weigh decisions against their personal value systems. Perceivers are always questioning ethics and reconsidering their position in their typical, open-ended way.[66]

The decisive, rule-following approach of thinkers/judgers is consistent with two studies finding that lawyers prefer a rule-based, rights-oriented approach to moral decision making. These studies are explored next.

Moral Development

A 1982 study using Harvard professor Lawrence Kohlberg's six-stage theory of moral development and methodology found that the responding attorneys were disproportionately clustered at the fourth stage of moral development, unlike the usual distribution of the general population across Kohlberg's six moral stages.[67] Kohlberg believed that individuals' moral development progresses through six stages. Most individuals never reach the final, sixth stage of moral development but stop developing at stage 3 or 4. The stages are based on the famous developmental psychologist Jean Piaget's stage theory of human development.[68]

Using Kohlberg's interview methodology, the 1982 study surveyed 900 randomly chosen, practicing attorneys in California, Wisconsin, and New York. Although a disappointingly small number of lawyers responded (195; 21%), the responding lawyers did not differ from the nonresponding lawyers on any observable criterion, so the researcher concluded that his small sample was typical of lawyers in general.[69] In this study, 90.3% of the responding lawyers operated at stage 4 and negligible proportions were at stage 5 (2.5%) and stage 3 (7.2%).[70] In contrast, other studies have found that adults are spread more evenly over stages 3, 4, and 5. Usually, 30 to 50% of adults, including university graduates, operate at stage 4.[71] By comparison, this lawyer study suggests that lawyers' moral reasoning is more uniform and (in some cases) less developed than other similarly educated individuals. Stage 4 is the social system and conscience (law and order) orientation. At this stage, laws, rules, and authority are upheld, the social order and system is maintained, and one fulfills one's fixed social obligations.[72] Stage 4 individuals primarily make decisions on the basis of rules, rather than in accordance with more universal, abstract concepts of right and wrong.[73] This is consistent with the decision-making style one might expect from thinkers/judgers.[74] In comparison, at less-developed stage 3, the mutual interpersonal expectations, relationships, and interpersonal conformity orientation, good behavior is that which has "good" motives, pleases or helps others, and is approved of by society; the individual conforms to stereotypes of nice, natural, or majority behavior.[75] At stage 5, the social contract or utility and individual rights orientation with law and rules remaining important, the individual is aware of the relative nature of personal values and rights. Thus, some nonrelative "values and rights like life and liberty . . . must be upheld in any society and regardless of majority opinion" or the law.[76] These nonrelative values and rights may conflict with the law and the individual may find it difficult to integrate them. Stage 5 has been referred to as the official morality of the American government and the U.S. Constitution.[77]

This 1982 study finding most lawyers in stage 4 is, however, inconsistent with my own study, conducted around 1992, which found that attorneys resolved professional ethical dilemmas on a case-by-case basis. They did not generally rely on rules and regulations. A stage 4 mentality would arguably be more consistent with a rules and regulations approach. Instead, in this study, attorneys' rationales for their decisions varied, depending on the situation, particularly on whether or not their actions would be subject to judicial scrutiny. They did not exclusively rely on laws, rules, and regulations when making decisions but also relied on other factors, such as personal moral beliefs and standards.[78] The inconsistent results of these studies are most likely to be the result of different methodologies used in the studies. However, it is possible that lawyers' professional decision making changed from 1982 to 1992, or that it differs from their personal decision making.

The second study (1994) used the theories of Harvard psychology professor Carol Gilligan to study lawyers' ethical decision-making preferences. Gilligan is well-known for her criticism that Kohlberg's stages of moral development do not adequately describe women's moral development and are thus gender-biased.[79] She believes, and empirical research has been performed to demonstrate, that Kohlberg's theory and methods improperly portray women as less morally developed than men.[80] Gilligan has asserted this is because women's moral reasoning differs qualitatively from men's; she claims that Kohlberg's work does not acknowledge these qualitative differences.[81] Although there is evidence that men and women make moral decisions differently, the research findings are not entirely conclusive, and the debate between Kohlberg and Gilligan has not been settled.[82]

Gilligan and others performed research that found that women more often make decisions based on an "ethic of care," whereas men more often decide on the basis of a "rights" orientation.[83] The ethic of care values interpersonal harmony, maintaining relationships, people's feelings and needs, and preventing harm.[84] It resolves conflicts by asking what best maintains relationships, what does each person need, and how not to hurt oneself or another.[85] It focuses on interdependence, social relationships, connectedness, community, and needs and sees people as connected by a network or web. It asks "How should I respond?"

In contrast, the rights orientation focuses on rights, rules, standards, individuality, independence, justice, fairness, objectivity, accomplishments, ambitions, principles, personal beliefs, and freedom from others' interference. It resolves dilemmas by impartially viewing competing claims, determining which values or rights are most important to uphold, and assessing the relative weight of the positive and negative consequences of a decision.[86] It focuses on hierarchies of rules and rights, individual rights, self, autonomy, and boundaries between people, and sees people as related hierarchically. It asks "What is just?"[87] The two orientations are not mutually exclusive, and the same person can use both, but people tend to use one over the other.[88]

This small, unpublished study in 1994 found a slight preference among lawyers toward the rights orientation.[89] In this study, 41% of all lawyers preferred a rights orientation, 32% preferred an ethic of care, and 27% were evenly balanced between the two approaches. Fifty percent of male lawyers preferred a rights orientation, whereas 43% of female lawyers preferred the ethic of care.[90] An exclusive focus on the ethic of care was rare (17%) among the male lawyers, but quite common (43%) among women lawyers.

Additional research is needed to explain the inconsistencies in the studies of lawyers' moral development. The studies do not unequivocally demonstrate that lawyers' moral reasoning differs from that of the general population, but there is some evidence, consistent with other studies of lawyers,[91] that the decision-making style of lawyers, particularly that of male lawyers, is significantly more uniform and more focused on logical, objective, rational analysis of rights, duties, and obligations.

Relationship Between Moral Development and Moral Behavior

How much does one's stage of moral development have to do with one's behavior? There is evidence that one's moral decision-making preference does not necessarily correlate with one's behavior in an actual ethical dilemma.

For example, two researchers in 1983[92] found that, although a certain Kohlbergian moral stage predicted one's moral intentions, it predicted actual moral behavior much less reliably, at least among college students. These researchers concluded that moral stage determines one's *intention* to engage in moral conduct, but that other variables (such as ego strength) are important in determining whether those intentions are translated into moral *conduct*.[93] Therefore, attorneys' stage of moral development may not necessarily accurately predict their behavior, particularly if their ego strength is low.

A 1985 study found that lawyers' actual behavior differed from what they said they did. Legal services lawyers' time sheets were compared to the lawyers' perceptions about their work.[94] Attorneys often claimed that they worked hardest on the most interesting cases and that they maintained independence in their work, yet their time sheets revealed that they worked constantly on cases that were "up against deadlines," indicating that they had less control over their work than they believed.[95]

Similarly, a 1978 source cited a study finding that civil commitment lawyers' descriptions of their lawyering style often did not match their actual behavior.[96] Civil commitment lawyers (i.e., lawyers who represent individuals who have been recommended for involuntary psychiatric hospitalization) described themselves as either "adversary" lawyers (actively opposing hospitalization) or "best interest" lawyers (allowing hospitalization to occur if it appeared to be in the client's best interests).[97] However, subsequent observation of these lawyers' civil commitment hearings revealed that the overwhelming majority of them functioned as best-interest lawyers in practice.[98] These studies suggest that attorneys' actual behavior may not match moral intentions, moral decision-making stage, or moral orientation.

Finally, attorneys' ethical decision making appears to be different than ethical decision making by mental health professionals.[99] Research has revealed that, when faced with hypothetical ethical dilemmas, what psychologists and other mental health professionals say they *should* do is consistently more ethical or requires more direct action than what they say they *would* do. Their intended behavior does not live up to their internal standards. Also, their more ethical choices are more often based on codified reasons, such as laws or ethic codes, suggesting that they see laws and ethics codes as setting a higher standard than their own personal values.

Similar research with attorneys yielded dramatically different results. First, what lawyers said they should or would do, and why, varied on a case-by-case basis, according to the particular situation presented. Second, lawyers often said they would do "more" than they should. Third, they appeared to see laws and ethics codes as a minimum for acceptable behavior, rather than as an ideal or maximum.[100]

ATTRIBUTES ASSOCIATED WITH EFFECTIVENESS AS A LAWYER

More time spent on cases and a more active attorney role may be associated with effective advocacy. A 1985 study looked at effectiveness among attorneys representing children in protection proceedings. Those attorneys whose involvement produced a beneficial effect differed from the rest in that they: (a) spent more time on their cases; and (b) displayed more independence in their role as the child's advocate.[101]

Finally, nonlawyers tend to think that aggression and gender in part determine one's effectiveness as a lawyer. A 1996 study found that undergraduate students were more likely to acquit a defendant in a criminal assault and robbery case when the defense counsel was either aggressive or was male.[102]

SUMMARY OF THE LAWYER ATTRIBUTES

In summary, lawyers are more competitive than people in other occupations. Lawyers are more often motivated by a need for achievement, which includes a need to compete against an internal or external standard of excellence (and thus can include the trait of competitiveness). Their goals and bases for evaluating settlement offers reflect a materialistic bent. They tend to display a disproportionate preference for the personality dimensions of introversion, intuition, thinking, and judging on the Myers–Briggs Type Indicator and tend to be more like each other in personality type than is

EXHIBIT 2.1
How Lawyers Differ From the General Population

As lawyers

Need for achievement

Extroversion and sociability
Competitiveness, masculinity, argumentativeness, aggression, dominance, cold
and quarrelsome, and less warm and agreeable

Low interest in people, emotional concerns, and interpersonal matters
Disproportionate preference for "Thinking" vs. "Feeling" on the Myers–Briggs Type
Indicator
Conventional, rules/rights-based morality

Materialism
Focus on economic bottom-line

Higher incidence of psychological distress and substance abuse

the general population. Women lawyers (in the literature to date) have been more achievement-oriented, masculine, competitive, and aggressive than other women professionals and laypersons.

There is evidence that lawyers' stage of moral development and decision-making styles are consistently and disproportionately focused on maintaining rules, regulations, social order, and conformity; however, there is also evidence that their stage of moral development does not differ from the moral development of other similarly educated adults. Some studies suggest that lawyers' moral reasoning differs depending on the situation presented. The proper measurement of moral development is the subject of current controversy, and gender differences in moral development also tend to confound results.

I created and began using the chart given in Exhibit 2.1 in an attempt to describe the lawyer personality. To me, the research conceptually coalesced into two groups of five traits: (a) a drive to achieve, evidenced by an achievement orientation; (b) dominance, aggression, competitiveness, and masculinity; (c) emphasis on rights and obligations over emotions, interpersonal harmony, and relationships; (d) materialistic, pragmatic values over altruistic goals; and (e) higher than normal psychological distress (which will be discussed in greater detail in chapter 5).

At last! There was a definable lawyer personality. Admittedly, the research is scanty, spotty, and at times conflicting. These generalizations may be much broader than any of the individual studies' conclusions. However, unlike other commentary on the profession, these generalizations do have some empirical basis.

In addition, the portrait of the typical lawyer seems to resonate with most lawyers and be useful. Many of the lawyers, law professors, and law students who hear this information say, "Yes, that describes me." Those who do not relate to the lawyer personality usually say, "No, I'm not like that but I've always felt odd, different, or set apart in the law and have often wondered what I am doing here." The information is usually helpful to listeners. By allowing them to identify themselves as a typical or atypical lawyer, it often sheds light on their place within the legal profession.

The next question that emerges is whether lawyers have the lawyer personality before coming to law school or whether law school itself instills and inculcates these attributes. In other words, do naturally aggressive, dominant, competitive individuals self-select into law school, or does the "paper chase"[103] experience, combined with law practice, engender these traits? The next chapter explores the roots of the lawyer personality.

NOTES

1. Most of the research on law students before 1980 involved predominantly male research participants. Gender differences begin to appear in the post-1970s studies. About 80% of women lawyers entered the profession since 1970, and the percentage of women in the law has risen from 3% in 1960 and 1971 to 23% in 1995. A.B.A. COMMISSION ON WOMEN IN THE PROFESSION, BASIC FACTS FROM WOMEN IN THE LAW: A LOOK AT THE NUMBERS 1 (Dec., 1995). The pre-1980s studies of law student attributes are still relevant today, because those law students have become the current population of senior, experienced attorneys in the United States. The attributes of those students are likely to be representative of these senior attorneys.

2. Darrin R. Lehman et al., *The Focus of Judgment Effect: A Question of Wording Effect Due to Hypothesis Confirmation Bias*, 18 PERSONALITY & SOC. PSYCHOL. BULL. 690, 695 (1992); Heather M. McLean & Rudolf Kalin, *Congruence Between Self-Image and Occupational Stereotypes in Students Entering Gender-Dominated Occupations*, 26 CAN. J. BEHAV. SCI. 142, 148–149 (1994). Re: competitiveness, see also John M. Houston et al., *Assessing Competitiveness: A Validation Study of the Competitiveness Index*, 13 PERSONALITY & INDIVIDUAL DIFFERENCES 1153 (1992).

3. John M. Houston et al., *Assessing Competitivness: A Validation Study of the Competitiveness Index*, 13 PERSONALITY AND INDIVIDUAL DIFFERENCES 1153, 1155 (1992).

4. Sue Winkle Williams & John C. McCullers, *Personal Factors Related to Typicalness of Career and Succession in Active Professional Women*, 7 PSYCHOL. WOMEN Q. 343, 350 (1983).

5. James M. Dabbs, Elizabeth Carriere Alford, & Julie A. Fielden, *Trial Lawyers and Testosterone: Blue-Collar Talent in a White-Collar World*, 28 J. APPLIED SOCIAL PSYCHOL. 84, 87–88 (1998), citing G. L. Schindler, Testosterone Concentration, Personality Patterns, and Occupational Choice in Women (1979)

(Dissertation Abstracts International, 40, 1411A University Microfilms No. 79-19403).

6. Dabbs et al., *supra* note 5, at 87–88.

7. *Id.*

8. *Id.*

9. Peter W. Hahn & Susan D. Clayton, *The Effects of Attorney Presentation Style, Attorney Gender, and Juror Gender on Juror Decisions*, 20 LAW & HUM. BEHAV. 533 (1996).

10. Leonard H. Chusmir, *Law and Jurisprudence Occupations: A Look at Motivational Need Patterns*, COM. L. J. May 1984, at 231–35.

11. *Id.* at 232, *citing* DAVID G. WINTER, THE POWER MOTIVE (New York: Free Press, 1973).

12. Notable exceptions are criminal lawyers, law librarians, and judges, who are motivated by a need for power rather than achievement. Chusmir, *supra* note 10, at 233–234.

13. Also, Chusmir theorized that because attorneys and judges have different needs, it is likely that happy judges were unhappy as attorneys. *Id.* at 234. Attorneys' jobs would require high needs for achievement to be satisfied; judges' duties would require high needs for power. This study determined which needs are associated with different legal positions by analyzing the duties performed by each position, rather than by surveying legal personnel and asking them about their perceptions of their own motivations.

14. *Id.* at 235. Finally, he noted that effective training is available to change people's "need profile" should lawyers or judges find themselves in jobs that they find unfulfilling.

15. Russell Korobkin & Chris Guthrie, *Psychology, Economics, and Settlement: A New Look at the Role of the Lawyer*, 76 TEX. L. REV. 77 (Nov. 1997).

16. Admittedly, because of high educational and socioeconomic levels, the participants of this study might not be representative of lawyers or litigants as a whole, and slightly less than a third of the attorneys approached agreed to participate, but the findings were still illuminating and consistent with studies suggesting materialism among law students. See *id.*

17. Korobkin & Guthrie, *supra* note 15.

18. *Id.* at 87.

19. ROBERT M. BASTRESS & JOSEPH D. HARBAUGH, INTERVIEWING, COUNSELING, AND NEGOTIATING: SKILLS FOR EFFECTIVE REPRESENTATION (Aspen Law & Business, 1990).

20. Tom R. Tyler, *The Psychological Consequences of Judicial Procedures: Implications for Civil Commitment Hearings*, in DAVID B. WEXLER & BRUCE J. WINICK, EDS., LAW IN A THERAPEUTIC KEY: DEVELOPMENTS IN THERAPEUTIC JURISPRUDENCE, 3–15 (Carolina Academic Press, 1996).

21. Jean R. Sternlight, *Lawyers' Representation of Clients in Mediation: Using Economics and Psychology to Structure Advocacy in a Nonadversarial System*, 14 OHIO ST. J. ON DISP. RESOL. 269, 321–331 (1999) and Korobkin & Guthrie, *supra* note 15, at 140.

22. Don S. Anderson et al., *Conservatism in Recruits to the Professions*, 9 Austl. & N.Z. J. Soc. 42 (1973)

23. *Id.* at 45. The study investigated motivations among students, how their attitudes changed and became more profession-centered and elitist during their training, and then how their attitudes changed in the first few years of professional practice, as the result of taking up a professional role. Their results from the first few years of practice were admittedly preliminary, because they only examined the first three years of professional work. *Id.* at 45. It is interesting to note how, in engineering, law, and medicine, the students' attitudes during training shifted toward a position "in which the profession and the autonomy of the individual practitioner become of central importance." *Id.* at 44.

24. Howard S. Erlanger, Charles R. Epp, Mia Cahill, & Kathleen M. Haines, *Law Student Idealism and Job Choice: Some New Data on an Old Question*, 30 Law & Soc'y Rev. 851, 853 (1996).

25. The job categories were defined as nontraditional, governmental–educational, other salaried position, solo practice, small firm, large firm. *Id.*

26. *Id.* at 851–865, 852–855 (1996) (reporting on data collected in 1985).

27. *Id.* at 858–859.

28. "Striving for Happiness," A.B.A. J., July 1995, at 41 (reporting results of a Bar Association survey of 1,975 lawyers in the St. Louis area).

29. *Id.* Other goals were to make a substantial income, serve the client, have control over work life, be respected, and be intellectually challenged.

30. *See supra* note 1.

31. Williams & McCullers, *supra* note 4, at 350–351.

32. *Id.* at 350. Women lawyers and doctors both scored higher on intellectual ability than women in more traditionally "feminine" jobs. *Id.* at 349. Masculinity was assessed by the Bem Sex-Role Inventory, S. Bem, *The Difference of Sexes Based on Self-Perception*, 8 Sex Roles 27 (1978) and the authors seem to link masculinity on this instrument with competitiveness and aggression. *Id.* at 347, 354. Although greater masculinity (i.e., aggressiveness and competitiveness) does distinguish women lawyers from women doctors, both groups were more masculine than women in more typical occupations. *Id.* at 354.

33. Williams & McCullers, *supra* note 4.

34. However, they may distinguish women in nontraditional careers (medicine, law) from women in more typical occupations (secretary, medical assistant). Williams & McCullers, *supra* note 4, at 351–354.

35. The authors concluded that a high level of intellectual ability is necessary to become a doctor or lawyer, but which career one chooses depends on "factors other than intelligence." *Id.*

36. Lawrence R. Richard, Psychological Type and Job Satisfaction Among Practicing Lawyers in the United States (1994) (unpublished PhD dissertation, Temple University).

37. Charlotte Chiu, *Do Professional Women Have Lower Job Satisfaction Than Professional Men? Lawyers as a Case Study*, 38 Sex Roles 521, 521–537, 530–531 (1998).

38. Connie J. A. Beck, Bruce D. Sales, & G. Andrew H. Benjamin, *Lawyer Distress: Alcohol Related Concerns Among a Sample of Practicing Lawyers*, 10 J. L. & HEALTH 1, 18 (1995–1996).

39. Bryna Bogoch, *Gendered Lawyering: Difference and Dominance in Lawyer–Client Interaction*, 31 LAW & SOC'Y REV. 677, 700–703 (1997).

40. *Id.*

41. *See* Paul Van R. Miller, *Personality Differences and Student Survival in Law School*, 19 J. LEGAL EDUC. 460 (1967); Frank L. Natter, *The Human Factor: Psychological Type in Legal Education*, 3 RES. PSYCHOL. TYPE 55 (1981); Vernellia R. Randall, *The Myers–Briggs Type Indicator, First Year Law Studies and Performance*, 26 CUMB. L. REV. 63, 80–81, 86–87, 91–92, 96–97 (1995–1996); and Richard, *supra* note 36.

42. *See* Richard, *supra* note 36, and SUSAN J. BELL & LAWRENCE R. RICHARD, DO YOU REALLY WANT TO BE A LAWYER? 152 (2d ed., Peterson's Guides 1992) [hereinafter BELL & RICHARD] for a description of thinking versus feeling on the Myers–Briggs Type Indicator.

43. Judith White & Chris Manolis, *Individual Differences in Ethical Reasoning Among Law Students*, 25 SOC. BEHAV. & PERSONALITY 19, 23 (1997).

44. *See generally* Richard, *supra* note 36, BELL & RICHARD, *supra* note 42, OTTO KROEGER & JANET THUESEN, TYPE TALK AT WORK (1992), and DAVID J. KEIRSEY, PLEASE UNDERSTAND ME II (Prometheus Nemesis Book Co., 1998).

45. Larry Richard, *How Your Personality Affects Your Practice—The Lawyer Types*, A.B.A. J., July 1993, 74, 75.

46. BELL & RICHARD, *supra* note 42, and KROEGER & THUESEN, *supra* note 44.

47. *See generally* Don Peters, *Forever Jung: Psychological Type Theory, The Myers–Briggs Type Indicator and Learning Negotiation*, 42 DRAKE L. REV. 1 (1993), and Don Peters & Martha Peters, *Maybe That's Why I Do What I Do: Psychological Type Theory, The Myers–Briggs Type Indicator, and Learning Legal Interviewing*, 35 N.Y.L. SCH. L. REV. 169 (1990).

48. This was done by psychologist and lawyer Larry Richard in the early 1990s and reported in 1994. Richard, *supra* note 36.

49. *Id.* at 29 & at 232, *citing* S. K. HIRSH & J. M. KUMMEROW, INTRODUCTION TO TYPE IN ORGANIZATIONAL SETTINGS (1987).

50. *Id.* at 233.

51. BELL & RICHARD, *supra* note 42, at 152. Richard also noted that the thinking–feeling scale is the most significant personality trait for predicting lawyer satisfaction, stating, "Those [lawyers] with a preference for Feeling are swimming against the tide." *Id.* at 153.

52. Richard, *supra* note 36. His results were published in summary form in Lawrence R. Richard, *How Personality Affects Your Practice*, A.B.A. J., July 1993, at 74.

53. Paul Van R. Miller, The Contribution of Non-Cognitive Variables to the Prediction of Student Performance in Law School (1965) (unpublished PhD dissertation, University of Pennsylvania) (on file with University Microfilms No. 66-4630) and cited by Richard, *supra* note 36 (bibliography).

54. Richard, *supra* note 36; *see also* Natter, *supra* note 41, and Randall, *supra* note 41.

55. Most of the studies done in the 1960s and 1970s excluded women from the population sampled, either because there were no women in the sample or the number was so small that they were excluded to factor out any gender influences. The 1990s studies, however, do include a reasonable proportion of women law students and lawyers. The Myers–Briggs findings did not change appreciably when women were included in the sample, even though more women in the general adult population can be classified into the feeling type (60%) rather than the thinking type (40%). In contrast, 45% of women lawyers are feelers, whereas 55% are thinkers. Debra C. Moss, *Lawyer Personality: Logical Problem Solvers Happiest, Consultant Claims*, A.B.A. J., Feb. 1991, at 34 (reporting statistics from Lawrence Richard's Philadelphia-based company, Lawgistics). Three studies of lawyers, in 1986, 1989, and 1994, respectively, found that 65–77% of lawyers preferred thinking to feeling; Richard, *supra* note 36, a study cited by Richard conducted by MacDaid in 1986, and Eric Y. Drogin, Psychological Type: Implications for Consultation to the Legal Profession (unpublished PhD dissertation, Hahnemann University, 1989) (on file with the author). The results of these three studies on lawyers and the MBTI are consistent. The 1986 and 1989 studies only surveyed 271 and 483 attorneys, respectively, and the 1994 study deserves much more attention because it administered the test to a nationwide sample of 1,220 attorneys (reflecting a 40% response rate). Notably, the first two studies used the same databank, a vast array of Myers–Briggs test scores collected from 1971 to 1984 and maintained by the Center for the Application of Psychological Type Myers–Briggs Type Indicator Data Bank in Gainesville, Florida. The third, larger study administered the MBTI in 1992 to 3,014 participants randomly drawn from the American Bar Association membership list.

56. Larry Richard, *How Your Personality Affects Your Practice—The Lawyer Types*, A.B.A. J., July 1993, at 74.

57. According to Richard: (a) about 75% of the adults in the United States prefer extraversion, whereas 57% of lawyers prefer introversion; (b) about 70% of the United States population prefer sensing, whereas 57% of lawyers prefer intuiting; (c) about 60% of all men and 35% of women in the United States prefer thinking, whereas 81% of male lawyers and 66% of female lawyers prefer thinking; and (d) about 55% of the U.S. population prefer judging, whereas 63% of lawyers prefer judging. Richard, *supra* note 56, at 74. Introversion and intuiting preferences are relatively stable across one's lifetime, suggesting that these characteristics are preexisting before law school. Personal communication with Larry Richard, August 24, 1995.

58. Richard, *supra* note 36, at 238, tab. 92; Drogin, *supra* note 55, at 104.

59. Taken from the title of John Gray's popular book, MEN ARE FROM MARS, WOMEN ARE FROM VENUS (HarperCollins, 1992).

60. Richard, *supra* note 36, at 232.

61. KROEGER & THUESEN, *supra* note 44, at 396.

62. DAVID KEIRSEY, PLEASE UNDERSTAND ME II, at 20 and 31 (Prometheus Nemesis Book 1998).

63. Drogin, *supra* note 55, at 113.

64. *Id.* at 117, citing ISABEL MYERS, GIFTS DIFFERING (Palo Alto, CA: Consulting Psychologists Press, 1980), at 6.

65. DAVID KEIRSEY, PLEASE UNDERSTAND ME II 20, 31 (Prometheus Nemesis Book 1998), attributing these adjectives to Isabel Myers, one of the creators of the Myers–Briggs Type Indicator test.

66. KROEGER & THUESEN, *supra* note 44, at 207.

67. Lawrence J. Landwehr, *Lawyers as Social Progressives or Reactionaries: The Law and Order Cognitive Orientation of Lawyers*, 7 LAW & PSYCHOL. REV. 39 (1982).

68. LAWRENCE KOHLBERG, THE PSYCHOLOGY OF MORAL DEVELOPMENT 7, 7–19, 621–639 (1984) [hereinafter KOHLBERG].

69. Landwehr, *supra* note 67, at 43 n.7. The response rate was 21%.

70. *Id.* at 44.

71. For example, a 1989 study found that 61% of university graduates (they were secondary schoolteachers) operated at stage 4, whereas 39% operated at stage 5; Diomedes Markoulis, *Postformal and Postconventional Reasoning in Educationally Advanced Adults*, 150 J. GENETIC PSYCHOL. 427 (1989). In a 1980 longitudinal study of undergraduates (all but one of whom received postgraduate degrees), approximately 65% were at stage 4 and approximately 35% were predominantly at stage 5; John M. Murphy & Carol Gilligan, *Moral Development in Late Adolescence and Adulthood*, 23 HUM. DEV. 77 (1980).

72. KOHLBERG, *supra* note 68, at 175, and Landwehr, *supra* note 67, at 40 n.2, *citing* Lawrence Kohlberg, *The Cognitive–Developmental Approach to Moral Education*, in READINGS IN MORAL EDUCATION 50–51 (P. Scharf ed. 1978) [hereinafter *Cognitive*].

73. This may also explain why laypersons are critical of lawyers, if lawyers and the general population approach moral dilemmas as differently as Landwehr's and Richard's data suggest.

74. *See* Randall, *supra* note 41, at 63; Richard, *supra* note 36; Natter, *supra* note 41; Miller, *supra* note 41. It is also consistent with the "rights orientation"; *see* Sandra Janoff, *The Influence of Legal Education on Moral Reasoning*, 76 MINN. L. REV. 193 (1991).

75. Landwehr, *supra* note 67, at 40 n.2, *citing Cognitive*, *supra* note 70.

76. KOHLBERG, *supra* note 68, at 175.

77. Landwehr, *supra* note 67, at 40 n.2, *citing Cognitive*, *supra* note 72.

78. Susan Daicoff, *(Oxymoron?) Ethical Decisionmaking by Attorneys: An Empirical Study*, 48 FLA. L. REV. 197 (1996).

79. CAROL GILLIGAN ET AL., *Contributions of Women's Elimination of Sex Bias in Moral Development Theory and Research*, Final Report to National Institute of Education (1982), cited in LAWRENCE KOHLBERG, THE PSYCHOLOGY OF MORAL DEVELOPMENT: ESSAYS IN MORAL DEVELOPMENT (VOL. II) (1984).

80. *Id.*

81. *Id.*

82. *Id.* at 338–361.

83. White & Manolis, *supra* note 43, at 33 (1997), *citing* Carol Gilligan, *Moral Orientation and Moral Development* in E. F. KITTAY & D. T. MEYERS (EDS.), WOMEN AND MORAL THEORY (Rowman & Littlefield, 1987).

84. Janoff, *supra* note 74, at 219–222.

85. *Id.*

86. *Id.* at 223–225.

87. *Id. See also* White & Manolis, *supra* note 43, at 27–30 (1997).

88. Janoff, *supra* note 74, at 231.

89. Erica Weissman, unpublished PhD dissertation, Yeshiva University, 1994. It surveyed only a small number of attorneys in New York who were personally known to the researcher.

90. *Id.* at 76 (1994). Fifty percent of male lawyers versus 35% of female lawyers were rights-oriented. Only 17% of male lawyers compared to 43% of female lawyers preferred the care orientation. Thirty-three percent of male lawyers and 22% of female lawyers were evenly balanced between the two orientations. *Id.* at 76.

91. *See, e.g.,* Randall, *supra* note 41; Richard, *supra* note 36; Miller, *supra* note 41; and Natter, *supra* note 41.

92. Richard N. Tsujimoto & Kathy A. Emmons, *Predicting Moral Conduct: Kohlberg's and Hogan's Theories,* 115 J. PSYCHOL. 241 (1983).

93. *Id.* at 243–244. This study investigated college students' moral stages, moral intentions, and actions, and found that they did not always do what they said they were going to do. Specifically, these researchers assessed the Kohlbergian moral stage of college students using Rest's DIT (*id.* at 242, citing J. R. Rest, *New Approaches in the Assessment of Moral Judgment.* In T. LICKONA (ED.), MORAL DEVELOPMENT AND BEHAVIOR (1976)) and also assessed the students based on another theory, Hogan's theory of moral development. *Id., citing* R. Hogan, *Moral Conduct and Moral Character: A Psychological Perspective,* 79 PSYCHOL. BULL. 217 (1973). Then they asked the students to volunteer to stuff envelopes for a charity and assessed moral behavior by whether or not the students who volunteered actually showed up for the envelope-stuffing. They found that Kohlberg's stage 5A (and Hogan's autonomy dimension) correlated positively and significantly with showing up, and that combining Kohlberg's and Hogan's measures predicted showing up better than did either theory alone. However, they also interpreted their findings as supporting Krebs's and Kohlberg's claim that "moral judgment stage is the major determinant of the intention to engage in moral conduct," but that "ego strength variables are important determinants of whether or not the intentions are actually translated into moral actions." Tsujimoto & Emmons, *supra* note 92, at 243, *citing* R. Krebs & L. Kohlberg, Moral Judgment and Ego Controls as Determinants of Resistance to Cheating (unpublished manuscript, Harvard University 1973). *See also* Leonard J. Haas, John L. Malouf, & Neal H. Mayerson, *Personal and Professional Characteristics as Factors in Psychologists' Ethical Decision Making,* 19 PROF. PSYCHOL. RES. & PRAC. 35, 39 (1988), *citing* A. Blasi, *Bridging Moral Cognition and Moral Action: A Critical Review of the*

Literature, 88 PSYCHOL. BULL. 1 (1980) (as noting the "nonequivalence of moral reasoning and moral behavior" on logical and empirical grounds).

94. Robert G. Meadow & Carrie Menkel-Meadow, *Personalized or Bureaucratized Justice in Legal Services: Resolving Sociological Ambivalence in the Delivery of Legal Aid for the Poor*, 9 LAW & HUM. BEHAV. 397 (1985). Legal services attorneys' perceptions about their autonomy from rules and regulations and their approach to lawyering were compared to the time sheets that recorded their daily tasks. How the lawyers described their approach to cases differed from the lawyering tasks they reported performing daily, suggesting that what lawyers think they do and what they actually do are not the same.

95. *Id.* at 407–408. They concluded that legal services attorneys do have some measure of autonomy, although it may not be over the types of tasks they think they have control over. Instead, it may reside "in the highly personalized ways in which attorneys deliver their services." *Id.* at 411. They say it "resides not so much in what they perform or who their clients are, but how they choose to perform" their tasks. Apparently, bureaucratic pressures and clients' demands played a large role in determining what the lawyers actually do. *Id.* at 409–410.

96. Lawrence P. Galie, *An Essay on the Civil Commitment Lawyer: Or How I Learned to Hate the Adversary System*, 6 J. PSYCHIATRY & L. 71, 78 (1978), *citing* a "forthcoming" 1978 publication by the University of Pittsburgh Law Review in volume 40. However, the cited study does not appear to have been published in volumes 39, 40, or 41 of such law review.

97. *Id.* at 78.

98. *Id.*

99. J. L. Bernard & Carmen S. Jara, *The Failure of Clinical Psychology Graduate Students to Apply Understood Ethical Principles*, 17 PROF. PSYCHOL. RES. & PRAC. 313 (1986); J. L. Bernard, Michael Murphy, & Marsha Little, *The Failure of Clinical Psychologists to Apply Understood Ethical Principles*, 18 PROF. PSYCHOL. RES. & PRAC. 489 (1987); Margaret A. Wilkins, John M. McGuire, David W. Abbott, et al., *Willingness to Apply Understood Ethical Principles*, 46 J. CLINICAL PSYCHOL. 539 (1990); Todd S. Smith, John M. McGuire, David W. Abbott, & Burton I. Blau, *Clinical Ethical Decision Making: An Investigation of the Rationales Used to Justify Doing Less Than One Believes One Should*, 22 PROF. PSYCHOL. RES. & PRAC. 235 (1991).

100. Daicoff, *supra* note 78.

101. Robert F. Kelly & Sarah H. Ramsey, *The Legal Representation of Children in Protection Proceedings: Some Empirical Finding and a Reflection on Public Policy*, 34 FAM. REL. 277, 282 (1985). Disappointingly, most of the attorneys appointed to represent the children had no beneficial effect on the outcome of the proceedings, according to the researchers. *Id.*

102. Peter W. Hahn & Susan D. Clayton, *The Effects of Attorney Presentation Style, Attorney Gender, and Juror Gender on Juror Decisions*, 20 LAW & HUM. BEHAV. 533 (1996).

103. THE PAPER CHASE (Twentieth Century Fox, 1973).

3

PRECURSORS TO THE LAWYER PERSONALITY

People who choose the law have some unique characteristics as children and as students. Many of their early characteristics foreshadow some of the lawyer attributes discussed in the second chapter of this book, suggesting that the lawyer personality develops long before the first day of law school. People with "lawyer attributes" appear to self-select into the law, perhaps attracted by the fit between their traits and the profession. This chapter explores studies establishing the profile of the prelaw individual.

THE LAWYER AS A CHILD: EARLY CHILDHOOD EXPERIENCES

Certain early memories and experiences distinguish law students from others. For example, the family background experiences of law students surveyed in 1960 differed significantly from that of dentists and social workers. Authoritarian male dominance, self-discipline, school achievement, reading, and activity were emphasized in law students' early childhood experiences, whereas emotions and concern for others' feelings were deemphasized.[1] These experiences may have been the seeds for lawyers' thinking preference, interest in dominance, and achievement orientations.

Portions of this chapter were adapted from an article by the author titled *Asking Leopards to Change Their Spots: Should Lawyers Change? A Critique of Solutions to Problems With Professionalism by Reference to Empirically-Derived Attorney Personality Attributes*, XI GEO. J. L. ETHICS 3 (1998). The author reserved the right to adapt and publish the material.

The author of this 1960 study expected lawyers' early childhood experiences to contain "the prominence of verbal aggression," a "concern with human justice," and "the exercise of privileged curiosity into the lives of others," but her results did not show this.[2] Parental emphasis on school achievement and pleasurable early school experiences were more frequently reported by law students.[3] Reading was important to and pleasantly remembered by the law students.[4] Law students more frequently remembered being read to and hearing stories as a child as pleasurable memories.[5] Finally, concern for emotional suffering and for the feelings of others were less emphasized in law students' families.[6]

A 1984 study found that the earliest memories of law students were significantly different from those of dental or clinical psychology students.[7] In particular, the law students' earliest childhood memories contained more nonfamily members and mentioned school as a setting more frequently, suggesting that school and people outside the family were more important to law students. In addition, the law students' memories contained more active than passive components, meaning situations in which the student decided to do something rather than react to decisions or actions of others.[8] From these results, the authors concluded that law students take more initiative in pursuing goals. This emphasis on active behavior, coupled with a school setting, is consistent with lawyers' primary need for achievement.[9] Also, because the law students (and dental students) less often reported fear or anxiety in their early recollections, the authors concluded that they "might be expected to see life in less emotional terms" compared to psychology students.[10] Even at an early age, lawyers may be geared toward dominance and achievement and away from emotions and others' suffering.[11]

Alfred Adler, a noted psychiatrist, believed that the early recollections and early childhood experiences of individuals explained their vocational choices. Specifically, he thought that people chose their jobs in an effort to master or conquer early feelings of discomfort resulting from uncomfortable early experiences.[12] For example, Adler claims he became a physician to compensate for and overcome feelings of inferiority and powerlessness stemming from his bad experiences with a medical problem as a small child.

One empirical study of female attorneys in the early 1980s supports Adler's ideas. Compared to female doctors, secretaries, and medical assistants, female attorneys had unhappier adolescences.[13] Adler might say that these women consciously or unconsciously chose law in an effort to overcome the pain they experienced as teenagers by becoming someone associated with dominance, competence, intelligence, status, and power. It is not known if this is true for these women only or for lawyers in general.

Very few studies have assessed prelaw college students or entering law students.[14] The scanty evidence that exists confirms a bent toward dominance and leadership and an aversion to being subordinate or feeling inferior.[15] Prelaw students typically also come from elite backgrounds, although this may be changing as the racial, ethnic, and gender makeup of the lawyer population diversifies.[16]

Demographic Attributes

In 1973, law students did not mirror the socioeconomic, racial, or religious makeup of the society from which they came; instead, they came from an elite background with a higher socioeconomic status than the general population.[17] They were more intellectually elite and more liberal in their political views than most people. More often, they were social scientists as college students.[18] This elite status may help explain lawyers' apparently materialistic focus. The stereotype of the well-heeled lawyer buzzing around in a BMW with a cell phone and personal assistant may represent everyday life for someone who grew up in a higher socioeconomic status than most. If one has enjoyed a privileged social status, one may simply be accustomed to it and therefore motivated to maintain it. However, the demographic makeup of law students is likely to have changed in the past 30 years because of the increasing diversity in the law student population after 1970. For example, the percentage of women in the law rose from 3% in 1960 and 1971 to 23% in 1995; law schools currently report that about half of the students are women.[19]

Psychological Needs

In 1971 the psychological needs of prelaw students were quite distinctive and differed significantly from the needs of engineering and premedical students. Prelaw students had definite needs to be leaders, to attract attention, and to avoid feeling inferior or taking subordinate roles.[20] Prelaw students scored highest on self-confidence, dominance, and exhibition scales, and scored lowest on abasement and deference scales of a standard psychological test.[21]

Perhaps even before law school, lawyers want to be dominant leaders. Perhaps we avoid situations where we would have to defer to others, consistent with the stereotype of lawyers as outgoing, confident, even arrogant and egotistical. This 1971 study suggests that these traits are not caused solely by law school or the practice of law; they are present before either experience. Perhaps lawyers are just hard-wired to lead, take charge, and take control.

Motives for Choosing Law

Law students' and lawyers' reasons for entering law are relevant because they indicate our values, goals, priorities, and ideals. Gender differences in these areas complicate the discussion; these gender differences began to appear after about 1970, when women entered the profession in greater numbers.[22]

"Uncertain"—Didn't Know What Else to Do

Law school has been called a residual graduate school. When I was attending a large state university in the late 1970s, almost every freshman was "premed." Once a big percentage flunked or bombed out in chemistry, those students became "prelaw." If the "prelaw" students' grades dropped, they turned into business majors. That was the informal hierarchy at this school, and it was well-known. At the time, I believed that prelaw was the default if you could not get into medical school; if you could not get into law school, your education was probably going to end with the bachelor's degree. It has been said that students often come to law school because they do not know what else to do. They have no particular vocational interests or goals other than further education,[23] and law preserves their options. Because a law degree can be used in business, government, and other positions, it does not pin one down vocationally, but it is a good bet for a prestigious, lucrative career. Law has been seen as a perfect career for the uncommitted, particularly for the well-to-do. This attitude can be summarized as: "I don't know what else to do, I need to maintain my current socioeconomic status, and I need to do *something* respectable." Also, because law requires no specialized preparation, the decision to go to law school can be and often is made at the last minute. One can almost painlessly "throw in" a few law school applications along with one's graduate school applications and job applications after college graduation.

Studies of law students' motives for going to law school support this uncertainty theory, particularly for the well-to-do—about 23% to more than half of law students consistently reported "uncertain career goals" as important to their decision to enter law school.[24] This uncertainty was more strongly associated with those in the highest income brackets.[25]

In addition, a 1968 study indicated that the Law School Admissions Test (LSAT), which is designed to predict academic achievement in law school and is almost universally used as an admission criterion to law school, was no more effective than any other comprehensive test of general achieve-

ment in predicting success in law school. This means that generic achievement ability is more relevant to success in law school than any particular
aptitude for law. Those who entered law school for no particular reason
could unwittingly excel at it, just because they are smart[26] and thus are
unlikely to be weeded out of law school for academic reasons. This uncertainty or lack of strong motivation for law may contribute to dissatisfied,
distressed, or simply unenthusiastic practicing lawyers. It may also result in
unprincipled or unethical lawyer behavior (because of a lack of clear values).

As a side note, all of these "uncertainty" studies date from the 1950s,
1960s, and early 1970s, when men were the vast majority of law students.
Toward the end of this period, young men were going to law school to
avoid the draft and thus many were understandably uncertain about their
career plans. Even so, the disturbing number of "uncertain" law students
supports my personal experience in college and the idea that law school is,
for some, a residual graduate school. Finally, however, despite uncertain
reasons for entering law, law students may have an aptitude for it, based
on one study of standardized vocational test results from 1976.[27]

Interest in Subject Matter, Altruism, and Materialism

Law students consistently report three top reasons for going to law
school: a desire for professional training—cited as "greatly important" to
an average of 54% of the students; an interest in the subject matter—greatly
important to 59% on average; and a desire for intellectual stimulation—
greatly important to 44% on average.[28] This was true for the classes of 1960,
1970, and 1972 at eight law schools.[29]

In this study, the desire to make money varied widely in importance,
depending on the law school studied; it was greatly important to 14%[30] to
58%[31] of the law students, with an average of about 32%.[32] The researcher
concluded that "a vast majority of all students surveyed indicated that
'prestige' was of some importance to them,"[33] and about a fourth said it was
of great importance to them in deciding to go to law school.[34] Money also
became more important in the decision to become a lawyer during the
1960s.[35] However, a desire to enter politics, to restructure society, and to
serve the underprivileged also became increasingly more important motives
for entering law, from 1960 to 1972, probably reflecting the effects of the
civil rights movement and the Vietnam War. Yet, overall, the desire to
serve the underprivileged was greatly important to only 17% of the students
on average, compared to 32% who focused on making money,[36] suggesting
that materialism outstrips altruism when it comes to reasons to choose law.

An Australian study looked at students in law, engineering, medicine,
and teaching in six Australian universities at about the same time as the
previous study was conducted.[37] It found two main reasons that law students

chose the law: professional orientation—consisting of an interest in the subject matter along with a desire to be of service, which the authors labeled intrinsic factors; and status concern—consisting of more extrinsic reasons, such as concern for security, prestige, and wealth.[38] Consistent with the American study, the Australian study found that altruistic concerns were a motivating factor for no more than 20% of entering law students and were less important to law students than to other professional students.[39]

These results were replicated in a 1979 study of Brigham Young University law students.[40] Their top three reasons for going to law school were desire for intellectual stimulation (65%), interest in the subject matter (63%), and desire for professional training (63%). Altruistic concerns were greatly important to 18 to 31%, although again prestige and financial rewards were greatly important to more (28–31%) of the students.[41]

These early studies consistently show that, at least for the predominantly male law student population studied in the 1960s and 1970s, interest in the subject matter of the law, a desire for professional training, and desire for intellectual stimulation were the top three motivators.[42] Money and prestige were also valued (albeit secondarily) and outweighed altruistic concerns.

Gender differences are striking in the area of motives. Most studies (with one exception) find that male law students are consistently more likely than female law students to say that a desire to make money motivated their decision to enter law.[43] Female students are more likely to cite altruistic reasons for becoming a lawyer[44] or desires to restructure society or serve the underprivileged.[45] However, this may be true for women as compared to men in general, not just in law. For example, in one study, status concern was more common for men than women in all professions.[46]

Why is this result so consistently found? Most researchers say that women are socially conditioned to deny a desire to make money—it traditionally has been seen as socially inappropriate for women—whereas men as "breadwinners" are expected to be financially motivated, so it is socially acceptable for men to admit materialistic goals. The gender difference may be simply an artifact of different social norms for men and women. Or female law students may be more altruistic than male law students.[47]

Even if women were more likely than men to go to law school for altruistic reasons, the most satisfied women attorneys are those who went to law school for pragmatic reasons. In 1977, later career satisfaction of women attorneys was associated with going to law school to develop existing talents, fulfill a personal goal, or fulfill realistic, materialistic goals.[48]

Summary of Attributes of Prelaw Students

In summary, law students appear to arrive at law school with a set of preexisting personality traits. They like school and reading. They prefer to initiate action affecting their environment rather than being passive or reactive. They are motivated toward leadership and social skills, even as elementary school children, and are less interested in emotions and the feelings of others. They have greater needs for leadership, dominance, and attention and dislike being subordinate or deferent. Their socioeconomic status is higher than average. They select the field of law primarily because they are interested in the subject matter and they desire intellectual stimulation; however, they also often come to law school for uncertain or materialistic reasons. Money and prestige are secondarily important to them, but they are more important than altruism or public service concerns.

THE LAWYER AS A LAW STUDENT

Law students tend to complain about their peers. They have said, "I am somewhat surprised to find out, although it seems logical to me now, what a really narrow group of people are actually attracted to law school," and "there's very little appreciation of creative intelligence or social intelligence, ability to deal with people and perceive situations really accurately."[49] They complain that their peers are homogeneous, unimaginative, and unexciting and they narrowly conform to a stereotype of intelligence.[50] These thoughts bring to mind a popular lawyer joke that runs: "What do lawyers use for birth control? Their personalities."

Research involving law students is plentiful but hodgepodge. There are about 30 studies dating from the late 1950s to the present. For the most part, the studies do not confirm or build on each other or use the same tests in any consistent fashion. Studies after the mid- to late-1970s should be considered separately from earlier studies, because the number of women and minorities in law school and in the legal profession dramatically changed after 1970.[51] As a result, women and minorities were often absent or intentionally excluded from the studies until the mid-1970s. Therefore, differences between early and later studies may simply reflect the different makeup of the profession. In the sections that follow, the research is presented chronologically, to allow consideration of demographic, social, political, and gender differences in law students over time.

Demographics

According to a study of eight law schools between 1969 and 1971,[52] women made up around 5 to 6% and non-Caucasians represented only about 2% of the student body.[53] These law students came from high socioeconomic, elite backgrounds.[54] If one compared the classes of 1960, 1970, and 1972, there was a trend toward increasing rejection of parents' religious beliefs in favor of atheism and agnosticism[55] and a trend toward homogenization of backgrounds.[56] Although law students in the 1950s were predominantly humanists in their undergraduate study, by the late 1960s they were predominantly social scientists in background.[57] Law students were relatively high academic achievers, because 50% ranked in the top quarter of their undergraduate classes.[58]

Most individuals with college or advanced degrees are more likely to be first-born or only children; this is also true of law students.[59] However, law students in 1983 were less likely than medical students were to be "following in their father's footsteps," meaning less likely to have a father in the same profession.[60] Finally, a 1983 study reported that law students were generally liberal in their political beliefs.[61]

Compared to Medical Students

One 1983 study found that law students were more politically liberal than medical students.[62] Two earlier studies, in 1967 and 1968, made a more comprehensive survey of law student personality.[63] These studies are important because they used one of the best psychological tests available, the Minnesota Multiphasic Personality Inventory (MMPI), a highly respected and widely used personality assessment and screening measure.[64] Many employers, such as police departments and suicide prevention centers, use the MMPI to screen out inappropriate employees. It is designed to distinguish abnormal personality characteristics from normal ones and is widely used in hospital, outpatient, and forensic settings.

Medical and law students differed significantly on the MMPI. Law students were more extroverted and sociable, more free from anxiety and insecurity, more ebullient and at ease in interpersonal relations, "more often accepted what our society considers to be a 'masculine' orientation," more cynical,[65] less humanitarian,[66] and more authoritarian[67] than the medical students. Medical students were more introspective, idealistic, prone to worry, socially perceptive, and "sensitive to the needs of others" and to interpersonal nuances than were the law students.[68] Unfortunately, no comparisons of either group with college students or adults in general were made. Pertinent to the professionalism crisis, law students scored higher than medical students on two scales, which measure, among other things, anger, ambition, high aspirations, amorality, and lack of concern about social and moral standards of conduct.[69]

Cold, Impersonal Attributes

Canadian law students in 1994 saw themselves as less "affiliative" than average, meaning less warm and agreeable and more cold and quarrelsome.

Their perceptions of themselves were even less affiliative than other graduate students' self-perceptions.[70] Also, the law students' perceptions of themselves did not fit the lawyer stereotype.[71] Students in other professions (i.e., engineer, physician, rehabilitation therapist, nurse, and teacher) described themselves in ways that fit better with those professions' stereotypes. Finally, the stereotypes and self-perceptions emerging from this study suggested that law was more like engineering than it was like nursing or teaching,[72] even though nursing, teaching, and law all deal with people and engineering does not. These findings partially explain the charge that lawyers are cold fish. They are also consistent with studies finding that lawyers have low needs to affiliate with others[73] and that our early childhood experiences deemphasize interpersonal concerns.[74]

Authoritarianism and Humanitarianism

Perhaps because *authoritarianism* and *humanitarianism* are used to mean different things, there are conflicting findings in this area. Some studies find law students are more humanitarian and less authoritarian than medical students or undergraduate students, and some find the exact opposite.[75] In general, when authoritarianism was used to mean dogmatism, conservatism, preference for law and order, or right-wing authoritarianism, it was not descriptive of law students. They were more likely to be politically liberal.[76] On the other hand, when authoritarian was used to mean accepting the concept of survival of the fittest, hero worship, rugged individualism, and the absence of humanitarian feeling, then it was more descriptive of law students.[77]

Competitiveness, Aggression, and Dominance

An extensive, multilaw school study in 1973 assessed perceived competitiveness, aggression, and congeniality among law students. First-term students were surveyed. Most of the law students said they expected to find high or moderate levels of aggression and competition among their peers,[78] but said they found as much cooperation and friendliness among their peers as they expected, less competitiveness than they expected, and less aggression than they expected.[79] However, the law students consistently mentioned that competitiveness still existed, although it may have been more subtle or taken the form of a self-induced, internal competitiveness rather than one resulting from peer pressure.[80]

Law students also viewed aggression as a favorable trait, seeing it as being "on the offensive" or "ambitious over the long run."[81] This is consistent with the stereotype of law students as competitive and aggressive; however, it does not indicate that they actually are more competitive or aggressive than others. A study conducted in 1983 suggested that they are.

In this assessment of a program designed to reduce stress in law students, the research measured competitiveness by scores on the Hard Driving scale of a psychological test.[82] The researchers claimed that as a result of the program, "students increased their knowledge and were able to use their knowledge effectively in their personal lives while retaining their competitive approach to life"; their scores on this scale were unchanged by the program.[83]

Consistent with the 1971 finding that prelaw students were more interested in dominance than other college students,[84] a 1978 study found that women law students described themselves as significantly more autonomous, aggressive, confident, and "internally motivated to succeed in pursuits of socially recognized significance" than did female undergraduate students.[85] These women law students saw themselves as having greater needs for achievement, dominance, autonomy, and aggression and with lower needs for nurturance, succorance, abasement, and deference, than did female undergraduates.[86] Yet even with this strong self-image, the women law students believed that the "ideal lawyer" would be even more persevering, interested in success and influence, knowledgeable, conscientious, serious, emotionally independent, competitive, distant from others, and objective than they were.[87] They also believed the ideal lawyer would be less aggressive and more nurturing than they were.

Notably, women in the law in the late 1970s and early 1980s were fewer and may have thought they had to be more dominant, aggressive, and masculine just to "make it" in a male-dominated profession such as law.[88] As a result, these findings may apply to neither male law students then nor law students today. For example, a 1994 Canadian study reported that, although dominance was associated with lawyers in general, only the female law students thought they were slightly more dominant than average; male law students actually thought they were less dominant than average.[89]

Cynicism and Machiavellianism

Cynicism and Machiavellianism began to be studied post-Watergate in the mid-1970s, probably in response to concerns in the legal community that the "sheer volume of new lawyers will make it more difficult to keep the dishonest out of the profession" and that the stereotype of the " 'crafty,' 'manipulative,' 'calculating,' 'Machiavellian' " lawyer had been revived.[90] At the same time, the American Bar Association increased its focus on monitoring attorney behavior.[91]

One study found that law students were more trusting than most adults and no more Machiavellian than undergraduate students in general.[92] In comparison, another study found that law students' cynicism increased during law school.[93] Twenty-five years later, a 1998 study found that law students were less trusting of the American legal system than were undergraduate students.[94] Changes in society from 1973 to 1998 may partially explain the results of these three studies, but because there are other early studies of law students' attitudes toward the ethics of lawyers that render opposite results,[95] no firm conclusions can be drawn in this area. The results may also be affected by the outcome of law school on law students' attitudes about the profession, which effects are explored later in this chapter.

Attributes Associated With High Grades

One commonly heard statement in my law school (particularly right after grades were posted each term) was that the "A" students would become law professors and judicial clerks and the "C" students would be successful practitioners and make a lot of money. There was a perception that, as compared to the top-ranking students, the "C" students were more realistic, practical, efficient people who would have more success in the private practice of law. The "A" students were viewed as perhaps more intellectual, abstract, obsessive–compulsive, exacting, and laborious than their lower-ranking peers. A number of studies have investigated what differentiates law students with high grades from those with lower grades. Some support this A student/C student myth. These studies do not establish any lawyer traits per se. They may indirectly indicate what personality traits are rewarded—and thus encouraged or inculcated—in law school, thus perhaps suggesting more about the effects of law school than about the lawyer personality.

It appears that law school grades are most strongly linked with one's general intelligence level, but personality traits are also part of the equation. In 1968, only two things distinguished students with the highest grades from those with the lowest grades: IQ score and "the bottom students exhibited a greater tendency towards heightened levels of unrealistic self-appraisal,"[96] which may simply indicate general psychological problems such as denial in the bottom-ranking students.

A 1976 study's findings echo the A student/C student perception. The top-ranking law students' interests were "clearly professional or artistic in nature,"[97] and the bottom students' interests were more "predominantly business or commercial in nature."[98] More pragmatic values seemed associated with lower grades whereas more intellectual or esoteric values were linked with higher grades; however, this is true of nonlaw students as well,[99] so it may not be peculiar to law. Women were excluded from this study because there were so few in law at the time of the study.[100]

Three studies suggest that individuals who are people-oriented and who care about interpersonal relations tend to make lower grades in law school. First, in 1968, one researcher found a trend for the lowest ranked law students to obtain higher humanitarian scores, which he dismissed as a result of chance without other confirmatory research. However, this trend is consistent with two later studies finding that individuals who prefer feeling on the Myers–Briggs Type Indicator[101] are more likely to either drop out of law school[102] or be dissatisfied as attorneys.[103] Humanitarianism in this context meant "a regard for the interests of mankind, benevolence, philanthropy."[104]

Second, in 1974, law students with higher grades reported preferring peer relationships that were competitive, task-related, and professional in tone. In contrast, the students with lower grades expressed doubt about being able to present the "right" image when interacting with peers and faculty and preferred more personally based relationships.[105] These results suggest that competitiveness and interpersonal distance are subtly encouraged in law school, whereas more intimate, personal relationships with peers are implicitly discouraged.

Third, a 1996 study of the Myers–Briggs type of first-year law students broke new ground when it found that the traits of introversion and thinking were related to grades.[106] The more the law student preferred introversion to extraversion and thinking to feeling, the better were the student's law school grades. The relationship between introversion and grades was only true for the female law students and was not true for males alone, suggesting that extraversion in males did not hamper their law school grades.[107] It is hard to understand why.

This study concluded that the findings on introversion and thinking were not surprising, because law school rewards the preferred learning style of introverts and thinkers. Introverts appreciate that most law school learning occurs in introverted, solitary, quiet, reading and reflecting activity and most testing is done in writing rather than orally. Legal analysis fits well with the cool, rational, impartial analysis thinkers prefer. However, this researcher noted that although thinkers might perform well in law school, thinking law students are "likely to undervalue factors, such as the importance of human relationships in legal problems, the human side of legal issues, the role of values in legal decision-making, and the art of communication."[108] These three studies, spanning 1968 to 1996, consistently suggest subtle pressure in the law to downplay human relationships, interpersonal communication, and emotional concerns.

Two recent studies shed a bit more light on personality traits that are linked to high law school grades. First, a 1995 study found that certain reading strategies were associated with higher law school grades. Specifically, the students with higher grades used a problematizing strategy where they would form a hypothesis about the ultimate conclusion and then work toward or away from it to solve the problem of understanding what they were reading. The students with lower grades tended to simply paraphrase, list, or restate what they were reading. The former strategy was more helpful than the latter when processing legal material. These two groups of students did not differ significantly on undergraduate GPA or LSAT scores, so they would have been expected to perform about the same in law school but did not.[109]

The final study, in 1997, was the most surprising. These researchers found that, in contrast to undergraduate students, pessimism was rewarded in law school.[110] Law students at the University of Virginia in 1987 whose attitudes were pessimistic outperformed optimistic students in earning grades, making law review, and serving on executive boards of the law review. Pessimism was investigated by looking at people's ideas about why events happen, or their attributional style or locus of control.[111] In this study, pessimistic law students tended to believe the causes of negative events were stable ("it will always be this way"), far reaching or global ("everything will be like this event"), and internal ("it's my fault"), and the causes of positive events were the opposite (external: "it's someone else's fault," unstable: "this will pass," and highly specific: "this is unusual and simply situational"). In other words, pessimists thought good things happened infrequently and by chance, whereas bad things were more likely to happen and were their own fault. In contrast, the optimistic law students thought that good things were more likely to happen and occurred because of their efforts, whereas bad things happened less frequently and for reasons unrelated to them.

Previous research with undergraduates had found that optimists did better in school, probably because they are more resilient, persistent, motivated, and aggressive, whereas pessimism had been linked to passivity, poor problem solving, helplessness, indecisiveness, and continued failure. Yet the opposite was true for law students.[112] The level of pessimism found in these higher ranking law students was even more extreme than the pessimism one typically finds in people with major depression who are receiving inpatient psychiatric treatment. This is significant because pessimistic beliefs are thought to contribute to or cause depression.

Struggling to interpret these results, the researchers thought that maybe pessimism in law school was helpful because it really indicated prudence, skepticism, and caution. Maybe, unlike undergraduates, it did not lead to passivity, helplessness, or failure in law students, because they were already highly motivated achievers who were unlikely to become paralyzed by these negative beliefs.[113] However, these researchers thought that even if this was true, the extreme pessimism they found might predispose some lawyers to develop depression.[114]

The pessimism may only be found in the top law students, however, because another study found no differences in locus of control or attributional style between law students and undergraduates at the University of

Washington in 1996.[115] This study suggests that law students' attitudes about why things happen are not radically different from those of other people.

"Thinking" Preferred to "Feeling"

Despite the scientific acceptability and credibility of the MMPI, a number of law student studies have used a different test, the Myers–Briggs Type Indicator (MBTI). Studies in this area since 1967 consistently establish that law students overwhelmingly prefer thinking to feeling on the MBTI. According to one of the preeminent researchers in this area, thinkers prefer "logical analysis, principles, cool and impersonal reasoning and cost/benefit analyses" and are "more tolerant of conflict and criticism."[116] Feelers prefer "harmonizing, building relationships, pleasing people, making decisions on the basis of [their own] . . . personal likes and dislikes, and being attentive to the personal needs of others" and like to avoid conflict and criticism.[117] The extremely consistent finding that law students prefer thinking, when added to previous studies described in this chapter, culminates in the conclusion that lawyers tend to downplay interpersonal, emotional, and people-oriented concerns.

By 1996 there were at least five published and eight more unpublished studies of the MBTI profile of law students, all confirming a strong preference for thinking among lawyers.[118] Because this preference for thinking over feeling was confirmed by a massive 1994 study[119] of lawyers, including women lawyers, this trait is particularly important. It appears to survive into law practice and has not been changed by the introduction of women into the profession.[120] Some of these studies will be examined in more detail below.

For example, a 1967 study[121] using the MBTI found no significant differences in the personality "types" of law students in their first week of classes at each of four law schools. All of the law schools attracted the same mix of students in terms of personality. However, law students had a marked (72%) preference for thinking over feeling.[122] In contrast, only 54% of male college students, about 60% of men, and about 35% of women in the United States prefer thinking.[123]

A 1981 study also found that law students preferred thinking to feeling.[124] This time the law students were enrolled in an elective, experiential legal process course—one that typical law students do not take—so they might not have been a typical group of law students. Still, 63% preferred thinking and 37% preferred feeling.

The 1967 study also found that more of the feeling law students dropped out of law school than did the thinking types, suggesting that feeling is incompatible with the study of law.[125] Perhaps the most striking finding was a perfect inverse relationship between the frequency of the personality types and their drop-out rates.[126] The type that was most prevalent in law school was the introvert–sensor–thinker–judger (ISTJ), who is typically "dependable and practical with a realistic respect for facts, who absorbs and remembers great numbers of facts and is able to cite cases to support his evaluations, and who emphasizes analysis, logic and decisiveness." The ISTJ type had a 6.7% drop-out rate.[127] The least frequently found type in law school was the extrovert–sensor–feeler–judger (ESFJ), described as "concerned chiefly with people, who values harmonious human contacts, is friendly, tactful, sympathetic, and loyal, who is warmed by approval and bothered by indifference and who tends to idealize what he admires." The ESFJ type had a drop-out rate of 28.1%.[128]

A bit of analysis on these two divergent types shows how important the thinking–feeling dichotomy is in law. David Keirsey, author of several books on the MBTI, believes that the 16 types actually group into four categories: rationals (intuitive–thinkers), guardians (sensor–judgers), artisans (sensor–perceivers), and idealists (intuitive–feelers). Guardians tend to rely on common sense; hold morally correct beliefs; protect and maintain order and society; and be economical, methodical, sensible, stable, dependable, and practical.[129] Under this theory, the two types described previously are both guardians (SJs) and would be quite similar except for the thinking–feeling and extraversion–introversion differences. Therefore, their vastly different drop-out rates in law school suggest that thinking and introversion must be important in law school. There is other evidence for this; a study conducted in the mid-1990s found that thinkers and introverts made higher grades in law school than did feelers or extroverts.[130]

In the 1967 study, likelihood of dropping out was not related to academic promise, based on grade point average and LSAT scores; rather, it was related to the MBTI personality characteristics.[131] One of the most ominous conclusions drawn by this researcher was his statement that "the only objective criteria [GPA and LSAT scores] now used to select students were impotent in predicting survival";[132] personality was more important. Job satisfaction research also suggests that it is important to match the job to the individuals' personality, interests, and motivations as well as to their skills, knowledge, talents, and abilities.[133]

A 1996 study of law students confirmed these earlier studies on the thinking–feeling preference of law students. In this study, law students preferred extroversion (51.3%), intuiting (51.9%), thinking (77.9%), and judgment (67.5%) to introversion, sensing, feeling, and perceiving, respectively.[134] Because most women in the general population prefer feeling to thinking,[135] this study is important because it indicates that the infusion of women into law school, which would be expected to dilute law students' preference for thinking, did not do so. It suggests that thinker women are particularly attracted to law school.

Left-Brained Analysis

A 1998 Canadian study found that law students preferred an analytical style of reasoning to an intuitive style of reasoning, when compared to management students.[136] The analytical mode included left-brained activity, mental reasoning, and detail, whereas the intuitive style involved right-brained activity, emphasized feeling, and adopted a global perspective.[137] The female law students were even more analytical than the male law students. Also, students interested in litigation were more analytical than those interested in corporate or commercial law in this study.[138] The researchers concluded that law attracts individuals who tend to be analytical. Despite the apparent similarity of this analytical, left-brained preference to thinking, other research cautions that traits like these that appear to be similar are not always the same.[139]

Moral Decision Making of Law Students

A fair number of studies have investigated the moral and ethical decision making of law students. These studies use different theories and methods to assess lawyers, including Harvard psychology professor Lawrence Kohlberg's stage theory of moral development, which was described in greater detail in chapter 2, and Harvard psychology professor Carol Gilligan's gender-sensitive theory of moral development.

Conventional Morality

A 1974 study found that law students' morality differed from the morality of college students, teachers, and prison inmates in that it was consistently more "conventional" and focused on maintaining social order and conformity.[140] Conventional thinking relies on formal rules and the moral conventions approved by the majority within the culture. In contrast, postconventional thinking emphasizes overarching moral principles such as justice, fairness, equality, and social utility, rather than the formal, societal rules.[141] Conventional thinkers would follow the rule whereas postconventional thinkers would disobey the rule if it was unjust or unfair. In this study, law students relied on formal rules and societal conventions more than other groups. They also appeared to be more like each other (e.g., homogeneous) in moral development than were other groups because of this conventional orientation.[142]

There is a perception that law students are a rather homogeneous group—that is, that law students are similar to each other with little diversity of background or attitudes. There are divergent findings on this, however. Some of the moral and ethical decision-making studies conclude that law students' decision-making styles are indeed uniform,[143] whereas others find they are more diverse,[144] and yet others find that law students' decision-making styles change depending on the context of the question presented.[145]

One explanation for these conflicting data is that law students have changed. Perhaps law students in earlier years mainly used conventional reasoning, but law students in the 1990s did not primarily use one stage of moral reasoning to solve problems.[146] This may be in part a result of the increases in the number of women and minority law students after 1980,[147] who may not share the more uniform moral reasoning of law students in the past.[148]

Kohlbergian Stage

Conventional morality is associated with Kohlberg's stage 3 and 4 moral reasoning, as described in the previous chapter. Postconventional thought is associated with later, more developed stages (such as stages 5 and 6).[149] The 1974 study found that law students' moral decision making operated predominantly in a fashion consistent with Kohlberg's stages 3 and 4.[150] In contrast, a later study found that law students at the University of Toledo in 1976 and 1978 were clustered in stages 4 and "5A," with relatively little stage 2 or 3 reasoning.[151] However, because of the different methods used in these two studies, the studies may be reconcilable. Stage 4 is associated with conventional reasoning, whereas stage 5 is usually associated with postconventional reasoning. However, stage 5A relies more on external norms (i.e., society's) to dictate right and wrong, whereas stage 5B relies more on the individual's internal values to determine whether rules are fair before following them. This focus on external norms suggests that what one study called stages 3 and 4 might have been what the other study called stages 4 and 5A; in both studies, law students may have preferred a "conventional," rule-following approach to moral decision making that conforms to societal or external norms or expectations. For example, if the rules conflicted with the law student's personal moral values, he or she would probably follow the rules. Because law students are presumably interested in society's rules, laws, and regulations, this simply makes sense.

However, the later study also found that the moral stage of law students was not different from that of students in other graduate schools,[152] whereas the 1974 study found that law students' morality was significantly more "conventional," meaning more rule-based, than that of other individuals.[153] So we cannot really conclude that law students are any different from other people in this area. However, several later studies do illuminate some distinct gender differences and indicate that important changes in one's moral orientation can occur during law school.

Gender Differences (and the Care Orientation)

Law student studies in the 1980s typically focused on gender differences, perhaps as a result of the influx of women into the profession during that decade. One of these studies was an extensive survey of gender differences among the entire population of students enrolled in Stanford Law School in 1986.[154] More than 45% of the students were women, in contrast to earlier studies in the 1960s and 1970s.[155] It found, among other things, support for Gilligan's contention that the moral reasoning of men and women differs. When asked to decide legal hypothetical situations and then asked to rate the importance of various factors in making their decisions, women law students more frequently rated contextual factors highly and men law students more frequently rated abstract factors highly.[156] Contextual factors were "factors based on relationships, care, and communication," whereas abstract factors were "factors relating to rights, logic, and abstract justice."[157]

The women law students' emphasis on contextual factors is consistent with Gilligan's concept of a style of moral reasoning referred to as an "ethic of care" or "distinct moral voice."[158] The care ethic values interpersonal harmony, maintaining relationships, people's feelings and needs, and preventing harm.[159] In contrast, Gilligan's "rights" or "justice" orientation focuses on rights, rules, standards, individuality, independence, justice, fairness, objectivity, accomplishments, ambitions, principles, personal beliefs, and freedom from others' interference.[160]

The ethic of care and rights orientation were directly investigated in a 1989 study assessing[161] the moral reasoning of first-year law students at Temple University Law School. It specifically asked whether Gilligan's categories of moral reasoning—the ethic of care and the rights orientation—existed among law students and found that female law students' moral reasoning more often reflected an ethic of care, whereas male law students more often used a rights orientation at the beginning of law school.[162]

Finally, a 1997 study of first-year law students explored whether the Myers–Briggs feeling preference and the ethic of care (and some other traits) might be related because of their conceptual similarities.[163] Despite their similar descriptions, they were not the same trait. Neither feeling nor communitarianism, which values common goals, social roles, unity, resolving problems one-on-one, and imposing restrictions on individual rights for the good of the community, were related to the care orientation.[164] However, female law students were more likely than were male law students to have an ethic of care, again demonstrating the strength of this gender difference.[165]

SUMMARY OF LAW STUDENT ATTRIBUTES

The four-decade research from 1960 to 1998 presented earlier, despite its scattered nature, portrays law students as dominant; competitive; leadership-oriented; socially confident; extroverted; sociable; ebullient; at ease in interpersonal relations; aggressive; "masculine";[166] achievement-oriented; of a higher than average socioeconomic class; motivated more by money and prestige than by altruism;[167] logical, rational, and analytical; cool-headed; and conforming to rules and externally based norms. Typical law students are not generally "concerned chiefly with people," do not value "harmonious human contacts," are not "friendly, tactful, sympathetic, and loyal, . . . warmed by approval and bothered by indifference," nor do they idealize what they admire.[168] To what extent do law students come to law school with these traits and to what extent does the socialization process of legal education create these characteristics? Little is known about this question. Some clues are found, however, in studies showing the effects of law school.

EFFECTS OF LAW SCHOOL

The drastic emotional effects of law school, particularly the first year, have been explored in books such as Scott Turow's *1L* and movies such as *The Paper Chase*. Anecdotes abound about law students who become estranged from friends, family, and spouses because of the changes wrought during the first year of law school. The often-cited rationale of legal educators for the brutal nature of law school is that law school has to be rough because "it's a shark fest out there," referring to law practice. Or law school is a sort of professional boot camp designed to beat preconceptions and attitudes out of students to teach them to "think like lawyers." Perhaps because it is intended to completely reform students' ways of thinking, it seems to have dramatic effects on their personalities as well. Law students' spouses are often the ones who complain the most about these effects, often saying that their mates have entirely changed since beginning law school.

Some commentators and researchers also believe that law school pressures law students to be more alike than different—in other words, homogenize or conform to a particular norm. It has been said that, more and more, students dress alike, share the same political views, and think alike as law school progresses. Certainly in my southeastern state law school in the early 1980s, by the end of law school, we were all wearing button-down oxford shirts, khaki pants, and leather topsiders. The most daring anyone got was to wear a *pink* button-down. Most of us, men and women, had finally succumbed to a short, clean-cut, professional haircut. Despite our original differences in appearance, attitudes, and undergraduate major, by the end of law school we had almost all begun to look like the group of people we thought we would soon join.

The next section explores what empirical evidence exists to show that law school does indeed mold and change people. This evidence helps us understand how much of lawyer personality predates law school. Also, the effects of law school are important to study because other research reveals that psychological distress among law students surfaces or intensifies in law school. These "distress studies" are developed in detail in chapter 5. The effects of law school may shed some light on the causes of this distress.

Homogenization

The data are conflicting as to whether law school tends to make law students more alike than different. For example, a 1979 study found that law students' opinions and personality did not become more homogeneous during the first year.[169] However, a 1996 study comparing attitudes of American and Korean law students and undergraduates found that in some areas the law students were more alike than were the two countries' undergraduates.[170] This study suggests that legal training has some similar effects even cross-culturally, particularly with respect to one's attitudes toward law, prisoners, and fault.[171] Finally, a 1991 Australian study found that, despite initial gender differences in this area, male law students tended to become less "authoritarian" and female students tended to become more "authoritarian" during law school.[172] Because of this effect, as training progressed, the men and women began to be more alike on this characteristic.[173] Perhaps homogenization occurs in law school, but only with respect to certain traits.

Changes in Attitudes

Some isolated early studies examined changes in attitudes during law school and found that law students became less cynical[174] and yet less idealistic[175] during law school. Their attitudes toward lawyers markedly worsened, becoming less certain, less positive, and more qualified,[176] although at the same time, they became more professionally oriented, or protective of the legal profession, during their training.[177] One later study in 1994 did confirm that, by the second year of law school, students had become more aware of the difference between law school and the real world, less idealistic about and more disillusioned and disenchanted with the legal system and lawyering, and more focused on descriptions of problem-solving methods.[178] This study assessed eight students before and during their first year and in their second year of law school in an attempt to determine what happens when someone is taught to "think like a lawyer."[179]

Changes in Values

A 2001 study found that Florida State University law students' value systems actually changed during the first few months of law school from intrinsic goals to more extrinsic rewards. By the end of the first year of law school, the law students had become less oriented toward personal "growth/ self-acceptance, intimacy/emotional connection, and community/societal contribution" and less likely to act for interest or inherent satisfaction. They had become "more oriented towards appearance/attractiveness" and "money/ luxuries, popularity/fame" and more motivated to please others.[180] This shift is consistent with the next change regarding interest in public service work.

Public Interest and Public Service

One fairly consistent finding is that, during law school, students' interest in public service and public interest work decreases in favor of an increased interest in private practice. Early studies in the 1950s about medical students suggested that altruistic impulses were strong among beginning students but dissipated as training progressed.[181] Perhaps consistent with this early work, a 1979 study at Brigham Young University found that law students became less interested in public service employment and more interested in employment with a small, private law firm during law school.[182] About half of the University of Wisconsin Law School class of 1976 had some interest in public interest work (meaning a job or field "with an explicit social reform component, such as poverty law, consumer or environmental protection, or affirmative action") before entering law school, but only 13% actually took a job in legal aid, as a public defender, or in a nonprofit organization.[183]

A later study of Harvard law students similarly found that their interest in public interest work all but evaporated during law school.[184] In 1986, although about 70% of the first-year Harvard law students expressed a desire to practice public interest law, only 5% of the graduating class ultimately entered government service or public interest work. One third-year student explained that, consistent with his or her initial interests, he or she could have taken a public interest job but just really did not want to live on $30,000 a year, nor was it obvious to this student what success looked like in the public interest area. This student was attracted to a mainstream corporate job instead, where success was well-defined, saying,

> I've gotten into the habit of going for the brass ring and so I don't want to slip. . . . I'm caught on a success treadmill. . . . If you get on a partner track at a large New York law firm then it's clear that you're still on track. I'm keeping my options open.[185]

Three obvious explanations for the decline in interest in public interest jobs are that such jobs are scarce; student debt is likely high by the end of law school and students therefore become more interested in higher paying jobs because of the pressures of mounting debt; and moral intentions often do not translate into actual behavior.[186] However, in the 1976 Wisconsin study, size of student debt did not entirely explain the discrepancy between intentions and first job. Those with the largest debt were indeed most likely to take traditional jobs, but those with the second largest debt were most likely to take nontraditional (public interest) jobs.[187] Only two factors explained a continuing, unflagging interest in public interest or nontraditional work: a strong political orientation and a history of political activism before law school.[188] Finally, in this study, an initial interest in public interest jobs appeared to be squashed by good law school grades (e.g., those with high grades tended to end up in traditional jobs).[189] This may be a result in part of the fact that traditional employers "court" high-achieving law students, whereas nontraditional employers may focus less on grades.

Changes in Personality Traits

A 1979 study investigated changes in personality traits during the first year of law school by administering a standard personality test before and after the first year.[190] Many personality changes are known to occur as a result of any type of further education (for example, increased tolerance for ambiguity, more aesthetic interests, and increased readiness to act); however, law school specifically differed from other forms of higher education; see Table 3.1 for examples.

Law school in this study did not change the students' religious orientation, interest in practical activities, gender orientation (masculinity/femininity), or degree of desire to make a good impression or present a good image. Unlike other higher education, it did make law students less philosophical and introspective; less interested in abstractions, ideas, and the scientific

TABLE 3.1
Personality Characteristic Changes in Law School

Effect of law school	Personality characteristic that changed
Less	Interested in reflective thought, ideas, abstractions, and academic activities versus action and practical applications
Less	Philosophical and introspective
Less	Dominant, confident, socially extroverted, preference for relating to people in a social context and for social activities
More	Socially alienated, emotionally disturbed, feelings of hostility, aggression, isolation, rejection
More	Tension, anxiety, and internal conflict
Less	Altruistic, trusting, and ethical in dealing with others, concerned for the welfare of others

method; less dominant, confident, and sociable; and more anxious and conflicted during the first year of law school.[191]

These results, particularly the increased anxiety and decreased social extroversion, are consistent with mid-1980s findings that law school intensified or resulted in various forms of emotional distress in law students (discussed in chap. 5). Although this study provides strong evidence of the fact that law school causes personality change, it should be noted that it surveyed Brigham Young University law students, 98% of whom were members of the Church of Jesus Christ of Latter Day Saints (Mormon). It is possible that this religious affiliation is significant, meaning that law students at different law schools might demonstrate different results; however, I am unaware of any data that suggest such differences. This study's findings on anxiety are clearly consistent with later studies on law student distress.

Increase in Psychological Distress

Dramatic increases in anxiety, depression, and other forms of emotional distress during law school have been widely documented by studies that will be described in chapter 5. Consistent with the 1979 Brigham Young study, law students experienced increases in these kinds of problems as a result of law school, even after the first year.[192] According to two studies, published in 1986 and in 2001, the first year of law school is particularly devastating to law students' psychological well-being.[193] In the 2001 study, at the beginning of law school, the law students' mental health was better than that of advanced undergraduates to which they were compared but significantly declined thereafter in the first year. These law students' scores "declined on every measure of positive well-being (i.e. positive mood, self-actualization, life-satisfaction), and increased on every measure of negative well-being (i.e. physical symptoms, negative mood, depression)."[194] Except for the 2001 study linking this decline in well-being to a shift in values, the causes of this increased tension, anxiety, and other distress are unknown, as is its relationship to the personality changes wrought by law school outlined earlier. One early study hints at a coping strategy law students likely use to deal with this increased stress.

Ambition and Aggression

This early study assessed third-year law students' ambition and aggression in 1973 in an attempt to determine the effects of law school.[195] The tenser the students felt and the more competitive they perceived law school to be, the more aggressive and ambitious they became.[196] Instead of coping with stress by soliciting help, for example, law students appear to cope by becoming more aggressive and ambitious (which may translate into working harder and being more dedicated to their studies).

Becoming more aggressive was independent of amount of time spent with faculty, quality of faculty–student interactions, number of hours spent studying, or frequency of informal discussions.[197] Instead, increased aggression and ambition were primarily related to how much competition and tension the law student experienced.[198] In addition, the warmer and closer relations with faculty the student had, the more likely he or she was to become more ambitious.[199] Finally, students who became more ambitious were also least likely to go into public defender, legal aid, or civil liberties work, indicating that this increased ambition was not channeled into public service.[200]

Ethical and Moral Decision Making

Research on the effects of law school on one's moral and ethical decision making is rather complex and often conflicting. Some theorize that "law school, especially during the stress of the first year, induces a regression in social and personal values which might be reflected in a regression on moral development measures or at least [retarded] growth,"[201] as well as "a decline in ethics and emotional sensitivity."[202] Only one study, however, supports the concept that law students regress morally during law school;[203] other studies typically find that law students' moral reasoning advances,[204] or does not change,[205] as a result of law school. For example, a 1969 study found that law students' responses to professional ethical dilemmas were more often "ethical" by the end of law school.[206] Another found in 1995 that only specific law school professional responsibility courses increased students' stage of Kohlbergian moral development.[207] However, both a 1974 and a 1981 study found no change in law students' moral reasoning during law school.[208]

Finally, a 1989 study found that law school actually changes individuals who come to law school with an "ethic of care," based on Gilligan's theory.[209] If true, the effects of law school found in this study may explain the conflicting results as to moral stage of law students and also shed some light on the gender differences in moral reasoning found in the 1980s studies.[210]

This study assessed the moral reasoning of law students enrolled in Temple University Law School as they entered law school and again at the end of their first year. Not surprisingly, it found that entering female law students' moral reasoning more often reflected an ethic of care, whereas entering male law students more often used a rights orientation. More important, however, it found a significant decrease in the amount of care orientation and a significant increase in the amount of rights orientation exhibited by the law students from the beginning to the end of the first year of law school.[211] Specifically, women's care orientations decreased and their rights orientations increased, whereas men's orientations did not significantly change in either direction.[212]

From these findings, the researcher concluded that law students, particularly women, "submerge" their orientation toward an ethic of care to "align with the rights assumptions of law school," and that law school tends to "silence" a voice of care.[213] In lectures, I sometimes joke that law school beats the ethic of care out of law students by the end of the first year.

This study hypothesized that law schools' attempt to teach students to "think like a lawyer" was responsible for the shift from an ethic of care to a rights orientation, because thinking like a lawyer means focusing on rights and placing oneself in an emotionally neutral state to be an advocate.[214] Therefore, it concluded that law school does not incorporate the relational side of human nature.

This study went on to make one final, important point. It suggested that people who come to law school with an ethic of care have to adapt to law school in one of three ways. They can submerge and deny their care orientation, "split" by using it only in personal settings and using a rights orientation in professional work, or keep it. The minority of law students chose the third, toughest route. For example, I had a colleague who identified with this research immediately. She said, "Yes, I have an ethic of care, I always have had it, and I kept it throughout law school and law practice. But, I felt like an outsider—I was definitely in the minority." She added that it had been challenging to maintain it, in law school and in the legal profession. So most individuals with an ethic of care probably submerge it or use it only in certain situations. Yet, it is these two strategies (submerging or subordinating the care orientation) that are most likely to cause personal angst. They may indeed explain why so many law students become so distressed by the end of the first year of law school.

Summary of Effects of Law School

Although law students come to law school with a variety of preexisting traits, such as a preference for dominance, leadership abilities, outgoingness, an interest in school and reading, and a deemphasis on emotional or interpersonal matters, law school appears to change people. It does not appear to change people as dramatically as most of the popular lore indicates, and in some areas, the data conflict as to whether changes even occur. However, there is evidence that law students become less idealistic about lawyers and the legal system; less interested in public service work; less motivated by intrinsic, internal values; more motivated by external rewards; and less philosophical, introspective, and interested in abstract ideas. Law students' moral decision making becomes crystallized at a conventional, rule-following, norm-obeying stage. Those with an ethic of care are likely to lose it during law school and shift instead toward a rights orientation. Finally, it is abundantly clear that people became much more anxious, insecure, and psychologically distressed in law school, compared to how they felt before classes began. The studies documenting this disturbing phenomenon will be explored in chapter 5.

As children, lawyers were focused on school; sought dominance, leadership, and attention; and preferred to initiate activities. Their families emphasized scholastic achievement, reading, self-discipline, and the channeling of impulses into expression. Their fathers were dominant and strong. They had good social skills but a low interest in emotions or others' feelings.

Law students have traditionally come from a socioeconomically elite and privileged background but, with the influx of women and minorities into the legal profession since 1970, this may have changed somewhat. Law students see themselves as more argumentative than others and may indeed be more competitive. Although law students seek leadership and dominance, which would imply "over others," these drives are not necessarily oriented toward other people. Rather, there is a need for personal excellence, material success, and perhaps the admiration of others from a distance. Across the board, prelaw students and law students are less interested in people, in emotions, and interpersonal concerns than are others. In fact, there is evidence that humanistic, people-oriented individuals often do not fare well, psychologically or academically, in law school or as lawyers. Both male and female law students and lawyers overwhelmingly display an orientation toward valuing rights and justice, logic, thinking, and rationality without regard to their personal values when making decisions. They do not apply their personal values to problems nor do they usually consider interpersonal harmony, relationships, or humanistic concerns in making decisions. There is evidence that some of this orientation may result from the socialization process of law school, occurring even as early as the first year (based on the shifts in values, motivations, and moral decision-making styles that occur during law school).

Although everyone who has been through it knows that law school has dramatic effects, there is empirical evidence to flesh out what actually changes when one learns to "think like a lawyer." People who come to law school with a rights orientation either keep it or it becomes more ingrained. Many of those who come to law school with an ethic of care appear to lose it and adopt a rights orientation by the end of the first year. Law students become less interested in community, intimacy, personal growth, and inherent satisfaction and more interested in appearance, attractiveness, and garnering the esteem of others. Cynicism about the legal profession increases and opinions of lawyers and the legal system become more guarded and negative by the end of the first year of law school, but an elitist protectiveness of the profession also emerges. Interest in public interest and public service

TABLE 3.2
Lawyer Personality Development

In early childhood	As prelaw students	Effects of law school
1. Scholastic achievement orientation, reading	No available research	Increased focus on external rewards and values
2. Leadership, authoritarian male dominance emphasis	Need for dominance, leadership, and attention	Increased aggression and ambition when under stress
Active approach to life, emphasis on self-discipline instead of submission to authority	Less subordinate and deferent, more authoritarian	Preference for competitive peer relations, failure to rely on peers for social support
3. Low interest in emotions or concern for others' feelings	Low interest in emotions, interpersonal concerns, and others' feelings	Increased "rights" focus (justice, rationality, etc.) as opposed to an "ethic of care"
4. No available research	Higher socioeconomic status; materialistic motives	Decreased altruism; increased focus on external rewards instead of intrinsic satisfaction
5. No available research	Normal levels of psychological distress	Increased psychological distress and substance abuse, increased tension and insecurity, pessimism rewarded in law school

work decreases as a result of law school. Students also become less intellectual (i.e., less philosophical and introspective and less interested in abstractions, ideas, and the scientific method), perhaps in favor of more realistic, practical values. Law school inadvertently discourages collaborative peer relationships, instead fostering more competitive interactions. It unintentionally rewards introversion and pessimistic attitudes. Finally, as chapter 5 documents, a variety of psychological problems dramatically emerge or intensify during law school. It is entirely possible, and in fact probable, based on very recent work, that at least some of these changes are responsible for law students' dramatic decline in psychological well-being during law school. The development of the lawyer personality is expressed in Table 3.2.

NOTES

1. Barbara Nachmann, *Childhood Experience and Vocational Choice in Law, Dentistry, and Social Work*, 7 J. COUNS. PSYCHOL. 243, 244 (1960).

2. Instead, compared to graduate social work students and dental students, law students' fathers were strong, dominant, adequate, authoritarian, and clearly masculine figures. Fathers were "both in word and deed the source of authority in the home." A strong male figure other than the father, such as an uncle or grandfather who was a lawyer, was more often an important influence or an admired figure to the law students. The dental students were emotionally and geographically closer to their fathers than were the law students. Law students more frequently reported that the goals of family discipline were self-discipline, in contrast to dental students' families who emphasized unquestioning submission to authority. Nachmann, *supra* note 1, at 244–248.

3. This was also true of the social work students, as compared to the dental students. *Id.* at 248.

4. Reading skills were taught at an early age in law students' and social work students' families, as compared to dental students', but law students more frequently reported having been read to and hearing stories as children as pleasurable memories than the other two groups. *Id.* at 248.

5. *Id.* at 248–249. Nachmann asserted that her findings were particularly reliable, because she carefully excluded research participants whose reasons for entering their chosen profession were related to prestige, money, expediency, and she included only those who were interested in the unique qualities of the work itself. *Id.* at 249. Channeling impulses into activity ("do") was more emphasized in law and social work students' families; dental students' families more often emphasized impulse repression ("don't"). *Id.* at 248–249.

6. *Id.* at 249. They were also deemphasized in dental students' families but not in social work students' families.

7. James L. Hafner & M. E. Fakouri, *Early Recollections of Individuals Preparing for Careers in Clinical Psychology, Dentistry, and Law*, 24 J. VOCATIONAL BEHAV. 236 (1984).

8. *Id.* at 240.

9. Leonard H. Chusmir, *Law and Jurisprudence Occupations: A Look at Motivational Need Patterns*, COM. L. J., May 1984, at 231–235 (finding lawyers are motivated to achieve); Sue Winkle Williams & John C. McCullers, *Personal Factors Related to Typicalness of Career and Success in Active Professional Women*, 7 PSYCHOL. WOMEN Q. 343, 350 (1983) (finding women lawyers more achievement-oriented than other women).

10. Hafner & Fakouri, *supra* note 7, at 239. This is perhaps consistent with the robust finding that lawyers are disproportionately thinking types, as compared to feeling types, using the Myers–Briggs Type Indicator nomenclature. *See generally* Lawrence R. Richard, Psychological Type and Job Satisfaction Among Practicing Lawyers in the United States (1990) (unpublished PhD dissertation, Temple University). Hafner and Fakouri relied heavily on Alfred Adler's ideas that events remembered from childhood are of great value in vocational guidance, because these events are "very near to the main interest of the individual." *Id.* at 240, citing ALFRED ADLER, WHAT LIFE SHOULD MEAN TO YOU (Capricorn Books 1931). They explained that "Adler suggests that a person's style of life is designed to overcome feelings of inferiority" and that his own first recollection,

a "traumatic medical experience," resulted in feelings of physical inferiority, which caused him to enter the field of medicine to conquer his somatic inferiority. Hafner & Fakouri, *supra* note 7. *See also* Adlerian Therapy in JAMES O. PROCHASKA, SYSTEMS OF PSYCHOTHERAPY: A TRANSTHEORETICAL ANALYSIS, 175–179 (1979) [hereinafter Adlerian Therapy].

11. Richard, *supra* note 10.

12. James L. Hafner & M. Ebrahim Fakouri, *Early Recollections of Individuals Preparing for Careers in Clinical Psychology, Dentistry, and Law*, 24 J. VOCATIONAL BEHAV. 236, 239 (1984) (summarizing Adler's ideas).

13. Sue Winkle Williams & John C. McCullers, *Personal Factors Related to Typicalness of Career and Success in Active Professional Women*, 7 PSYCHOL. WOMEN Q. 343, 350–351 (1983).

14. Martin J. Bohn, *Psychological Needs of Engineering, Pre-Law, Pre-Medical, and Undecided College Freshmen*, 12 J. C. STUDENT PERSONNEL, 359, 359–361 (1971); Robert Stevens, *Law Schools and Law Students*, 59 VA. L. REV. 551 (1973); and G. Andrew H. Benjamin, Alfred Kazniak, Bruce Sales, and Stephen B. Shanfield, *The Role of Legal Education in Producing Psychological Distress Among Law Students*, AMERICAN BAR FOUNDATION RESEARCH J. 225 (1986) [hereinafter Benjamin et al. 1986].

15. Bohn, *supra* note 14.

16. Stevens, *supra* note 14. *See* A.B.A. COMMISSION ON WOMEN IN THE PROFESSION, BASIC FACTS FROM WOMEN IN THE LAW: A LOOK AT THE NUMBERS 1 (December 1995) (noting that the number of women in the law rose from 3% in 1960 and 1971 to 23% in 1995; most entered after 1970).

17. Stevens, *supra* note 14, at 598.

18. *Id.* Even the minority students had a more elite background, financially and educationally, than most. *Id.* at 600–601.

19. About 80% of women lawyers entered the profession since 1970, and the percentage of women in the law has risen from 3% in 1960 and 1971 to 23% in 1995. A.B.A. COMMISSION ON WOMEN IN THE PROFESSION, BASIC FACTS FROM WOMEN IN THE LAW: A LOOK AT THE NUMBERS 1 (December 1995).

20. Bohn, *supra* note 14, at 359, 361.

21. *Id.* at 360. The test used was the Adjective Check List (*id.* at 361, citing H. G. GOUGH & A. B. HEILBRUN, JR., MANUAL FOR THE ADJECTIVE CHECKLIST (Consulting Psychologists 1965)); it was scored for 15 psychological needs according to a standardized system. The engineering and premedical students' scores were close to the mean on all the scales. Also, the prelaw students' scores were the mirror image of the undecided students' scores (e.g., high on abasement and deference and low on self-confidence, dominance, and exhibition), indicating that college freshmen who are undecided about their career choices have the opposite needs of those who expect to enter law school.

22. *See* A.B.A. COMMISSION ON WOMEN IN THE LAW, BASIC FACTS FROM WOMEN IN THE LAW: A LOOK AT THE NUMBERS 1 (December 1995) (80% of women lawyers entered the profession after 1970).

23. For example, Stephen Reich stated in 1976: "It is a well-observed fact that law frequently attracts students who are very uncertain about their ultimate

occupational goals." Reich, *Strong Vocational Interest Blank Patterns Associated With Law School Achievement*, 39 PSYCHOL. REP. 1343, 1344 (1976). Because law prepares one for so many business and government positions, he says, "students feel they can study law without pinning themselves down vocationally. . . . [Because there are no particular prerequisites for admission to law school, [t]he decision to study law can thus be made (and is frequently made) at the last hour of undergraduate training and the resultant law student body is thus a mixture of students with clear vocational goals and students who are ambivalent about their occupational future." *Id.* at 1344, 1346. *See also* Stevens, *supra* note 14, at 623 n.131 and accompanying text, citing commentators from 1957 to 1965 who asserted that law is a career for the uncommitted, because it preserves options rather than requiring a decision to pursue a particular goal. Stevens in 1973 reported that uncertainty about career goals was prevalent among law students; however, it appeared to be associated more strongly with those in the highest income brackets; those in the lower income brackets appeared to be less uncertain. *Id.* at 616. An average of about 25% of the law students surveyed indicated that they were "uncertain of career plans; [they thought] law a good bet" and this was of "great" importance to their decision to enter law. *Id.* at 583 (average compiled from tab. 19 data). Stevens asserted that law schools are indeed becoming residual graduate schools, although his data should be evaluated in light of the Vietnam War. He studied law students in the classes of 1960, 1970, and 1972; thus, the latter two classes may have included a large number of individuals who entered law school to avoid the war and thus were quite uncertain of their career plans.

24. Stevens, *supra* note 14, at 623–624 (slightly more than half of the law students surveyed indicated uncertain career plans as of great or some importance in their decision to enter law school); *id.* at 623 n.131, citing Wagner P. Thielans, Jr., *Some Comparisons of Entrants to Medical and Law School*, in THE STUDENT PHYSICIAN 140–141 (ROBERT K. MERTON, GEORGE G. READER, & PATRICIA L. KENDALL, EDS., 1957) (reporting that 23% of law students reported indecision as in part important to their decision to enter law).

25. Stevens, *supra* note 14, at 616.

26. Thomas M. Goolsby, Jr., *Law School Selection and Performance and Subsequent Admission to Legal Practice*, 28 EDUC. & PSYCHOL. MEASUREMENT 421 (1968). Thus, if these uncertain students achieve highly in general, they are unlikely to be weeded out for academic reasons in law school, and may go on to become dissatisfied or distressed practicing lawyers.

27. Jean Campbell, *Differential Response for Female and Male Law Students on the Strong–Campbell Interest Inventory: The Question of Separate Sex Norms*, 23 J. CONSULTING PSYCHOL. 130 (1976) (investigating gender differences in vocational testing and finding incidentally that the first-, second-, and third-year law students surveyed scored the highest on the lawyer scale of the Strong–Campbell Interest Inventory (a widely used vocational test) compared to the other scales of the test; the sample studied appears to be law students at Texas Tech University).

28. Stevens, *supra* note 14, at 575–577.

29. *Id.*

30. This percentage was found at Yale University among the law school class of 1970. *Id.* at 577.

31. This percentage was found at the University of Southern California among the law school class of 1970. *Id.*

32. *Id.* at 576–577 (averages roughly compiled from tabs. 8–11).

33. *Id.* at 578.

34. *Id.* at 624.

35. Stevens, *supra* note 14, at 577.

36. *Id.* at 578–579. Average compiled from data reported in tab. 14 at p. 579. This is not surprising, given the political and social events occurring during this time. The effects of the events of this decade may be one of the reasons altruism receives inconsistent findings among law students studied from 1960 to date.

37. Don S. Anderson et al., *Conservatism in Recruits to the Professions*, 9 AUSTL. & N.Z. J. SOC. 42 (1973).

38. *Id.* at 43. Not surprisingly, status concern was not present as a motivation among the teacher trainees.

39. Altruistic concerns were a motivator for 25% of entering engineering and medical students and for 35% of teacher trainees. *Id.* at 43.

40. James M. Hedegard, *The Impact of Legal Education: An In-Depth Examination of Career-Relevant Interests, Attitudes, and Personality Traits Among First-Year Law Students*, AM. B. FOUND. RES. J. 791, 814 (1979).

41. *Id.* at 814.

42. For example, Stevens found that more than 95% of law students surveyed indicated that the desire for intellectual stimulation or an interest in the subject matter motivated them to enter law school. Stevens, *supra* note 14, at 614. Subject matter interest was of great importance more often for the women (65.6%) than for the men (57.4%). *Id.*

43. Stevens found in 1973 that 54.7% of women law students surveyed indicated that financial rewards had been of no importance to their decision to enter law school, whereas only 13.6% of the male law students said it had been of no importance. Stevens, *supra* note 14, at 612. Also, the vast majority of all law students surveyed indicated that prestige was of some importance in their decision; *id.* at 578; and the importance of money in the decision to become a lawyer apparently increased during the 1960s. *Id.* at 577.

44. Anderson et al., *supra* note 37 (a 1973 study); Stevens, *supra* note 14 (a 1973 study); Georgina W. LaRussa, *Portia's Decision: Women's Motives for Studying Law and Their Later Career Satisfaction as Attorneys*, 1 PSYCHOL. WOMEN Q. 350 (1977); Janet Taber et al., *Project—Gender, Legal Education, and the Legal Profession: An Empirical Study of Stanford Law Students and Graduates*, 40 STAN. L. REV. 1209 (1988). Women (and minorities) were significantly more likely than men to enter law school to restructure society or serve the underprivileged. Stevens, *supra* note 14, at 613. An extensive study done with students and graduates of Stanford Law School as of December 1986 found that, among other things, significantly more male than female students indicated they went

to law school because of (a) a desire to make money and (b) an interest in politics. Graduates were slightly different. Female graduates more often reported (a) a desire to serve society and (b) the need for additional education to obtain a job as motivations to go to law school. Male graduates more often cited (a) a desire to make money and (b) an interest in going into business as motives for law school. There is no comparison of these motives with motivations of students or graduates of other professional schools; however, it can be noted that there were clear gender differences between the law students and lawyers as to their motives for choosing the law. More male students than female students cited an interest in politics (39.2% versus 20%) or a desire to make money (38.7% versus 20.6%) as an incentive for going to law school. More female graduates of Stanford Law School than male graduates cited a desire to serve society (81.5% versus 69.3%) or the need for additional education to obtain a job (50% versus 31.4%) as a motivation for going to law school. Male graduates were more likely than female graduates to admit desire to make money as a motivator for law school (49.5% versus 38%). *See* Taber et al. *supra. But see also* James J. White, *Women in the Law*, 65 MICH. L. REV. 1051, 1069–1070 (1967) (finding that women are not more motivated to enter law for altruistic reasons than are men and that they are also motivated by money, contrary to expectations).

45. Stevens, *supra* note 14, at 612–613. For example, in the 1973 American study by Stevens, 54.7% of women said financial motives were of no importance to their decision to go to law school, whereas only 13.6% of men said such motives were of no importance to them. These results were replicated in a 1986 study at Stanford University Law School, Taber et al., *supra* note 44. This Stanford study found that more male students went to law school to make money or because of an interest in politics. More male graduates went to make money or because of an interest in business or politics, whereas more female graduates went to serve society or to get additional education to get a job. Finally, a 1967 study of women in the law found that they were not more often motivated to enter law for social worker-type, altruistic reasons but were also motivated by money. James J. White, *Women in the Law*, 85 MICH. L. REV. 1051, 1069 (1967); *see also* Georginna W. LaRussa, Portiás Decision: Women's Motives for Studying Law and Their Later Career Satisfaction as Attorneys, 1 PSYCHOL. WOMEN Q. 350, 350–364 (1977).

46. Anderson et al., *supra* note 37, at 43.

47. This could be true; other research has found that female lawyers are somewhat more likely to have an ethic of care than are male attorneys, which focuses more on helping others. Taber et al., *supra* note 44; and Erica Weissman, Gender-Role Issues in Attorney Career Satisfaction (unpublished PhD dissertation, Yeshiva University, 1994).

48. LaRussa, *supra* note 44. In this study, women's motives for entering law fell into eight categories, in order of frequency: altruistic (helping society or others), realistic (practical, utilitarian, materialistic), self-enhancement (increased personal image), stimulation (intellectually challenging, difficult), self-fulfillment (developing existing talents or fulfilling personal goal), professional identifica-

tion (wanted to be a lawyer), action-oriented (interest in the tangible results of lawyering), and theoretical interest (interest in law for its own sake as a scholarly discipline). More than 50% of the women mentioned altruistic or realistic motives.

49. Stevens, *supra* note 14, at 608–609.

50. *Id.* at 609.

51. For example, in 1970, there were fairly few women in the law; in 1999, the number of entering women law students in U.S. law schools came close to the percentage of women in the U.S. population as a whole. *See* A.B.A. COMMISSION ON WOMEN IN THE LAW, BASIC FACTS FROM WOMEN IN THE LAW: A LOOK AT THE NUMBERS 1 (December 1995) (documenting the rising percentage of women in the law). Also, beginning in the late 1970s, there were a number of studies investigating gender differences among law students and lawyers.

52. Stevens, *supra* note 14.

53. *Id.* at 571–572.

54. *Id.* at 572–574. A similar result was also reported in a 1965 book about law students. S. WARKOV & J. ZELAN, LAWYERS IN THE MAKING (National Opinion Center 1965), *cited by* Lawrence Dubin, *The Role of Law School in Balancing a Lawyer's Personal and Professional Life*, J. PSYCHIATRY & L. 57, 61 n.8 (Spring, 1982).

55. Stevens, *supra* note 14, at 574. Of course, this may have been true of most young people at the time, given the political and social climate of the 1960s.

56. *Id.*

57. At the least this indicates a change in their intellectual approaches to life. *Id.* at 575. Stevens also demonstrated that law students are relatively high academic achievers, because 50% of law students ranked in the top quarter of their undergraduate classes.

58. Stevens, *supra* note 14, at 575.

59. A 1974 study found that law students were more often first-born or only children, but then admitted that this was also true of medical students, college undergraduates, and graduate students in general. Kay Standley et al., *Family Constellations of Law and Medical Students*, 26 J. LEGAL EDUC. 241, 242, 246, 242 (1974). *See also* Williams & McCullers, *supra* note 9, at 351 (finding that women lawyers and physicians are more likely to be first-born or only children and to share other similarities) and S. WARKOV & J. ZELAN, LAWYERS IN THE MAKING (Chicago National Opinion Research Center 1965), *cited by* Lawrence Dubin, *The Role of Law School in Balancing a Lawyer's Personal and Professional Life*, J. PSYCHIATRY & L. 57, 61 n.8 (Spring, 1982) (asserting that law students come from higher social and economic levels than do other college graduates, which may be consistent with the idea that they seek to achieve a socioeconomic level equal to their parents').

60. Standley et al.'s 1974 study also found that medical students were more likely to have a father who was a physician than law students were likely to have a father who was an attorney. Standley et al., *supra* note 59, at 244–245. The authors suggested that maybe sons of physicians have a clearer idea of what

their fathers do on a daily basis at work than do sons of attorneys. This is consistent with Stephen Reich's ideas that prospective law students have a poorer idea of what attorneys do than do students in medicine, engineeering, psychology, and dentistry. Reich, *supra* note 23, at 1344. Also, the 1974 study excluded female students because of the small number of women in the sample studied. Their preliminary results with the women students suggested that these same results may not be true for women medical and law students. Standley et al., *supra* note 59, at 245.

61. Marilyn Heins et al., *Law Students and Medical Students: A Comparison of Perceived Stress*, 33 J. LEGAL EDUC. 511, 516 (1983).

62. Heins et al., *supra* note 61.

63. Norman Solkoff, *The Use of Personality and Attitude Tests in Predicting the Academic Success of Medical and Law Students*, 43 J. MED. EDUC. 1250–1253 (1968) [hereinafter Solkoff]; Norman Solkoff & Joan Markowitz, *Personality Characteristics of First-Year Medical and Law Students*, 42 J. MED. EDUC. 195 (1967) [hereinafter Solkoff & Markowitz]. These studies were done while Dr. Solkoff was an associate professor of psychology within the Department of Psychiatry at the State University of New York, Buffalo School of Medicine.

64. For example, police departments and suicide prevention centers often use the MMPI to screen out inappropriate employees. The MMPI was designed to distinguish abnormal personality characteristics from normal ones, in contrast to the Myers–Briggs Type Indicator (MBTI), which was developed to distinguish among normal personality types and does not indicate whether dysfunction is present or not. The MMPI is used in clinical settings; the MBTI is more often used as a counseling tool. The MBTI has been used in many seminars and workplace interventions designed to help people understand their "psychological type" and work more effectively with one another. It has also been introduced into the law office and legal education; *see, e.g.*, Don Peters, *Forever Jung: Psychological Type Theory, The Myers–Briggs Type Indicator and Learning Negotiation*, 42 DRAKE L. REV. 1 (1993); Don Peters & Martha Peters, *Maybe That's Why I Do What I Do: Psychological Type Theory, The Myers–Briggs Type Indicator, and Learning Legal Interviewing*, 35 N.Y.L. SCH. L. REV. 169 (1990).

65. *Cynicism* was defined from the dictionary as "a contemptuous disbelief in man's sincerity of motives or rectitude of conduct characterized by the conviction that human conduct is suggested or directed by self-interest or self-indulgence." Solkoff & Markowitz, *supra* note 63, at 197.

66. *Humanitarianism* was also defined from the dictionary as "a regard for the interests of mankind, benevolence, philanthropy." *Id*. at 197. This is somewhat similar to the definition of feeling types in Miller's 1967 study, Paul Van R. Miller, *Personality Differences and Student Survival in Law School*, 19 J. LEGAL EDUC. 460 (1967) [hereinafter Van R. Miller].

67. Authoritarianism was similarly defined as acceptance of the idea of survival of the fittest, hero worship of acquaintances, and rugged individualism. Solkoff & Markowitz, *supra* note 63, at 197.

68. Solkoff & Markowitz, *supra* note 63, at 199.

69. In particular, the law students' Pd (psychopathic deviate) and Ma (hypomania) scores were significantly higher than those of the medical students, whereas the medical students' D (depression) and Mf (masculine–feminine) scores were higher than those of the law students. *Id.* Other interpretations of these scales are: Pd measures trouble with the law, lack of concern about social and moral standards of conduct, family discord, authority problems, social alienation, self-alienation, social imperturbability (often thought of as anger); and Ma measures overambitiousness, extroversion, high aspirations, amorality, psychomotor acceleration, imperturbability, and ego inflation. S. R. HATHAWAY & J. C. MCKINLEY, MINNESOTA MULTIPHASIC PERSONALITY INVENTORY–2: MANUAL FOR ADMINISTRATION AND SCORING, 29–30 (University of Minnesota Press, 1989).

70. Heather M. McLean & Rudolf Kalin, *Congruence Between Self-Image and Occupational Stereotypes in Students Entering Gender-Dominated Occupations*, 26 J. BEHAV. SCI., 142, 153–154 (1994).

71. *Id.* at 154–155. This correlation was only 0.14, which was the lowest correlation between self-description and stereotype for all the occupations studied: engineer, law, physician, rehabilitation therapist, nurse, and teacher.

72. *Id.* at 155.

73. *See generally* Leonard H. Chusmir, *Law and Jurisprudence Occupations: A Look at Motivational Need Patterns*, COM. L. J., May 1984, at 231–235.

74. *See generally* Nachmann, *supra* note 1.

75. In the 1967 and 1968 studies, law students were more authoritarian and less humanitarian than medical students. *See generally* Solkoff and Markowitz, *supra* note 63. In this study, authoritarianism meant accepting the survival of the fittest, hero worship of acquaintances, and rugged individualism. However, one study found that law students were actually more humanitarian than medical or undergraduate students. A 1991 Australian study looked at authoritarianism, which it defined as the absence of humanitarian feeling. Richard Pestell & J. Richard B. Ball, *Authoritarianism Among Medicine and Law Students*, AUSTL. AND N.Z. J. PSYCHIATRY 265, 267 (1991). Authoritarianism meant having dogmatic beliefs, a hierarchical approach to interpersonal relationships, significantly greater distrust and suspicion, interpersonal manipulativeness, and material rather than social values. Among doctors, it had been associated with poor treatment of certain disadvantaged patients. *Id.* at 256–266. Despite the 1967 and 1968 findings, this study found that Australian law students were less authoritarian than medical students. Although men in both fields were more authoritarian than women, there was a trend for these groups to converge—the men to become less authoritarian and the women to become more so—as school progressed. The researchers thought that this occurred because women in medicine and law simply became more masculine and adopted a male gender-role stereotype as the training programs progressed. Caution is warranted in applying these results to American law students, because Australian training for medicine and law is done at the undergraduate level, unlike the American system. A later study comparing Korean law and undergraduate students to American law and undergraduate students also found the law students to be

less authoritarian than the undergraduates. Eun-Yeong Na & Elizabeth F. Loftus, *Attitudes Toward Law and Prisoners, Conservative Authoritarianism, Attribution, and Internal–External Locus of Control: Korean and American Law Students and Undergraduates*, 29 J. CROSS-CULTURAL PSYCHOL. 595, 598–599, 601–602, 605, and 611 (September 1998). In this study, students from the University of Washington School of Law in 1996 had the lowest "conservative authoritarianism" of all four groups, meaning they were the most liberal in their views. However, authoritarianism does not always mean the absence of humanitarianism. In this study, authoritarianism meant dogmatism, conservatism, preference for law and order, or right-wing authoritarianism, which may not be the same as the earlier studies' use of the term to mean accepting the survival of the fittest, hero worship, rugged individualism, and absence of humanitarian feeling. Therefore these studies may or may not be comparable.

76. Heins et al., *supra* note 61.

77. *See* discussion in *supra* note 75.

78. Stevens, *supra* note 14, at 673–675.

79. *Id.* at 671–675. Competitiveness may have been lessened in this study by one law school's elimination of grades and institution of a pass–fail system during the study.

80. *Id.* at 674.

81. *Id.* at 675.

82. Janet S. St. Lawrence et al., *Stress Management Training for Law Students: Cognitive Behavioral Intervention*, 1 BEHAV. SCI. & L. 101 (1983). This test was the Jenkins Activity Scale.

83. *Id.* at 106.

84. *See generally* Bohn, *supra* note 14.

85. Jane W. Coplin & John E. Williams, *Women Law Students' Descriptions of Self and the Ideal Lawyer*, 2 PSYCHOL. WOMEN Q. 323, 327–332 (1978).

86. *Id.* at 329.

87. *Id.* at 329–331. This study used the Adjective Check List to determine needs as well as personality traits. There was one interesting "reversal," in that women law students described themselves as more aggressive and less nurturing than their ideal lawyer, perhaps as a result of overcompensation and deemphasis on feminine traits. *Id.* at 331.

88. *See, e.g.*, Williams & McCullers, *supra* note 9 (empirical study of successful women professionals).

89. Heather M. McLean & Rudolf Kalin, *Congruence Between Self-Image and Occupational Stereotypes in Students Entering Gender-Dominated Occupations*, 26 CAN. J. BEHAV. SCI. 142, 153–154 (1994).

90. Quotations from Alan N. Katz & Mark P. Denbeaux, *Trust, Cynicism, and Machiavellianism Among Entering First-Year Law Students*, 53 J. URB. L. 397, 398 (1976).

91. *Id.*

92. Katz & Denbeaux, *supra* note 90, at 401–405.

93. *See generally* Anderson et al., *supra* note 37.

94. Na & Loftus, *supra* note 75, at 604–605.

95. Katz & Denbeaux, *supra* note 90, at 410–411 (finding that law students believed lawyers were more honest and ethical than were people in general), citing Thielens, The Socialization of Law Students: A Case Study in Three Parts (1965) (unpublished PhD dissertation, Columbia University), at 195 (finding that law students rated lawyers' ethical standards as generally superior to those of typical nonlawyer adults); Campbell, *The Attitudes of First-Year Law Students at the University of New Mexico*, 20 J. Legal Educ. 71 (1967) (finding that 91% of the 69 law students surveyed rated the honesty of doctors above that of lawyers); and The Gallup Poll Index, September 1975, at 13 (a poll of 904 undergraduates in which 66% rated the honesty and ethical standards of doctors as high or very high, whereas only 40% gave a similar ranking to lawyers).

96. Solkoff, *supra* note 63, at 1252. This latter characteristic was evidenced by higher L (lie) scores on the MMPI among the lower ranked students. Solkoff's findings are fairly consistent with a later study by Reich in 1976 in which no relationships between personality dimensions (measured by the California Psychological Inventory) on first-year law school academic achievement were found. Stephen Reich, *California Psychological Inventory: Profile of a Sample of First-Year Law Students*, 39 Psychol. Rep. 871, 872 (1976). In general, it appears that there are few *personality* attributes that accurately predict law school academic performance. Solkoff's finding that, of the academic measures, only IQ score accurately predicted academic performance is supported by a later study finding that the LSAT correlates only about .35 with law school grades, which is not particularly high. Goolsby, *supra* note 26. Goolsby concluded that "any comprehensive test of achievement would serve as well as the LSAT as a predictor of success in law school." *Id.* at 425. These studies suggest that IQ may be more closely associated with success in law school than are undergraduate grade point average or LSAT score, which are the two criteria currently used for admission to law school.

97. Reich, *supra* note 23, at 1343–1346. The top students scored significantly higher on the Strong Vocational Interest Blank scales named physician, psychiatrist, psychologist, biologist, artist, musician–performer, lawyer, and author–journalist. The bottom students scored significantly higher on the public speaking, business management, merchandising, office practices, mechanical, religious activities, production manager, accountant, office worker, purchasing agent, banker, pharmacist, funeral director, salesman, president–manufacturing, credit manager, and business education teacher scales. This means their interests were most similar to the interests of individuals in those professions. *Id.* at 1344.

98. Reich, *supra* note 23, at 1344.

99. *Id.* at 1344. According to Reich, these results are consistent with other studies of medical, engineering, and male and female undergraduates; top students generally score higher on professional or intellectual scales and bottom students score higher on business or commercial scales.

100. *Id.*

101. Van R. Miller, *supra* note 66, at 460–467.

102. *Id.*

103. Richard, *supra* note 10, at 233–234.

104. Solkoff & Markowitz, *supra* note 63, at 197.

105. Michael J. Patton, *The Student, the Situation, and Performance During the First Year of Law School*, 21 J. LEGAL EDUC. 10, 43–45 (1968).

106. Vernellia R. Randall, *The Myers–Briggs Type Indicator, First Year Law Students and Performance*, 26 CUMB. L. REV. 63, 80–81, 86–87, 91–92, 96–97 (1995–1996).

107. *Id.* at 81.

108. *Id.* at 93.

109. Dorothy H. Deegan, *Exploring Individual Differences Among Novices Reading in a Specific Domain: The Case of Law*, 30 READING RESEARCH Q. 154, 154–170 (April/May/June 1995).

110. Jason M. Satterfield, John Monahan, & Martin P. Seligman, *Law School Performance Predicted by Explanatory Style*, 15 BEHAV. SCI. & LAW 95 (1997).

111. An external locus of control means you believe things just happen by chance—others or situations cause events. An internal locus of control means you believe it is your fault, that you cause events. A more positive explanation is that an internal locus of control means you believe you are capable of affecting your world, whereas an external locus of control means you feel that events and forces act on you. DAVID G. MEYERS, SOCIAL PSYCHOLOGY, 2D ED. (McGraw-Hill, 1987), at 104–105.

112. Satterfield et al., *supra* note 110, at 100–104. In addition, pessimism plus undergraduate GPA predicted law school GPA better than did undergraduate GPA alone, suggesting that pessimism is an important variable determining one's law school grades. *Id.*

113. *Id.*

114. *Id.*

115. Na & Loftus, *supra* note 75, at 601–612 (1998) (reporting data collected in 1996).

116. Richard, *supra* note 10, at 233.

117. *Id. See also* SUSAN J. BELL & LAWRENCE R. RICHARD, FULL DISCLOSURE: DO YOU REALLY WANT TO BE A LAWYER? (2d ed. Peterson's Guides 1992) (1955), at 152. Richard also notes that the thinking/feeling scale is the most significant personality trait for predicting lawyer satisfaction, stating, "Those with a preference for Feeling are swimming against the tide." *Id.* at 153.

118. Paul Van R. Miller, *Personality Differences and Student Survival in Law School*, 19 J. LEGAL EDUC. 460 (1967); Frank L. Natter, *The Human Factor: Psychological Type in Legal Education*, 3 RES. PSYCHOL. TYPE 55 (1981); Vernellia R. Randall, *supra* note 110, at 80–81, 86–87, 91–92, 96–97 (1995–1996); and Richard, *supra* note 10, at 238 (one of the unpublished studies, summarizing the results of a study published in 1991 by Thorne and Gough and eight other unpublished studies ranging from 1965 to 1993 conducted by Cole, Davis, Liebman, and Miller).

119. Richard, *supra* note 10.

120. All of the early (1967–1968) studies excluded women from the sample studied.

121. Done in 1963 with students in their first week of law school at four law schools, this study measured drop-outs after the first year of law school and attempted to find correlates among academic predictors and personality type (using the Myers–Briggs Type Indicator). It found that dropping out from the first year of law school is unrelated to academic promise as a law student, based on undergraduate grade point average and Law School Admissions Test (LSAT) scores. Miller, *supra* note 118, at 460–467.

122. 72% of the law students preferred thinking and 54% of the male college students studied preferred thinking over feeling. *Id.* at 465.

123. *See id. See also* Lawrence R. Richard, *How Your Personality Affects Your Practice*, 79 A.B.A. J., July 1993, at 74.

124. Frank L. Natter, *The Human Factor: Psychological Type in Legal Education*, 3 RES. PSYCHOL. TYPE 55, 56 (1981).

125. Feeling may also be incompatible with the contented practice of law. *See, e.g.*, Richard, *supra* note 10, at 233–234, and BELL & RICHARD, *supra* note 117.

126. An overrepresented type is one that is more prevalent in the law student sample than it is in the general population (i.e., it was self-selected into law school). Van R. Miller, *supra* note 66, at 466.

127. This is the ISTJ type, reflecting a preference for introversion, sensing, thinking, and judging.

128. This is the ESFJ type, reflecting a preference for extroversion, sensing, feeling, and judging. *Id.* at 466.

129. DAVID KEIRSEY, PLEASE UNDERSTAND ME II, 18–20, 75–115 (Prometheus Nemesis Book Company, 1998) (basing his four types on Isabel Myers's four categories of personality types).

130. Randall, *supra* note 106, at 81, 92.

131. Miller, *supra* note 118, at 467.

132. *Id.* at 467. He goes on to say that "presumably, the purpose of a law school is to train future lawyers and not to titillate the faculty by supplying them with intellectually able first-year students—although the two are not, of course, mutually exclusive." *Id.* The objective criteria referred to are the undergraduate grade point average and the LSAT score.

133. Chusmir, *supra* note 9.

134. Randall, *supra* note 118, at 80–97.

135. Larry Richard, *How Your Personality Affects Your Practice: The Lawyer Types*, 79 A.B.A. J. 74, 76 (1993). About 35% of women in the general population prefer thinking to feeling; about 65% of men in the general population prefer thinking to feeling, according to Richard. *Id.* at 76.

136. Pauline A. Doucette & William E. Kelleher, *Cognitive Style and Law Students in Eastern Canada: Preliminary Findings*, COLLEGE STUDENT J. 206 (1998) (participants were 284 full-time Canadian law students in all three years of law school).

137. *Id.* at 207.

138. The third-year law students were more intuitive than first- or second-year students, but this was to be expected, because people usually become more intuitive as they get older, according to researchers. *See id.* at 208, 210.

139. Judith White & Chris Manolis, *Individual Differences in Ethical Reasoning Among Law Students*, 25 Soc. Behav. & Personality 19, 21–30, 33, 39–41 (1997) (finding that having a feeling preference did not necessarily predispose one to endorse the ethic of care; the two appeared to be unrelated).

140. June Louin Tapp & Felicia J. Levine, *Legal Socialization: Strategies for an Ethical Legality*, 27 Stan. L. Rev. 1, 22–23 n.86 (1974) (investigating the moral stage of graduating law students and using open-ended questions to elicit a general discussion and then evaluating the law students' responses scientifically).

141. *See id.* at 30. Postconventional thinking weighs compliance with the law "against the inherent rightness or morality of the rule." *Id.* at 26.

142. *See generally* Tapp & Levine, *supra* note 140.

143. Because of the conventional morality, Tapp and Levine in 1974 concluded that law students' morality was homogeneous; *see* Tapp & Levine, *supra* note 140, at 29–31. *See also* Sandra Janoff, *The Influence of Legal Education on Moral Reasoning*, 76 Minn. L. Rev. 193, 238, 229–230 (1991) (finding that law students began to move toward a uniform rights orientation by the end of the first year, even if they had an ethic of care at the beginning of law school). *Compare* Landwehr's 1982 study, Lawrence J. Landwehr, *Lawyers as Social Progressives or Reactionaries: The Law and Order Cognitive Orientation of Lawyers*, 7 Law & Psychol. Rev. 39 (1982), finding that 90.3% of the lawyers surveyed were clustered at Kohlberg's stage 4 "law and order" morality.

144. For example, Willging and Dunn in 1981 found that law students were clustered in Kohlberg's stages 4 and what they called 5A, but this was not different from the general population or from graduate students in other professional schools. Thomas E. Willging & Thomas G. Dunn, *The Moral Development of the Law Student: Theory and Data on Legal Education*, 31 J. Legal Educ. 306, 354, 356 (1981).

145. *See, e.g.*, Kurt M. Saunders & Linda Levine, *Learning to Think Like a Lawyer*, 29 U.S.F. L. Rev. 121 (1994) (finding that law students' level of moral development differed depending on the context); and Taber et al., *supra* note 44, at 1277 (finding that law students do not adopt a global approach to solving legal hypotheticals but rather use a case-by-case approach in which various factors are weighted, depending on the situation). Saunders and Levine conducted an in-depth study of eight law students and observed that the students did not appear to reason at any particular level and instead jumped from stage to stage. For example, their reasoning might use postconventional thought in one situation and conventional thought in another. Saunders & Levine, at 181.

146. Specifically, Tapp & Levine, *supra* note 140, and Willging & Dunn, *supra* note 144, discussed *supra* notes 142 and 143.

147. A.B.A. Commission on Women in the Profession, *Basic Facts From Women in the Law: A Look at the Numbers* (Author, 1995).

148. *See, e.g.*, Janoff, *supra* note 143.

149. Willging & Dunn, *supra* note 144, at 323, 343.

150. Tapp & Levine, *supra* note 140.

151. Willging & Dunn, *supra* note 144.

152. *Id.* This study used a paper and pencil, multiple-choice test that was created to quickly assess people's Kohlbergian stage of moral development. The test presents moral dilemmas and asks the participants to choose what they would do and then rank 12 arguments in order of importance to their decision. Each argument represents a moral stage of reasoning. The test then yields a score that corresponds roughly to a Kohlbergian stage. Earlier empirical studies with this test indicated that these scores consistently increased as people got older but leveled off after they left college or another academic environment. The average scores of entering law students were not different from those of other graduate and professional (e.g., medical) students. The researchers did not appear to perform any statistical analysis to determine whether law students' test scores differed significantly than other graduate students' scores; they simply reported the average scores for various groups and stated that "there does not appear to be much difference." Willging & Dunn, *supra* note 144, at 356.

153. Tapp & Levine, 1974, *supra* note 140.

154. Taber et al., *supra* note 44.

155. *Id.* at 1230.

156. *Id.* at 1249–1251. These results were found somewhat consistently for two hypothetical situations presented to the students, fact patterns involving media law and the law of standing. However, not all contextual factors were important to the women surveyed, indicating that maybe the women law students engaged in a case-by-case analysis of each factor or used an individualized approach to weighing each factors' importance. The authors explain the results by reference to Gilligan's idea that women's morality focuses on people. Women law students may have weighted different contextual factors differently because some factors were heavily people-oriented and some were not. Alternatively, the women students and graduates might have been sufficiently socialized by legal training so that they no longer stereotypically responded to all contextual factors or ignored all abstract factors, as women in general might do. *See* Taber et al., *supra* note 44, at 1249–1250. This latter idea is supported by later research by Sandra Janoff. *See* Janoff, *supra* note 143. Instead, perhaps they displayed a mix of the ethic of care and rights orientation in their decision making. This study also found that women followed legal precedent just as often as did men, contrary to the researchers' expectation. Taber et al., *supra* note 44, at 1250.

157. *Id.* at 1248. The two situations involved media law and the law of standing.

158. CAROL GILLIGAN, IN A DIFFERENT VOICE: PSYCHOLOGICAL THEORY AND WOMEN'S DEVELOPMENT (Harvard University Press, 1982). This concept is more fully discussed in the previous chapter. The ethic of care typically emphasizes interpersonal concerns and is believed to be characteristic of women. Unsatisfied with the appropriateness of Kohlberg's theory of moral development to women, Gilligan and others performed research that found that women more

often make decisions out of an ethic of care whereas men more often decide on the basis of a rights orientation. *See* White & Manolis, *supra* note 139, at 33, citing Carol Gilligan, *Moral Orientation and Moral Development in* E. F. KITTAY & D. T. MEYERS (EDS.), WOMEN AND MORAL THEORY (Rowman & Littlefield, 1987).

159. Janoff, *supra* note 143, at 219–222.

160. *Id.*

161. *Id.*

162. *Id.* at 218, 222, and 226. The methods used were a sentence completion test compiled from the Washington University Sentence Completion Test, the Real-Life Moral Conflict and Choice Interview, and a demographic information questionnaire. *Id.* at 211–212. The sentence completion test and interview were coded and scored for a care orientation versus a rights orientation. Resulting data were then statistically analyzed for significant differences. Although men displayed both orientations, they tended to favor rights orientations overall. Janoff explained that the two orientations are not mutually exclusive and the same individual can express sentiments consistent with both orientations but generally prefers one over the other. *Id.* at 231.

163. White & Manolis, *supra* note 139, at 21–27, 39–41. In this study, law students were assessed on five apparently similar dimensions: concrete versus abstract learning styles; thinking versus feeling; world view (organicism versus mechanism); communitarian versus consequentialist attitudes; and the ethic of care versus a justice orientation. Only three things were empirically related to having an ethic of care—being female, preferring abstract learning, and having an organicist world view. Abstract learners prefer to rely on intellect, rationality, logic, and distanced knowing, whereas concrete learners prefer to rely on personal experience and intuition. Organicists focus on concepts and see the world as active and changing and people as active, autonomous, and part of the social environment. Mechanists focus on sensory data and see the world as static and stable and people as objective, reactive, passive, and determined by their environment. Communitarianism values common goals and values, social roles, unity, resolving problems one-on-one, and imposing restrictions on individual rights for the good of the community, whereas consequentialism values the greatest good for the greatest number and defines what is good by the consequences of the action. *Id.*

164. *Id.*

165. *Id.*

166. Solkoff & Markowitz, *supra* note 63, at 197. *See also* Hedegard, *supra* note 40, at 803 (summarizing research before 1979 as indicating that law students were more confident, expressive, dominant, assertive, socially outgoing, introspective, and philosophical in outlook than other students).

167. Results on cynicism among law students are inconsistent. *See, e.g.,* Solkoff & Markowitz, *supra* note 63; Katz & Denbeaux, *supra* note 90, *citing* Wagner P. Thielens, The Socialization of Law Students: A Case Study in Three Parts (1965) (unpublished PhD dissertation, Columbia University); and Anderson et al., *supra* note 37. *See also* Hedegard, *supra* note 40 (regarding altruism).

168. Van R. Miller, *supra* note 66, at 466.

169. Hedegard, *supra* note 40, 804–805, 866.

170. Na & Loftus, *supra* note 75, at 595–615.

171. *See id.* at 611. The law students' attitudes toward fault were assessed by investigating their locus of control, or attributional style, which generally looks at why people think things happen, what causes events, who is responsible, and who is to blame.

172. Pestell & Ball, *supra* note 75, at 266, 268.

173. *See id.* (their scores on a measure of authoritarianism converged, where they had differed before).

174. This was a 1958 study comparing cynicism among medical students and law students. The medical students' cynicism increased and the law students' decreased, by their senior year of training. Solkoff & Markowitz, *supra* note 63, at 198, *citing* L. D. Eron, *The Effect of Medical Education on Attitudes: A Follow-Up Study*, 33 J. MED. EDUC. 25 (1958). Several investigators into the effects of law school on law students cite Eron's early work, which suggested that altruistic impulses are strong among incoming medical students, but these tend to dissipate as medical training progresses. Some then argue that the replacement of idealism with cynicism is a natural product of all education, not just medical school, so that this shift should be present in law students but not unique to legal education. Anderson et al., *supra* note 37, at 42–43, *citing* L. D. Eron, *Effect of Medical Education on Medical Students*, 10 J. MED. EDUC. 559 (1955) and L. D. Eron, *The Effect of Medical Education on Attitudes: A Follow-Up Study*, J. MED. EDUC. 33 (1958). However, this idea conflicts with the results of Eron's 1958 study, described earlier.

175. *See, e.g.*, Anderson et al., *supra* note 37.

176. *See* Hedegard, *supra* note 40, at 832 (1979), finding that, although law students' perceptions of attorneys were fairly positive during orientation week before law school, their perceptions of lawyers deteriorated by the end of their first year of law school. Their attitudes almost uniformly became "less certain, more qualified, and less positive," *id.* at 832. This related more to how they thought lawyers actually were than to how they thought lawyers should be, however, suggesting that their ideals changed less than did their perceptions of what exists.

177. *See* Anderson et al., *supra* note 37, at 44. This was true, however, of graduate students in engineering, law, and medicine. In all three fields, the students' attitudes during training shifted so that the profession and the autonomy of the individual practitioner assumed central importance.

178. *See* Saunders and Levine, *supra* note 145, at 146. The loss of idealism and increase in disillusionment and disenchantment with the legal system and lawyering even occurred after a summer clerkship experience; *id.* at 148. These results are consistent with the increasing pragmatism and increasing cynicism about the legal profession found by Hedegard in 1979; *see* Hedegard, *supra* note 40. The students in the 1994 study also became more tolerant of the role of interpretation and ambiguity, but this appears to be characteristic of additional education in general and not specific to law school.

179. Saunders and Levine, *supra* note 145.

180. Lawrence S. Krieger & Kannon M. Sheldon, Does Law School Change Law Students? Values, Motives, and Well-Being in a First Year Class (unpublished manuscript, 2001) (studying the emotional well-being of Florida State University law students and comparing it to that of advanced undergraduate students at the University of Missouri).

181. Anderson et al., *supra* note 37, at 42–43, *citing* L. D. Eron, *Effect of Medical Education on Medical Students*, 10 J. MED. EDUC. 559 (1955); and L. D. Eron, *The Effect of Medical Education on Attitudes: A Follow-Up Study*, J. MED. EDUC. 33 (1958).

182. Hedegard, *supra* note 40, at 805 n.34, 825 (finding this shift occurring in Brigham Young University law students from their orientation week of law school to the end of their first year).

183. Howard S. Erlanger, Charles R. Epp, Mia Cahill, & Kathleen M. Haines, *Law Student Idealism and Job Choice: Some New Data on an Old Question*, 30 L. & SOC'Y REV. 851–864, 854–854 (1996).

184. Robert Granfield, *Learning Collective Eminence: Harvard Law School*, 33 SOC. Q. 503, 518 (1992).

185. *Id.*

186. Richard N. Tsujimoto & Kathy A. Emmons, *Predicting Moral Conduct: Kohlberg's and Hogan's Theories*, 115 J. PSYCHOL. 241 (1983) (finding that moral development does not correlate neatly with moral behavior).

187. Erlanger et al., *supra* note 183, at 857–859. This study suggests that it excluded non-Whites from its sample, although it included women. *Id.* at 852–853 n.3.

188. *See* Erlanger et al., *supra* note 183.

189. *See id.*

190. *See* Hedegard, *supra* note 40, at 810, 836–837. The test used was the Omnibus Personality Inventory, a 385-item questionnaire consisting of 14 scales: thinking introversion (liking for reflective thought, ideas, abstractions, and academic activities; in contrast, extroverts like action and value practical applications); theoretical orientation (preference for theoretical concerns and for the scientific method, logical, analytical and critical in approach); estheticism (diverse interests in the arts, literature, music, and drama; highly responsive to such stimuli); complexity (experimental and flexible orientation instead of a fixed way of viewing events, high tolerance of ambiguity, uncertainty, and new situations); autonomy (liberal, nonauthoritarian thinking, a need for independence, realistic, liberal, and nonjudgmental); religious orientation (skeptical of conventional religious beliefs); social extroversion (preference for relating to people in a social context and for social activities); impulse expression (readiness to express impulses and to seek gratification, active imagination, may also feel rebellious and aggressive); personal integration (socially alienated or emotionally disturbed, feelings of hostility, aggression, isolation, rejection); anxiety level (presence of tension or anxiety); altruism (trusting and ethical in dealing with others, concerned for the welfare of

others); practical outlook (interest in practical, applied activities, materialism, value is placed in immediate utility, often authoritarian, conservative, and nonintellectual); masculinity–femininity (degree of adherence to typical gender stereotypes); and response bias (attempt to make a good impression or present a good image). *Id.* at 810–812. During the first year of law school, thinking introversion, theoretical orientation, social extroversion, and altruism all decreased, whereas impulse expression, anxiety, personal integration, autonomy, complexity, and estheticism all increased. *Id.* at 835. The other traits did not change. However, some of these changes were typical of further education in general, because they were typically seen in undergraduates as they go through college. Thus, the study discarded law students' tendencies to become more expressive and assertive, tolerant of ambiguity and complexity, and interested in aesthetic things as a general result of further education and not specific to legal education. *See id.* at 835–837.

191. Hedegard, *supra* note 40, at 836–837.

192. Benjamin et al., 1986, *supra* note 14 (finding that depression skyrockets during the first year of law school and does not return to prelaw school levels even after graduation).

193. Benjamin et al., 1986, *supra* note 14, and Krieger & Sheldon, *supra* note 180 (studying the emotional well-being of Florida State University law students and comparing it to that of advanced undergraduate students at the University of Missouri).

194. Krieger and Sheldon, *supra* note 180.

195. Stevens, *supra* note 14.

196. *Id.* at 678. Of the third-year students, those who felt a high level of tension throughout law school were more likely to believe that they had become more aggressive as a result of law school. Also, more of those who described the law school atmosphere as very competitive, as opposed to cooperative, reported that they had become more aggressive.

197. Thus Stevens concludes that self-reported "increased aggression is related primarily to perceived competition and [felt] tension." *Id.* at 678.

198. *Id.* at 678–679. Students who felt tense throughout law school were more likely to say they became more ambitious as law school progressed. Students who saw the law school atmosphere as very competitive were more likely to say they became more ambitious as a result of law school. Students who perceived faculty–student relations as warmer and more frequent were also more likely to become more ambitious during law school. *Id.*

199. *Id.* at 679.

200. *Id.* at 681.

201. Willging & Dunn, *supra* note 144, at 322, 349.

202. *Id.*

203. Willging & Dunn, *supra* note 144, at 349–350 and 354 (finding a trend for Kohlberg's stage 5B reasoning to decrease and stage 5A to increase, suggesting a slight regression toward more conventional reasoning as a result of law

school). Willging and Dunn explained that Kohlberg described stage 5A as "normative and utilitarian, with judgments based on external sources," whereas stage 5B "includes an awareness of rules combined with an internal evaluation of their fairness." *Id.* at 322, citing Lawrence Kohlberg, *Moral Stages and Moraliation: The Cognitive–Developmental Approach.* In MORAL DEVELOPMENT AND BEHAVIOR: THEORY, RESEARCH, AND SOCIAL ISSUES (T. Lickona, ed., 1976), at 40–41. In this study, maybe the stage 5B law students, who in stage 5B were willing to evaluate rules and regulations by reference to their own personal values, moved back to stage 5A during law school, meaning that they emphasized rules and regulations and externally imposed, societal norms without regard to their internal beliefs. This is consistent with the idea that law students operate at predominantly a conventional, rule-following stage 4 or stage 5A level of moral reasoning and suggests that this is partially a result of law school.

204. *See, e.g.,* Steven Hartwell, *Promoting Moral Development Through Experimental Teaching,* 1 CLINICAL L. REV. 505, 522–530 (1995). He found that specific law school professional responsibility courses had a substantial positive effect on the law students' Kohlbergian moral stage, as measured by the Defining Issues Test, a pencil and paper test of one's Kohlbergian moral stage. To further verify his results, he administered the Defining Issues Test (DIT), a test developed by James Rest, *id.* at 511-512, citing JAMES R. REST, GUIDE FOR THE DEFINING ISSUES TEST 20 (1987, rev. 1990), to students in five other experientially taught clinic courses, before and after each course; none of the mean precourse DIT scores differed significantly from the mean postcourse scores for these five courses. Hartwell's results were independent of the manner in which the DIT was administered and of whether Kohlberg's theory was presented in the course. Hartwell, at 522–530. *See also* Wagner P. Thielens, *The Influence of the Law School Experience on the Professional Ethics of Law Students,* 21 J. LEGAL EDUC. 587, 590–591 (1969), finding that law students' responses to professional ethical dilemmas were more often ethical by the end of law school, where *ethical* meant conforming to the ethics code or code of professional responsibility. Yet the number of unethical responses was still disappointingly high, indicating a disparity between professional ethical norms and their acceptance by law students. Also, this study compared law students to practicing attorneys and found that the percentage of unethical responses of the lawyers (47.2%) was higher than that of even first-year law students (45.6%), suggesting a regression in ethics after graduation. Third-year law students had the lowest percentage of unethical responses, at 39.2%. *Id.*

205. *See, e.g.,* Tapp & Levine (1974), *supra* note 140, at 25–26 (moral reasoning did not appreciably change during law school); Willging & Dunn (1981), *supra* note 144, at 348 (no significant differences in law students' Kohlbergian moral stage before and after their first year and before and after a comprehensive third-year ethics course); and Saunders & Levine, *supra* note 140 (no law student was observed to progress through the stages of any educational model of moral development during law school, including Kohlberg's). Saunders and Levine, for example, began by asking entering law students to illustrate

their concept of the law in a map or diagram and to describe what it means to think like a lawyer. *Id.* at 144. Eight of the 94 entering students were reinterviewed about these ideas during their first year and once in their second year. *Id.*

206. Thielens, *supra* note 95.

207. Hartwell, *supra* note 204, at 522–530, who concluded that these three third-year professional responsibility courses taught by him in 1988, 1990, and 1992 were an effective, specific intervention technique having a substantial positive effect on the law students' moral development. In contrast, there were no differences in the students' moral stage before and after other experientially taught clinic courses, so these results appear to be specific to the professional responsibility courses themselves. Or they may have been specific to the professor teaching the courses. This professor thought that his students changed because his courses were "student-centered" rather than "teacher-centered," meaning he was not just a talking head in front of the class, like most law school courses. In his courses, his role was primarily to record and clarify student participation, to encourage the students to seek self-revelation and self-knowledge, and not to offer or defend opinions. He thought that moral development occurred because the students had a chance to step out of the role of advocate and arguer and into the role of decision maker, which he called "moral discourse." This is an appealing but unconvincing argument, because a 1990 study found that even a teacher-centered course, in this case an undergraduate ethics course, produced a significant increase in the students' Kohlbergian moral stage. William Y. Penn, Jr., *Teaching Ethics—A Direct Approach*, 19 J. MORAL EDUC. 124 (1990). In response, Hartwell, *supra* note 204, at 534, suggested that perhaps Penn's course was less teacher-centered than was reported. To conclude, it is unclear precisely what caused the increase in moral stage in Hartwell's law students.

208. Tapp and Levine, *supra* note 140, and Willging and Dunn, *supra* note 144.

209. Janoff, *supra* note 143.

210. *Id.*

211. *Id.* at 226.

212. *Id.* at 229–232. Women's care orientations decreased and rights orientations increased; men's did not show a significant change in either direction.

213. *Id.* at 227. Janoff also concluded that law school does not incorporate the relational side of human nature. However, this may be a result of law students' preexisting tendency to ignore relationships and interpersonal concerns. There is a consistent empirical finding that law students prefer the decision-making style known as thinking as measured by the Myers–Briggs Type Indicator (versus feeling) before they come to law school (more than does the general population); Vernellia R. Randall, *The Myers–Briggs Type Indicator, First Year Law Students and Performance*, 26 CUMB. L. REV. 63 (1995); *see also* Frank L. Natter, *The Human Factor: Psychological Type in Legal Education*, RESEARCH IN PSYCHOLOGICAL TYPE (1981), and Miller, *supra* note 66, at 460 (1967). Law professors are likely to predominantly prefer thinking; Lawrence R. Richard, Psychological Type and Job Satisfaction Among Practicing Lawyers in the

United States (1994) (unpublished PhD dissertation, Temple University); thus the fact that legal education ignores relationships and human issues may simply reflect preexisting characteristics of the individuals who make up the law schools. Richard suggested that preferences for thinking are fixed personality traits rather than being situationally induced attributes. *Id.*

214. Janoff, *supra* note 143, at 228.

4

LAWYER PERSONALITY AND THE PROFESSIONALISM AND PUBLIC OPINION CRISES

If indeed a distinct lawyer personality exists, as developed in chapters 2 and 3, then what light does it shed on the current problems in the legal profession? I believe it explains a great deal about why we have developed a legal culture of competition, interpersonal distance (if not outright incivility), and poor public image. First, this chapter explores the first two facets of the tripartite crisis in light of the lawyer personality in an attempt to understand why these problems exist. Second, the chapter briefly explores whether, if we want to change the legal culture, we should seek to change lawyers' personalities and inner traits or if we should simply accept attorneys as we are.

LAWYER PERSONALITY AND LOW PUBLIC OPINION

Did you hear that the post office had to recall its series of stamps depicting famous lawyers? People were confused about which side to spit on.

Two attorneys go into a diner and order drinks. They pull sandwiches out of their briefcases and start to eat. The owner marches over and

---

Portions of this chapter were adapted from an article by the author titled *Asking Leopards to Change Their Spots: Should Lawyers Change? A Critique of Solutions to Problems With Professionalism by Reference to Empirically-Derived Attorney Personality Attributes*, XI GEO. J. L. ETHICS 3 (1998). The author reserved the right to adapt and publish the material.

says "You can't eat your own sandwiches in here!" The attorneys look at each other, shrug their shoulders, and then exchange sandwiches.[1]

Lawyers have a different way of viewing the world than do nonlawyers. Our technical, analytical, logical way of looking at the world makes things seem appropriate to us that other people find silly, appalling, or nonsensical (as in the last joke). Nowhere is this more evident than in the study finding that lawyers and nonlawyers evaluated settlement options differently. In this study, the nonlawyers were affected by noneconomic, psychological factors and the lawyers were completely oblivious to them.[2]

Lawyers' preference for introversion, thinking, and objective analysis and lack of sensitivity to human, emotional, interpersonal concerns may also hamper relationships with clients. Lawyers' preference for introversion suggests an indifference to the outer world, including other people, and their preference for thinking implies a cool, impersonal attitude, both of which suggest that they may not sympathize with other people, including clients. There is evidence that lawyers are actually more like engineers than they are like nurses or teachers, being logical and unemotional.[3]

Unfortunately, unlike engineers, lawyers' work is inextricably involved in interpersonal conflicts and issues. These lawyer attributes, although they may be adaptive for the practice of law because they allow the lawyer to avoid feeling unduly emotional about his or her clients' cases, may be maladaptive in the client counseling part of legal practice. Clients are likely to say their lawyers have a terrible "bedside manner" and lawyers are likely to wonder, "What do they mean? What more do they want from me?"

The movie Erin Brockovich[4] portrays the cold-fish lawyer well in its character Teresa. Teresa is a young woman associate attorney employed by the prestigious expert law firm. This firm is brought in on the case when the toxic tort class action becomes too complex for its original, solo practitioner attorney. Teresa attended the "right" law school, has the ultimate professional clothing and demeanor, and engenders the respect and awe of most of the first-year law students in my Contracts I class. In fact, with no real basis for this opinion other than her looks, demeanor, and the prestige of her firm, they often opine that she is quite competent as an attorney. However, the contrast between the clients' reactions to Teresa and their reactions to the down-to-earth, people's person, nonlawyer Erin Brockovich, is striking. After one of Teresa's stilted visits, in which she admonishes the clients (huddled on their couch with their fatally ill child between them) to tell her the facts of their case, leaving out any emotions, they actually call Erin and ask that Teresa not be sent out to their house again. They complain that she is stuck up and she makes them nervous. The unfortunate (perhaps true) message is that the more competent the attorney, the worse his or her bedside manner is likely to be. The nonlawyer in the story is the most personable, likable, and compassionate of all the legal personnel involved (and the least knowledgeable about the law).

Teresa's style can be explained in part by the lawyer personality. There is a gap in understanding, even a difference in values and morality, between lawyers and nonlawyers. This gap can cause lawyers to seem cold, dispassionate, uncaring, overly logical, fact-driven, aggressive, competitive, ruthless, and even amoral to more feeling-type clients. Clients may perceive lawyers as cold, uncaring, unsympathetic, disinterested in anything but the "relevant facts," overly rule-oriented, aggressive, competitive, and hard-driving because they actually *are* more that way than are most people. In addition, lawyers' use of the Myers–Briggs Type Inventory (MBTI) thinking style and tendency toward conventional, stage 4 or 5A moral reasoning may well appear odd, rigid, and even amoral to a public who uses both thinking and feeling and who reasons at Kohlberg's stages 3, 4, and 5 (including postconventional reasoning).

Another way to say this is that lawyers, regardless of gender, typically embody the "masculine" ideals of rationality and impartiality. However, they lack the counterbalancing "feminine" ideals of compassion and care, unlike the American public, which uses both.

This gap likely promotes misunderstanding and mutual criticism. Clients may view lawyers as cold, unemotional, and inhuman, whereas lawyers may view clients as illogical, emotional, and frustrating to deal with. At best, these lawyer characteristics set lawyers apart from people generally and cause the public to see lawyers as a special, strange breed of individuals. One of my family members (who does not have the lawyer personality!) has often complained about the cold, rational, unemotional, and excessively verbal way in which I argue, usually saying, "don't pull that lawyer stuff on me again."

This gap probably does not exist between corporate executives and their lawyers. The MBTI personality type of corporate executives is strikingly similar to that of lawyers—people at the top of organizations are overwhelmingly thinkers (95%) and judgers (87%), just like lawyers.[5] It is possible that top corporate executives are not complaining about their lawyers because they are just like them. They understand them. It may be the more plentiful criminal defendants, divorce clients, and small business people, whose personalities are more likely to mirror the general public's, who find their lawyers to be strange.

LAWYER PERSONALITY AND DEPROFESSIONALISM

The very traits that make us "lawyerlike" may also be characteristics that, in the extreme, have led to several aspects of the professionalism crisis.

The lawyer personality appears to be related to the prevalence of the Rambo[6] litigator, extreme competition, materialism, and a business-like approach to lawyering.

Unprofessional, Rambo Behavior and Lawyer Misconduct

> There's a true story about a convicted con man who was recently found to be impersonating a lawyer in New York City. The judge remarked, "I should have suspected he wasn't a lawyer. He was always so punctual and polite."[7]

> A woman and her daughter were visiting the grave of the little girl's grandmother. On their way through the cemetery back to the car, the little girl asked, "Mommy, do they ever bury two people in the same grave?" "Of course not, dear," replied the mother, "Why would you think that?" The girl replied, "The tombstone back there said, 'Here lies a lawyer and an honest man.'"

> A lawyer was on vacation in a small farming town. While walking through the streets, a car was involved in an accident. A large crowd gathered, and the lawyer was eager to get to the injured, but couldn't get near the car. Being a clever sort, he started shouting loudly, "Let me through! Let me through! I'm the son of the victim!" The crowd made way for him. Lying in front of the car was a donkey.[8]

The lawyer traits responsible for the professionalism crisis are probably our demonstrated competitive, aggressive, and masculine traits; our need for achievement and material success; some law students' uncertainty about career goals; and the high levels of psychological stress lawyers exhibit. Unprofessional, discourteous, and uncivil behavior and lawyer misconduct, materialism, and commercialization of the law may simply be products of these typical lawyer attributes.

As the number of lawyers has dramatically increased, competition for clients and fees has correspondingly increased. Lawyers' competitiveness and need for achievement and dominance could easily lead to competitive, aggressive, hostile, and overreaching behavior in a tight market, particularly if achievement after law school is defined in terms of professional prestige and material success. Competitiveness and a need for achievement could also foster an undue desire to win cases, which could intensify unprofessional behavior.

These traits appear to be present in prelaw students, thus they are unlikely to change solely as a result of changes to legal education or to the profession. Further, legal education appears to foster extrinsic rewards as opposed to intrinsic motivations, further emphasizing competition for outward measures of success. Unless the legal profession can successfully redefine "success" and "achievement" away from materialism and "winning" and toward more intrinsic, community-oriented values, the natural competitiveness, preference for dominance, and achievement orientation of lawyers are likely to continue producing unprofessional behavior as long as there is competition for clients. In short, it *is* a sharkfest out there.

In fact, some lawyers may even have a biological basis for competitive, aggressive behavior. The fact that both male and female trial lawyers' testosterone levels equaled those of blue-collar workers (and were much higher than those of nontrial lawyers and other white-collar workers) suggests that at least trial lawyers are biologically destined to be aggressive, energetic, persistent, competitive, and perhaps even a bit antisocial and angry.

The disturbing proportion of law students who come to law school for uncertain career goals may also explain part of the unprofessional behavior exhibited by modern attorneys. This argument is a little complex, but goes like this: If these individuals are uncertain about becoming lawyers, they may be similarly uncertain about their values, standards, morals, and ideals. When they face moral dilemmas in practice, they may develop unethical and unprincipled habits in their legal practices simply because they are not clear about what to do and what not to do. As uncertain and undeveloped people, they may also be unduly susceptible to the peer pressure of law school and may adopt the materialistic, competitive, achievement-oriented, impersonal, and objective values present in other law students. Unchecked, these values can indirectly encourage unethical behavior. Whether legal education or the legal profession can instill other values promoting ethical behavior in these individuals remains to be seen. Whether law school can or does promote moral development is also unclear.[9] Finally, even if law school did promote moral development, moral development does not always result in moral behavior,[10] so fixing this problem could be quite difficult.

Empirical data hints at a conflict between law students' outer confident, socially ascendant image and their inner view of themselves as awkward, defensive, and insecure.[11] When they become lawyers, this conflict may be inadequately resolved. As a result, the conflict may emerge as defensiveness, unwillingness to admit mistakes or change attitudes, or aggression toward others as ways to compensate for the inner insecurity. These defensive, compensating characteristics may lead to discourteous, uncivil behavior.

Some lawyers may experience another conflict. Individuals who do not resemble the lawyer norm in terms of values and decision-making approaches appear to change during law school to fit the norm. These atypical individuals may experience conflict as a result of this transformation.[12] They may have adopted one set of values but lost their own values and ideals in the process. This submerged conflict may surface in behavior that is unethical or unprofessional simply as a result of confusion about the individual's true values.[13]

Finally, the high levels of anxiety, depression, alienation, and dissatisfaction among law students and lawyers can cause unprofessional behavior. The next chapter explores lawyer distress and its relationship to deprofessionalism and low public opinion in more detail.

Materialism

> It was so cold last winter.... (*How cold was it?*) .... I saw a lawyer with his hands in his own pockets.

> A lawyer opened the door of his BMW, when suddenly a car came along and hit the door, ripping it off completely. When the police arrived at the scene, the lawyer was complaining bitterly about the damage to his precious BMW. "Officer, look what they've done to my Beeeemer!" he whined. "You lawyers are so materialistic, you make me sick!" retorted the officer. "You're so worried about your stupid BMW, that you didn't even notice that your left arm was ripped off!" "Oh my gawd. . . .", replied the lawyer, finally noticing the bloody left shoulder where his arm once was, "Where's my Rolex?!!"

About 30% of law students admit that a desire for money and prestige was an important motivation for going to law school. It may be even more prevalent than that; materialistic goals may be hidden in this more palatable, popular reason for going to law school: "desire for professional training." These research findings support the common perception that materialism and financial motivation are widespread in the legal profession.

Lawyers make more money than they did 25 years ago. Could it be that law is simply attracting more materialistic individuals? Empirical data show that about the same percentage of students were motivated by money and prestige to enter law in the 1960s and the 1970s but that these motives became more prevalent in the 1980s.[14] However, financial success and status-oriented life goals became much more important to all students, not just law students, in the 1980s, so this may simply reflect a widespread cultural phenomenon or national trend. We as a society may have become more materialistic in recent years; lawyers may simply reflect society. It is also possible that, as practicing lawyers became more overt about their materialism (consistent with the rest of society), the contrast with our past image of lawyers as public servants was simply too stark not to be noticed.

Not only may lawyers seek to maximize their own incomes, but they also evaluate options for clients based primarily on the economic "bottom line." Empirical data demonstrates that lawyers tend to evaluate settlement options based solely on the probability of monetary return. Unlike litigants, lawyers make dispassionate decisions based simply on maximizing income. However, there are many cases in which the litigants want something other than money. In cases where clients want the legal system to vindicate psychological or emotional needs, lawyers may appear unsympathetic and money-grabbing because they ignore these factors in their assessments.[15]

To conclude, materialism among lawyers does appear to be present, even if it simply is a reflection of a more materialistic society in general. It is possible that the combination of materialism, competitiveness, and need for achievement and dominance has contributed to Rambo litigation tactics and uncivil and discourteous behavior among lawyers. Again, the question is, Why have these traits become a problem now, if they have been present for decades? One can only point to increased competition, a dramatic increase in the number of lawyers, and overcrowded dockets as external factors that may have activated the negative potential of these traits.

LAW AS A BUSINESS

Have you hear about the lawyers' word processor? No matter what font you select, everything comes out in fine print.[16]

The charges that law has become too much of a business and no longer a profession and that lawyers do not render enough pro bono or community service are also consistent with the lawyer personality. In this case it is lawyers' impersonal orientation (e.g., thinking on the MBTI) and materialism that may contribute to the phenomenon. Lawyers, being logical, rational, and not people-oriented, may not see public service as necessary to their success. They are not likely to be motivated to provide public service simply for the benefit of others or for the emotional gratification of the work, because of their thinking or rights orientation, unless it is logical or rational to do so. Also, lawyers' materialism likely discourages them from pro bono work and other nonlucrative community service that preempts paying, private clients' matters. Although these two traits are partially present before law school, law school appears to magnify them, as evidenced by students' waning interest in public interest work during law school.

It is unclear if these traits were present 50 years ago. Studies suggest that thinking has been overwhelmingly preferred by lawyers since the 1960s, suggesting that lawyers have consistently had a preference for logic, rationality, and objective analysis and a disinterest in interpersonal concerns since then. Yet there was a shift in undergraduate preparation of law students from humanistic studies in the 1950s to the social sciences in the late 1960s, suggesting a move away from humanism. Also, materialism appears to have increased in recent years. The current combination of logical decision-making preferences with increased materialism may explain why law has become more of a business and less of a profession.[17]

SHOULD WE CHANGE?

In summary, the public opinion crisis may in part result from lawyers' preferences for introversion and thinking, rights orientation, possibly conventional or stage 4 or 5A morality, competitiveness, aggressiveness, need for dominance, and drive to succeed. These traits may, in the extreme, contribute to a gap in understanding and communication between lawyers and clients or the public. They prevent lawyers from developing more humanistic traits, which might enhance their interpersonal interactions with others and with clients. However, these are precisely the characteristics needed to be a modern lawyer. They allow lawyers to practice with a minimum of emotional conflict. Thus, these characteristics, some of which appear to be preexisting before law school, are likely to be resistant to change. In addition, law school appears to intensify some of them. Changing them may be neither possible nor desirable.

The public opinion and professionalism crises may in part result from lawyers' competitive, aggressive, ambitious, dominant, achievement-oriented, and materialistic natures. The law's emphasis on rationality and objectivity, and its lack of emphasis on humanism, fail to provide any checks on the behavior engendered by these traits. As a result, these lawyer traits may have intensified to the point that they are now causing tension between lawyers and discord between lawyers and the public at large.

In some part, low public opinion and lawyers' dissatisfaction with other lawyers are based on the perception that lawyers are nothing but hired guns who are willing to represent immoral and unethical causes and clients. However, attorneys' willingness to advocate for such causes and clients is entirely consistent with lawyers' preferred ethical decision-making styles (thinking and the rights orientation). Because lawyers tend to overwhelmingly prefer a manner of ethical decision making that separates their personal values from what they consider to be fair, just, rational, and logical, they are naturally able to represent personally repugnant clients and causes in furtherance of their professional duty to render competent representation. This ability to divorce one's personal feelings or values from one's professional duty and be a morally neutral advocate is the very trait that allows lawyers to do their work effectively and with a minimum of personal angst. It is empirically supported by the data on lawyer personality. And yet when this trait enables lawyers to zealously represent clients and causes that many consider to be immoral or unethical, it contributes to the perception that lawyers themselves are willing to be immoral or unethical. The public may judge us by the company we keep, whereas we judge ourselves by the competence of our representation rather than by the moral value of the ultimate ends of our clients.

One law professor describes this beautifully. First, he explains how many lawyers view their roles. Many lawyers act like a car mechanic who has been engaged to fix a car. The mechanic does not ask the customer about the morality of the uses to which the car will be put once it is fixed.[18] For example, the car mechanic does not say to the client, "You mean, you are going to take this car as soon as I fix it, drive across the country and abandon your wife, taking the family car with you at a time when your wife is nine months pregnant and needs the car to get to the hospital? Well, in that case I refuse to repair your vehicle." Most lawyers believe they should simply "fix the car," regardless of the morality of the client's ultimate aim in engaging the lawyer's services. With this approach to the lawyer's professional role, lawyers can end up representing immoral clients and causes without censure and in fact with societal approval, because they are simply doing their jobs.[19]

The professor also points out that the school of jurisprudential thought known as legal realism, which has predominated in American legal education for the past 30 years or so, compounds the problem. Legal realists see the law as vague, amorphous, uncertain, manipulable, and "dependent upon the client's situation, goals, and risk preferences." Legal problems are analyzed by the potential risks and costs to the client. Rather than a "source of moral limits," the law is seen as a "potential constraint, as a problem, or as data to be factored into decisions as to future conduct." He says,

> Thus, if one combines the dominant "legal realism" understanding of law with the traditional amoral role of the lawyer, *there is no moral input or constraint in the present model of the lawyer–client relationship* [Emphasis in original].[20]

In other words, lawyers adopting an amoral role in today's legal environment have no moral constraints on their behavior; because of legal realism, clients have no moral constraints on their actions. Thus the lawyer personality, the amoral professional role, and legal realism have combined to erode the integrity of the law and the legal profession.

Should we change? Some of the lawyer traits are so deeply ingrained, even perhaps predating law school, that they are likely to be unbending. For example, a disinterest in emotions and in interpersonal concerns appears to exist in early childhood long before law school, even though it seems to intensify during law school. Even if legal education were changed, these long-ingrained tendencies may resist change. It may not be possible to ask lawyers to change, personality-wise.

Second, many of the lawyer traits are actually essential and desirable in the practice of law. For example, some people believe that clients will not patronize lawyers who are not competitive, aggressive, and ruthless. I have had a cartoon on my office door for years now that shows a lawyer explaining to his new client that he is not a Rambo-style, scorched-earth litigator. He says, "I'm *not* one of those lawyers who will stab my opponent in the back. Or one who'll manufacture facts or evidence. I'm also *not* one of those lawyers who'll pummel a witness mercilessly merely for a client's personal satisfaction. Any questions so far?" The client replies, "Can you give me the number of one of *those* lawyers?"[21]

Lawyers' impersonal attributes (specifically, a preference for introversion and thinking, a rights orientation, and possibly conventional, or stage 4 morality) may be the very traits that American society appears to need and insist on in its lawyers. First, some believe that lawyers who are the ideal thinkers or rights-oriented individuals, who can put aside their personal values and feelings to vigorously and zealously represent a client or cause whose values might conflict with the lawyers' own, are the most effective lawyers.[22] Second, these impersonal qualities may be necessary for lawyers to be able to mete out impartial justice and provide legal representation to all, even unpopular or repugnant clients.[23] Maybe society has to give up interpersonal sensitivity, caring, compassion, and emotionality in lawyers to preserve lawyers' ability to be rational, logical, oriented toward rights, attuned to rules, and able to effectively advocate for their clients.[24] Our entire system of justice may depend on its administrators, who are lawyers, to be logical, rational, objective, unemotional, and impartial to administer the laws "fairly"[25] and in a predictable way. If so, then society will want to consider carefully the consequences of asking all lawyers to be less impartial, objective, and rights-oriented before urging us to change.

Objectivity and rationality in lawyers may actually be necessary for the evolution of justice and necessary social change through the laws as our society evolves and changes. If lawyers are unwilling to represent unpopular causes and clients, then certain factions of society might never be heard. Monroe Freedman pointed this out in the context of the civil rights revolutions of the 1960s, asserting that law and society would never change if lawyers were unwilling to represent unpopular causes and clients. If lawyers could not represent causes and clients that conflicted with the lawyers' own personal values, then the legal system would simply perpetuate the values of lawyers as a whole—a group whose socioeconomic status is usually above average and which is not necessarily a representative cross-section of the United States.

However, because of widespread dissatisfaction with and in the legal profession, a number of commentators on the tripartite crisis have criticized our tradition in the profession of an amoral professional role or "hired gun/zealous advocate" approach to lawyering. They argue that this morally neutral advocate stance provides no obstacle to lawyers representing immoral clients and causes. Because it provides no moral check on our associations, it can lead to our profession becoming associated in the public's mind with immorality and ruthlessness. We were praised for our objectivity in the 1960s, when our efforts led to civil reform, but now are criticized for our objectivity when our efforts are seen as obtaining unfair legal advantages for only those who can afford us. Because of these difficulties with the hired gun role, several commentators have proposed discarding the amoral professional role in favor of a style of lawyering they have called moral lawyering or caring lawyering.[26]

Moral lawyering requires lawyers to infuse their own personal values and beliefs into the representation of clients, thus sometimes turning down cases and clients that conflict with those values and beliefs. This would allow lawyers to act in ways that are consistent with their own personal values, thus providing a moral check on attorney behavior and possibly reducing inner values conflicts for lawyers. Caring lawyering refers to a panoply of suggestions, including lawyering with an ethic of care, collaborative problem-solving, empathetic listening, and a more holistic approach to client representation. This would enhance lawyers' interactions with each other, clients, and society in general, thus improving lawyers' standing and relationships with others. Despite the bedside manner appeal of these suggestions, however, the lawyer personality developed in chapters 2 and 3 clashes with these two solutions for most lawyers. If lawyers are indeed constitutionally oriented toward a decision-making style that does not take into account their own personal values, and if they are, even as children, less interested in interpersonal relationships, emotions, and concerns, then these two proposals are asking lawyers to develop skills they do not normally have. These are skills that appear to be scarce before law school and all but disappear during law school. Therefore, these proposals are unworkable for the majority of lawyers given the intractability of the lawyer personality attributes and the fact that these attributes directly conflict with the skills these proposals would require.

Absent a consideration of the problem of lawyer distress, therefore, it would be easy to conclude that lawyers should not change. The typical lawyer personality appears to be adaptive to the practice of law, if not almost necessary. Asking lawyers to change may be about as successful as asking leopards to change their spots.[27] Instead of asking lawyers to change, perhaps society should simply stop complaining about the personality of its lawyers, appreciate the unique personality that is required to be a modern lawyer, and accept lawyers as they are. However appealing this answer may be, it does not take into account the disturbing phenomenon of lawyer distress and dissatisfaction. The next two chapters look squarely at this problem and its relationship to lawyer traits, before the final chapter explores possible changes to the legal profession.

NOTES

1. http://www.ohyesuare.com/lawyerjokes/lawyershorts.shtml (retrieved August 4, 1999).

2. Russell Korobkin & Chris Guthrie, *Psychology, Economics, and Settlement: A New Look at the Role of the Lawyer,* 76 Tex. L. Rev. 77 (Nov. 1997).

3. Heather M. McLean & Rudolf Kalin, *Congruence Between Self-Image and Occupational Stereotypes in Students Entering Gender-Dominated Occupations,* 26 J. Behav. Sci. 142 (1994).

4. Erin Brockovich (Universal Pictures 2000).

5. Otto Kroeger & Janet M. Thuesen, Type Talk at Work 396 (1992) (in contrast, among trainers and educational specialists in organizations, only 42% were thinkers and 57% were judgers).

6. "Rambo" is a reference to Sylvester Stallone's macho character in the 1982 movie Rambo: First Blood (Orion Picture Corporation 1982), which became a popular media icon. The label *Rambo litigator* became used to refer to a no-holds-barred, nail-the-opponent-to-the-wall approach to litigation.

7. http://www.apc.net/ia/law.htm © Alan C. Baird (retrieved July 6, 1999).

8. This joke and preceding joke from http://www.ohyesuare.com/lawyerjokes/lawyershorts.shtml (retrieved August 8, 1999).

9. *See* Steven Hartwell, *Promoting Moral Development Through Experimental Teaching,* 1 Clinical L. Rev. 505, 522-530 (1995). In addition, researchers have not isolated the features of these courses that appear to have caused the improvement, thus we do not yet know exactly how to improve students' moral development. *Id.* at 531–535. *See also* William Y. Penn, Jr., *Teaching Ethics—A Direct Approach,* 19 J. Moral Educ. 124 (1990) (empirical study finding that undergraduate students' "P" scores on the Defining Issues Test of moral development significantly increased as a result of an undergraduate ethics course that integrated the study of logic, developmental theory, and philosophy and taught the skills of logic, role-taking, and justice operations). The Defining Issues Test was used by Hartwell, *supra* this note, at 511–512, citing James R. Rest, Guide for Defining Issues Test 20 (1987, rev. 1990). Hartwell explained that this test presents hypothetical moral dilemmas to the research participant and then yields P scores, which are a measure of "the degree to which a [participant] chooses 'principled moral reasoning,' characteristic of State Five, in responding to the dilemma presented." Hartwell, *supra* this note, at 512 and n.31. It appears that higher P scores indicate higher Kohlbergian-stage moral reasoning.

10. Richard N. Tsujimoto & Kathy A. Emmons, *Predicting Moral Conduct: Kohlberg's and Hogan's Theories,* 115 J. Psychol. 241 (1983) (finding that moral development does not correlate neatly with moral behavior).

11. Stephen Reich, *California Psychological Inventory: Profile of a Sample of First-Year Law Students,* 39 Psychol. Rep. 871 (1976).

12. Sandra Janoff, *The Influence of Legal Education on Moral Reasoning,* 76 Minn. L. Rev. 193 (1991).

13. Rand Jack & Dana Crowley Jack, Moral Vision and Professional Decisions, 130–155 (Cambridge University Press, 1989) (describing the three ways in which atypical individuals resolve this conflict—none of which is a satisfactory resolution, according to the authors).

14. *See* Robert Stevens, *Law Schools and Law Students*, 59 Va. L. Rev. 551, 598, 652–663 (1973), and Michael J. Patton, *The Student, the Situation, and Performance During the First Year of Law School*, 21 J. Legal Educ. 10, 43–45 (1968); respectively, and Alexander Astin, *Prelaw Students—A National Profile*, 34 J. Legal Educ. 73 (1984).

15. *See* Jean R. Sternlight, *Lawyers' Representation of Clients in Mediation: Using Economics and Psychology to Structure Advocacy in a Nonadversarial System*, 14 Ohio St. J. on Disp. Resol. 269, 321–331 (1999); and Russell Korobkin & Chris Guthrie, *Psychology, Economics, and Settlement: A New Look at the Role of the Lawyer*, 76 Tex. L. Rev. 77, 140 (November 1997).

16. http://www.ohyesuare.com/lawyerjokes/lawyershorts.shtml (retrieved August 4, 1999).

17. A fourth topic is advertising, but its relationship to lawyer attributes is unclear. Advertising may also have developed a crass and perhaps distasteful flavor because of lawyers' lack of sensitivity to interpersonal concerns. Lawyers, being rational and logical, may see direct advertising as sensible, and may be blind to the human or emotional impact it may have on others. Thus, what lawyers tolerate in their own profession may appear to the public as unprofessional and insensitive. It may be logically reasonable to the attorneys, as business people, but emotionally unpleasant to the public. However, there is evidence that attorneys actually view lawyer advertising more negatively than do clients, suggesting that attitudes toward advertising are not well understood and not easily related to lawyer attributes.

18. Stephen L. Pepper, *The Lawyer's Amoral Role: A Defense, A Problem, and Some Possibilities*, 1986 Am. B. Found. Res. J. 613, 624 (1986) (providing philosophical support for an amoral lawyer role, based on the values of autonomy, diversity, and equal access to justice); *but see* David Luban, *The Lysistratian Prerogative: A Response to Stephen Pepper*, 1986 Am. B. Found. Res. J. 637, 639 (1986) (disagreeing with Pepper's defense of the amoral role); *and* Andrew Kaufman, *A Commentary on Pepper's "The Lawyer's Amoral Ethical Role,"* 1986 Am. B. Found. Res. J. 651, 652 (1986) (adopting neither Pepper's support of the amoral role nor Luban's criticism of it; instead admitting a preference for "eclectic views on the theoretical issue that divides" the two scholars and suggesting that a more contextual, case-by-case analysis is appropriate).

19. *See generally* Pepper, *supra* note 18, at 624–626.

20. *Id.* at 626.

21. Bill Moore, *Attorney at Law by Pat Rice* (cartoon; Future Features Syndicate, 1996).

22. I developed this idea based on comments of my former colleague at Capital University Law School, clinical law professor Roberta Mitchell, suggest that that law students in the clinic who were less effective were those who could

not adequately divorce their own personal feelings about the case from their work as a lawyer on the case.

23. Impartial lawyers are important so that each litigant receives legal representation (otherwise, some litigants' positions would be so unpopular that no lawyer would represent them).

24. Although these two groups of qualities are not mutually exclusive, they have usually been viewed as dichotomous categories rather than extremes. For example, thinking and feeling on the MBTI are usually viewed as dichotomous categories rather than as extreme ends of a continuous trait. Lawrence R. Richard, Psychological Type and Job Satisfaction Among Practicing Lawyers in the United States (1994) (unpublished PhD dissertation, Temple University), at 61, *citing* I. B. MYERS & M. H. McCAULLEY, MANUAL: A GUIDE TO THE DEVELOPMENT AND USE OF THE MYERS–BRIGGS TYPE INDICATOR (Consulting Psychologists Press, 1986).

25. In fact, it is possible that some of the current emphasis on logic, rights, rational analysis, and so forth in legal education and the legal profession, noted by Daniel R. Coquillette, *Professionalism: The Deep Theory,* 72 N.C. L. REV. 1271, 1273–1276 (1994) (arguing that the profession's emphasis has shifted from "justice" to simply serving as a means to achieving the client's ends) has come from a reaction to perceived injustices worked by the American legal system before the events of the 1960s (such as the civil rights movement).

26. Regarding lawyering with an ethic of care, *see* Carrie Menkel-Meadow, *Is Altruism Possible in Lawyering?* 8 GA. ST. U. L. REV. 385 (1992) (arguing that lawyers should become more altruistic); Carrie Menkel-Meadow, *Review Essay: Moral Boundaries: A Political Argument for an Ethic of Care by Joan C. Tronto,* 22 N.Y.U. REV. L. & Soc. CHANGE 265 (1996). Regarding moral lawyering, *see* Robert M. Bastress, *Client Centered Counseling and Moral Accountability for Lawyers,* 10 J. LEGAL PROF. 97 (1985) (arguing that lawyers need to become more client-centered in the Rogerian sense as well as morally accountable in their representation of clients and arguing for lawyering that requires the lawyer to discuss his or her personal morals and beliefs with the client and to refuse to take actions that are inconsistent with these morals and beliefs—i.e., "moral accountability").

27. Susan Daicoff, *Asking Leopards to Change Their Spots: Should Lawyers Change? A Critique of Solutions to Problems With Professionalism by Reference to Empirically-Derived Attorney Personality Attributes,* 11 GEO. J. LEGAL ETHICS 547.

5

LAWYER AND
LAW STUDENT DISTRESS

The existence of lawyer distress, as evidenced by inordinate levels of depression, anxiety, alcoholism, job dissatisfaction, and other problems among lawyers, was documented in chapter 1. This chapter expands this discussion by exploring first how much of this stress is present before law school, how much exists during law school, and how much develops after graduation and in practice. It then examines potential causes and correlates of law student and lawyer distress in an attempt to determine what is causing these excessive amounts of psychopathology in the legal profession.

LAW STUDENTS IN DISTRESS

Despite the confident, active, competitive, rational, logical, and clear-headed image of the law student presented in chapter 3, the inner world of the law student appears to be quite different. Many studies report disturbing findings about the inner psyche of the law student, consistent with the lawyer distress documented in chapter 1. These studies hint at a chink in the formidable armor presented by the otherwise dominant, capable, and outgoing picture of the typical law student.

The Chink in the Armor: Evidence of Internal Distress

A particularly revealing study in 1976[1] found that law students' outward images clashed with their internal feelings. These (mostly male) law students' consistent scores on a personality test[2] indicated that they

> tend to be seen as aggressive, persuasive, having leadership potential and initiative, as being socially ascendant and self-seeking, quick, spontaneous, as having an expressive, ebullient nature, as intelligent, outspoken, sharp-witted, and possessing self-confidence. . . . [They would have] great interest in and enthusiasm for social role-playing, and for competitive, sharp-witted and self-seeking social relations. It is the picture of a group which projects itself or attempts to project itself, as socially successful, as possessing a high degree of social polish, and at least the appearance of great self-confidence, poise, and leadership.[3]

This description is entirely consistent with the studies discussed in chapter 3, finding law students to be at ease socially, ebullient,[4] and initiative-taking,[5] compared to others. However, it appears simply to be an outer shell.

In sharp contrast to these qualities, these same law students also scored significantly lower than average on a Sense of Well Being scale,[6] indicating that they were also "seen as self-defensive and apologetic, as awkward, cautious, and as constricted in thought and action."[7] If there had been no other scores like this, the researcher would have concluded only that this score was puzzling and interpreted it with caution. However, the students' scores on another cluster of scales[8] indicated that they were "seen as awkward, moody, dogmatic, under-controlled, impulsive, defensive, self-centered, suspicious, aloof, inhibited, cautious, nervous, and as having internal conflicts and problems."[9] The researcher concluded that this "gives some evidence of a flaw in the social armor of the law students; it may be an indication that on an inner level, on the level of self-doubt, the law student does not see himself as a polished, aggressive, successful, and dominant person"[10] and that "on an intrapersonal and inner level, the law students are insecure, defensive, distant, and lacking in maturity and socialization."[11]

His explanation of these conflicting findings is fascinating. He theorized that these law students wore a social mask—inwardly they felt awkward, defensive, and nervous and yet outwardly they sought to project a strong, active, enthusiastic, definite image, perhaps to fulfill a social role they had adopted or felt society expected from them. Perhaps law students chose the law to counteract feelings of inadequacy and uncertainty. Law was the perfect choice because it allowed them to adopt a social role that was "dominant, clear-cut, and ascendant." Being a role-playing profession, law allows inwardly insecure people to ignore inner discomfort and instead don the role of the professional lawyer. In this role, lawyers can champion the rights of other people and focus on others' problems instead of their own. Law allows lawyers to avoid dealing with their genuine feelings or resolving this internal discomfort, according to this researcher.[12]

He also concluded that law school would only make the problem worse, because it does not encourage law students to explore themselves but fosters role-playing. Finally, he noted that the profession of law actually validates and rewards the mask one can wear of "demonstrations of public vigor and dominance while being privately anxious and uncertain."[13]

Later studies support the existence of this chink in the armor. The studies discussed in the next section consistently find that, despite law students' positive, confident images, they experience unduly high levels of psychological distress.

General Psychological Distress

Three studies in the late 1950s and 1960s reported that law students were less depressed than were medical students.[14] In sharp contrast, however, a series of well-designed studies of law student distress in the mid-1980s and one in 2001 all found significant distress among law students.[15] These later studies were not plagued with the inconsistent methods, low response rates, and methodological problems of the earlier studies.

In the 1985 study, law students in all three years of law school were given a comprehensive, standard psychiatric test.[16] Overall, law students had a higher rate of psychiatric distress than either medical students or people in general. They scored significantly higher than average for anxiety, depression, hostility, obsessive–compulsivity, interpersonal discomfort, phobic anxiety, paranoid thoughts, psychoticism, overall distress, intensity of symptoms, and total number of symptoms. In this study, first-, second-, and third-year students did not differ (except that second-year students experienced more hostility-related symptoms), suggesting that the distress stayed constant throughout law school. Twelve percent of the law students were depressed enough to warrant psychiatric evaluation and intervention. In comparison, only about 3 to 9% of adults in Western civilized nations are so depressed.[17] The study concluded that "the law students are overall quite distressed."[18]

The 1985 study did not determine whether the psychological distress predated law school, whether people with a higher potential to develop psychiatric distress under stress were disproportionately attracted to law school, or whether law school caused the distress.[19] It also did not establish whether the psychiatric distress impaired social and occupational performance or led to lawyer impairment such as substance abuse, psychiatric disorders, malpractice, or ethical violations after law school.[20] To date no follow-up research has explored any of these questions except for a second study in 1986 that tested law students before, during, and after law school.[21]

This 1986 study is perhaps the most comprehensive, systematic, and well-designed study of law students and lawyers to date.[22] Its findings are dramatic. Whereas law students in the summer before law school reported normal levels of psychiatric distress, their distress significantly increased above average during the first year of law school, rocketed to alarming levels during law school, and never returned to prelaw school levels, even two years after graduation.[23]

The second study used the same tests as the 1985 study—validated, proven measurement instruments—but improved on the 1985 study by retesting the same individuals during their law school career.[24] Consistently, prelaw students had the lowest amount of distress, alumni next lowest, first-year students second to highest, and third-year law students highest. Like the 1985 results, 17 to 40% of the law students reported significantly elevated levels of depression and 20 to 40% reported other significantly elevated symptoms, such as obsessive–compulsiveness, interpersonal discomfort, anxiety, hostility, paranoid thoughts, and social alienation and isolation.[25] The law students' most severe symptoms fell into the areas of obsessive–compulsiveness and paranoia.[26]

However, the prelaw students appeared almost normal. Only 10.3% of the prelaw students suffered from clinically significant depression,[27] not unlike the typical 3 to 9% frequency of depression among adults in Western industrialized nations.[28] For example, a 1998 World Health Organization survey indicated that an average of 7% of men and 12.5% of women in 14 countries in Europe, Africa, Asia, and the Americas are depressed.[29]

A 2001 study confirmed these results. Entering law students' well-being and mental health was normal or above average, yet it greatly declined by the end of the first year in law school.[30] By April of the first year of law school, "Every measure of positive well-being (i.e. positive mood, self-actualization, life-satisfaction)" had significantly decreased and "every measure of negative well-being (i.e. physical symptoms, negative mood, depression" had significantly increased for these law students as a group.

These more recent studies indicate that law students do not necessarily experience more neurosis or psychological distress than most people before coming to law school. One explanation is that, just before law school starts, these students are at the top of their game. Most of them have just graduated from undergraduate school at the top of their classes, are hopeful, and are eagerly anticipating their new endeavor in the law. Their needs for dominance, attention, and leadership could be well-fulfilled at this point and this time in their life could be the least depressing for them. The drastic increase in depression thereafter suggests that something happens during law school to produce extreme distress among law students.

The 1980s studies' authors drew some interesting conclusions. First, they openly concluded that more law students and new lawyers suffered from impaired psychological well-being than did most people. Second, they blamed law school—it seems to have had a pervasive, socializing effect, somehow causing law students to become unduly paranoid, hostile, obsessive–compulsive, and so forth.[31] However, they also wondered whether people self-select into law school who, although not overtly depressed on entrance have predisposing characteristics that put them at risk for developing depression when under stress. Because we know that pessimism (which is related to depression) is associated with making high grades in law school,[32] it is possible that either (a) law school subtly encourages a pessimistic and therefore depressive outlook or (b) pessimistic, depression-prone individuals tend to do well in law school and thus are drawn to it.

Anxiety and Tension

Like the 1985 and 1986 studies described earlier that found law students to be more anxious than most people,[33] two studies 40 years apart (in 1957 and 1997) found that law students were more stressed than were medical students.[34] In the 1957 study, law students were not overall more stressed than medical students, but they felt more stress associated with academic demands and more stress "related to personal reactions to the academic environment" than did medical students.[35] These comparative findings are interesting when one considers that medical students work about 30% more hours per week than do law students.[36]

In the 1997 study, Canadian law students were less satisfied with their vocations, less healthy, less able to relax, more anxious and hostile, more driven to accomplish something constructive and achieve, and more stressed than were medical students. Compared to people in general, the law students were significantly less vocationally satisfied, worked against deadlines more often, and were more depressed and anxious.[37] A 1991 study similarly found that law students at Loyola University School of Law in New Orleans were significantly more anxious than undergraduate students.[38]

Tension or anxiety is not necessarily maladaptive or dysfunctional. Although too much or too little anxiety can interfere with good performance, an optimal amount of anxiety or stress is actually required for optimal performance, such as "at the top of your game."[39] Stress is sometimes defined as "physical, mental, or emotional strain or tension" or, physiologically, "any stimulus, such as fear or pain, that disturbs or interferes with the normal physiological equilibrium of an organism."[40] A 1968 study demonstrated the desirable qualities of optimal stress in the first semester of law school.[41] In this study, the most and least anxious students failed to achieve first-semester law school grades equal to their grades as predicted from their Law School Admission Test score and undergraduate grade point average, whereas middle-level anxious students achieved grades closer to their predicted grades.[42] In law school, an optimal level of anxiety appears to be associated with reaching one's academic potential.

Even if stress is helpful, however, the amount of stress and other problems experienced by law students as documented in the mid-1980s studies appears excessive and undesirable. For example, although it has not been tested, obsessive–compulsiveness and perhaps even hostility may be helpful if they motivate law students to achieve. Conditions such as depression and paranoia, in contrast, are not likely to be helpful but are more likely to be paralyzing and debilitating.

It is interesting to note that a 1973 study found than tension actually decreased as law school progressed, despite the results of the other studies finding inordinate and increasing anxiety and tension among law students.[43] In this study, law students' feelings of tension declined sharply by the third year of law school, as did the amount of time they spent studying. Although only 12% of the first-semester students felt relaxed, 75% of the fifth-semester students felt relaxed and 30% were actually bored and unchallenged. Only 5% of the fifth-semester students felt tense or found their studies difficult. Most fifth-semester students reported a two-day work week and part-time intellectual participation in law school.[44]

In part, this may just reflect the phenomenon of "senioritis" that exists in most graduate and undergraduate programs.[45] A better explanation, however, is that the tension and anxiety of the first year gives way to boredom, alienation, dissatisfaction, and disengagement by the third year of law school. Law students may still be actually psychologically distressed and even depressed (i.e., the *quantity* of distress does not change) but the outward symptoms of the distress change from the first to the third year of law school. This idea is echoed by the results of a University of Michigan law student study discussed in the following section.

Alienation and Dissatisfaction

One final law student distress study looked not at psychologically defined distress but at negative attitudes among law students.[46] This 1977 study was motivated by the 20% first-year dropout rate at the University of Michigan Law School. It revealed several types of negative attitudes among law students including alienation and dissatisfaction.[47]

One in seven Michigan law students (14%) manifested "a very strong tendency towards alienation."[48] *Alienation* meant the student had become disinterested, disengaged, "turned off," uncaring, indifferent to the idea of law reform, and suspicious of peers and alumni.[49] It was described as a special brand of cynicism directed toward the school, faculty, peers, and law. Alienated students tended to spend little effort on studying, received lower grades, and admitted more frequent acts of antisocial conduct, such as vandalism.[50] The researchers asserted that the alienated students detracted from law school morale, were more likely to be a menace to their clients, and were more likely to be indifferent to professional standards of conduct.[51]

No demographic factors explained the alienation. It appeared to cut across race, gender, age, and socioeconomic lines, with one exception: Students who had worked during undergraduate school were more likely to be alienated in law school.[52] Because alienation was not correlated with family income, the researchers theorized that these students worked because they wanted to, not because they needed to, and thus law school was unfulfilling for them because their goals were more practical and less academic.[53]

A slightly higher percentage, 15.67%, of law students or almost one in six reported being "dissatisfied," which is different from alienation.[54] Dissatisfied students were angry at faculty, peers, and alumni and worried about their grades. The researchers said the dissatisfied student was "not 'turned off,' he is 'teed off.' "[55] Dissatisfaction decreased during law school, being highest during the first year.[56] It did not affect academic performance or diligence, but it did correlate positively with alcohol and drug use. Although both alienated students and dissatisfied students used alcohol and drugs more than the norm, dissatisfied students engaged in substance use more than did alienated students.[57]

The researchers concluded that the dissatisfied students were "not themselves particular ethical risks";[58] however, they could be risks to themselves and, later, to clients because of the ways they coped with their dissatisfaction—alcohol and drug use and continuing to strive in law school despite feelings of hostility and anger, which indicates an ability to ignore feelings. The fact that dissatisfaction decreased over time suggests that it is not a stable personality trait predating law school.

The study did not indicate whether there was any overlap between alienation and dissatisfaction. It simply concluded that both states, alienation and dissatisfaction, were too prevalent and very damaging to the law student and the law school environment.[59] They could ultimately affect the legal profession because of the negative behavior and attitudes they foster. Alienation and dissatisfaction could also cause or coexist with anxiety, depression, and other mental distress.[60]

As this study points out, law students' ways of coping with distress and psychological discomfort are discouraging and may even ultimately exacerbate the distress.

Ways of Coping With Stress

Law students' usual methods of coping with stress involve isolating socially, abusing alcohol and drugs, working harder, and being more ambitious and aggressive. In a 1957 study comparing law students to medical students, law students indicated that they managed to cope with their stress but were far less inclined to seek help from anyone to deal with it (usually using "no one") compared to medical students.[61] A 1973 study found that those law students who felt more tense as law school progressed also said they had become more aggressive and ambitious during law school, suggesting that law students cope with tension through aggression and ambition, perhaps by working harder and achieving more.[62]

Suicide, however, may be less popular. Despite reports of increased stress, depression, anxiety, and general psychiatric distress among law students, a 1983 study reported that "law students commit suicide significantly less frequently than age-matched peers,"[63] medical students, and graduate students in general.[64] Although the frequency of suicides increased slightly during the third year of both medical school and law school, law student suicide rates still remained lower than medical students'.[65]

Substance Abuse

Substance abuse is both a method of coping with stress and a sign of psychological distress itself. It is a long-standing problem in the law. For example, in 1957, law students reported a greater frequency of objective symptoms of stress than did medical students, including excessive alcohol use.[66] A 1994 report by the American Association of Law Schools found that law students began depending on alcohol more frequently as law school progressed,[67] perhaps to deal with the stress and anxiety they experienced. Although law students' current drug and alcohol usage did not differ appreciably from that of college graduates of similar age, they did report higher usage rates of alcohol and psychedelic drugs other than LSD over their lifetime, past year, and past month, and higher usage rates of tranquilizers and barbiturates in the past month. Past month usage is important because substance abuse specialists generally believe that past month usage is a reliable indicator of regular use.[68] Law students also used barbiturates, LSD, other psychedelic drugs, marijuana, and cocaine more often than medical students. Finally, law students said they used alcohol in a maladaptive fashion "to relieve stress or tension," possibly foreshadowing later, more severe substance abuse problems as practicing lawyers.[69]

Law students also accept alcohol use and abuse on campus as "normal." A 1997 survey of 3,000 law students at 15 law schools concluded that alcohol use by law students is common and is seen as a major part of social activities.[70] More than half of the law students reported drinking more than they planned to on occasion, and one third said they drove while intoxicated. Finally, this 1997 survey found that about a third of law students said that law professors get drunk around them, thus implicitly endorsing excessive drinking.[71] However, in 1990, law students also reported feeling concerned about their alcohol use; this concern significantly and steadily increased during law school and the first few years of law practice.[72] Some law schools have banned alcohol from law school events because of problems with overconsumption and concerns about substance abuse in the legal profession.

Gender Differences

Despite a plethora of gender difference studies[73] concluding that women law students are more stressed than men law students, these gender differences may be simply an artifact of the way that men and women report stress. A general psychological phenomenon is that women tend to overreport stress and men tend to underreport it.[74] As noted earlier, this just illustrates the "women are from Venus, men are from Mars" differences in the sexes.[75] Dramatically, when researchers in a mid-1990s study adjusted their data for this effect, women lawyers were not more stressed than their male counterparts. In fact, the male lawyers emerged as actually more distressed than the female lawyers.[76]

However, women do report different reasons for feeling stressed in law school.[77] In 1994, women law students' stress was not caused by being socially isolated, frustrated academically, stressed by the Socratic method, pressured to find a job, or feeling unsupported by faculty or administration. Instead, they related their stress to nonacademic factors such as perceived sexism and the lack of time for themselves and their partners.[78]

Possible Causes of Law Student Distress

Little empirical research exists to explain the inordinately high levels of distress experienced by law students in general. However, the scant evidence that is available suggests that this distress is not related to environmental pressures nor is it explained by demographic features. Instead, it appears to be related to attitudes, values, and motivations and changes that law students undergo as early as the first year of law school.

For example, in the 1980s studies, no demographic or descriptive differences differentiated those who developed severe distress from those who did not. Neither age, undergraduate grade point average, law grade point average, hours devoted to undergraduate studies, nor hours devoted to law school studies explained or was related to the distress.[79]

In the 1986 study, elevated distress levels were associated with interpersonal concerns.[80] These researchers therefore concluded that the distress was caused by law school's "unbalanced development of student interpersonal skills." Indeed, legal education does not assist or encourage students to acquire interpersonal skills;[81] instead it often concentrates exclusively on the development of analytical skills. As a result, it may deemphasize the social and concrete consequences of decisions. The traditional argument is that law students must develop certain analytical or rational qualities to successfully "think like a lawyer," but these may be the very qualities responsible for law student distress.

The 1977 Michigan study discovered a third group of distressed law students who were described as "sociable." These sociable law students generally tended to wish for more personal contact with faculty, peers, and lawyers. They found law school lonely and believed it was too doctrinal and not focused sufficiently on public policy. They desired more emotionally satisfying relationships in law school. The researchers concluded that these sociable law students became distressed in law school because these desires were unlikely to be fulfilled by law school.[82]

A 1979 study at Brigham Young University[83] confirmed that law students became more anxious and internally conflicted during law school[84] and found that the students who experienced the greatest psychological conflict and feelings of isolation and alienation were those who were interested in abstract, jurisprudential issues or in "helping the underdog." The study concluded that students who are willing to tackle such issues pay a psychological price for doing so.[85]

Finally, a 2001 study found a relationship between certain changes in law students' values and motivations and the dramatic decline in students' psychological well-being during the first year.[86] In particular, the Florida State University law students in this study "became *less* oriented towards community, intimacy, and personal growth ('intrinsic' values . . .), and *more* oriented towards appearance/attractiveness (an 'extrinsic' value . . .)." They also became less likely to act "for interest or inherent satisfaction" and more externally motivated, or "motivated to please others." Specifically, the more externally motivated (i.e., by others) the students became and the more they valued extrinsic things such as "money/luxuries, popularity/fame, and beauty/attractiveness" (and the less they valued intrinsic things such as "growth/self-acceptance, intimacy/emotional connection, and community/ societal contribution"), the more distressed they became. These shifts were empirically associated with a decline in well-being. Also, previous research indicated that these shifts were likely to continue to cause decreased "well-being and life satisfaction."[87]

The 2001 study's authors noted that these changes occur in the first few months of law school and concluded that law school fosters changes in values and motivations in law students that " 'won't make them happy,' regardless of their level of achievement."[88] Their results point to law school as the culprit; however, they did suggest that law students may come to law school with a slightly materialistic focus and noted that this focus may predispose law students toward reduced mental health.[89]

Law school's unbalanced emphasis on extrinsic values and on rational, logical analysis; its deemphasis of interpersonal and relational concerns; as well as certain personality traits such as altruism, a desire to help the underdog, or an emphasis on human relationships may foster law student distress. Perhaps individuals with altruistic, humanistically oriented traits experience pressure in law school to change their values and adopt a more rational, pragmatic, or materialistic style. This pressure leads them to either change their values or retain their atypical views; but either response may cause distress. Changing may entail internal conflict, whereas refusing to change may result in alienation and ridicule.[90]

Conclusions About Law Student Distress

Despite a panoply of dominant, confident, and self-assured attributes found in both prelaw students and law students, law students appear to be internally conflicted. They outwardly project a self-confident image while internally feeling awkward, defensive, and insecure. It is likely that this conflict develops in law school. Since 1970, law students have consistently reported an unusually high level of psychological distress in law school. This distress primarily manifests as anxiety, depression, obsessive–compulsive symptoms, isolation, paranoia, and substance abuse. Depression levels are relatively normal before law school, but dramatically increase during the first year of law school, peak in the third year of law school, and do not return to prelaw school levels after graduation. Law students appear to deal with this stress via increased substance abuse (but not suicide) and by becoming alienated or more aggressive and ambitious as law school progresses. Additional research is necessary to determine the causes of these high levels of psychiatric distress.

Data link law student distress to an orientation toward interpersonal relationships, helping others, warm emotional relations with others, and broad issues of public policy. It is also linked to shifting one's value system during law school from more intrinsic satisfactions toward values based on external rewards, appearance, attractiveness, and others' esteem. Law student distress is also associated with a failure to use social systems as support (despite traits of sociability and extroversion) and possibly the overuse of thinking and rational analysis as coping strategies.

Finally, some of this data suggests that impaired people have not simply self-selected into law school. If the findings regarding depression are true for other forms of law student distress, then law students are mostly "normal" on entry to law school. The first year of law school itself appears to cause the distress (or trigger it) and, surprisingly, it does not abate after graduation. One might conclude that law school somehow irretrievably damages 10 to 20% of its graduates. Some graduates and critics of legal education would probably agree.

LAWYERS IN DISTRESS

In chapter 1, the existence of lawyer distress and job dissatisfaction was documented. However, possible reasons for the distress and dissatisfaction have only been hinted at. No studies have established what causes lawyer distress, but several studies have determined correlates of lawyer distress in an attempt to explore possible causes.

Correlates of Lawyer Distress

Correlates are conditions that coexist along with lawyer distress without clearly being either caused by or causing it. To date, correlates of lawyer distress are somewhat obvious and therefore fairly unenlightening.

For example, lawyer distress is related to attorney job dissatisfaction. In one 1995 study, the most dissatisfied attorneys reported the highest levels of distress, whereas the most satisfied reported the lowest levels of distress. Even though this study did not establish whether dissatisfaction causes distress or vice versa, or whether they simply coexist,[91] the researchers concluded that, although work environment is not the sole cause of lawyer mental and physical distress, it is an important contributing factor. My own empirical work in 2000 confirmed that lawyer distress was highly correlated[92] with lawyer job dissatisfaction, but again did not reveal whether distress causes dissatisfaction or vice versa, or whether they simply coexist.[93]

At first blush, this finding appears self-evident. Distressed lawyers are simply miserable in general, thus they are unhappy with their work as part of their general malaise. However, this finding does suggest one important feature of lawyers. For lawyers, perhaps "work is life," so that if they are unhappy at work, they are distressed in general. If this is so, then perhaps lawyers' well-being is overly dependent on work, suggesting an imbalanced, workaholic-type life view.[94]

A 1995 study linked lawyer distress to anger and marital dissatisfaction.[95] In this study, lawyers reported feeling more stress and anger and more dissatisfaction with their primary (marital) relationships than the general population. In addition, whereas both male and female lawyers were angrier than most people, male lawyers tended to feel more stressed and female lawyers tended to be unhappier in their primary relationships.[96] These researchers hypothesized that lawyers' anger might be a product of the adversarial, hostile environment in which they spend the majority of their days and said that perhaps they cannot "turn off" the anger and hostility when they are not at work.

The researchers also noted that people who are unhappy in their significant relationships are more susceptible to stress; social support and satisfying personal relationships tend to reduce one's vulnerability to stress. So, the fact that distressed attorneys also reported unhappy primary relationships made sense. However, this again seems circular or self-evident, much like saying distressed lawyers are distressed!

Is it really the work environment that causes lawyer distress? Commentators disagree about how to interpret the data in this area. In 1985, the distress experienced by lawyers two years postgraduation was not related to the number of hours worked, passing the state bar examination, or the size of the law practice.[97] This suggests that perhaps the often-quoted environmental reasons for lawyer dysfunction and distress—long hours and large law firms—are not supported by the data.

Similarly, little data exist on factors associated with lawyer depression. One study found that, for male lawyers, depression changed with age over the career span, but did not indicate exactly how.[98] Another study investigated feeling "in control" of one's work and discovered that both physicians, with an almost zero depression rate, and lawyers, with a high depression rate, felt out of control of their work. This study therefore concluded that feeling out of control of one's work did not accurately predict whether individuals in various occupations would be depressed.[99]

Correlates of Lawyer Job Dissatisfaction

Much more is known about one of the correlates of lawyer distress, attorney job dissatisfaction. Most of the studies on lawyer dissatisfaction have explored the relationship between dissatisfaction and demographic factors, such as practice setting, length of time practicing law, area of specialty, gender, race, and income level. However, the results have been inconclusive; almost no one factor (except perhaps age or income level) has consistently emerged as associated with dissatisfaction.

The one consistent finding is that the higher one's age or income level, the more satisfied the attorney is with his or her job. However, this is true for all people in general; previous research has found that the older you are, the more satisfied you are likely to be with your job. An American Bar Foundation (ABF) study of Chicago lawyers in 1998 found that the older the lawyer was and the more money he or she made, the more satisfied he or she was as a lawyer.[100] Similarly, the 1990 American Bar Association's

Young Lawyers' Division's (ABA/YLD) survey stated, "While 19% of all lawyers in private practice are dissatisfied, when we look just at lawyers who graduated law school after 1967, the percentage dissatisfied rises to 31%."[101] As one would expect, the newer lawyers, who are likely to be younger and making less money, were more dissatisfied.[102]

Some conflicting and unconfirmed findings involving demographic attributes include the following. The 1990 ABA/YLD survey found that significantly more female attorneys in private practice were dissatisfied with their jobs than were male attorneys,[103] and another researcher found identical job satisfaction among male and female attorneys in private practice in 1994.[104] The 1998 ABF study found that government practice and African American race were associated with dissatisfaction.[105] In contrast, in 1994 another researcher found no significant differences in job satisfaction related to work setting (military, legal aid/public defender, corporate counsel/legal department, government agency, private practice, judicial clerkship, and other), except for military lawyers and legal aid/public defenders, who reported the highest job satisfaction.[106]

He also found that attorneys in labor law, matrimonial/family law, and criminal law reported greater job satisfaction than attorneys in real estate law, corporate/business/commercial law, and general practice. Criminal lawyers reported greater job satisfaction than did litigators and those not specifying an area of practice. Those with the highest job satisfaction were criminal and family lawyers; those with the lowest were real estate and corporate/commercial/business lawyers.

Size of firm was explored in a survey of the University of Michigan Law School class of 1987. This survey found that dissatisfaction was higher at larger firms:

> Only 28 percent of those working in law firms of 50 or more attorneys report being "quite satisfied with their careers overall"—down from 53 percent for the classes of 1976 and 1977. Smaller firms fared better. But dissatisfaction still was high: 39 percent of those working in firms of fewer than 50 attorneys were quite satisfied, down from 45 percent of the classes of 1976 and 1977.[107]

Second-generation lawyers may fare better. Children of lawyers who followed in their parent's footsteps were more satisfied than most lawyers. A 1989 national study of multigenerational lawyer families looked at lawyers who had a lawyer parent and found that 87% would choose law as a career over again, if they could. Only about 9% of these second-generation lawyers were neutral or dissatisfied with their careers in 1989, as compared to the 24% found by the 1990 ABA/YLD survey of all lawyers. This means that more than 90% of these lawyers were very or somewhat satisfied with their choice of career; less than 1% were quite dissatisfied and only 3.6% were somewhat dissatisfied. No one factor was related to this satisfaction (such as specialty, when they first thought of law as a career, going directly to law or taking time off before law school, staying in one's first job, having a public job), except those who had worked with their parent in the same firm were more likely to be quite satisfied than those who had not. Almost half were working with their parent. Even among these lawyers, however, recent graduates were less satisfied than those who had been in practice longer, confirming the consistent finding that satisfaction increases as age or income level increases.[108]

Nondemographic Characteristics, Personality Traits, and Dissatisfaction

There are also links between attorney job satisfaction and several nondemographic attributes. First, the ABF study found that "lawyers who indicated greater latitude in selecting clients" and "respondents who had expressed no conflict between career and personal demands" were more likely to express high job satisfaction. These researchers concluded that autonomy and lack of perceived role conflicts were related to satisfaction.[109]

Second, a 1994 study found that the most satisfied lawyers were those who preferred the Myers–Briggs dimensions of extroversion, thinking, and judging, which were described in detail in chapters 2 and 3. Although the finding regarding extroversion was unexpected, the relationship of thinking and judging to lawyer job satisfaction made sense, given that these individuals are likely to prefer "logical analysis, principles, cool and impersonal reasoning, and cost/benefit analyses," to be "tolerant of conflict and criticism" (thinking), and prefer work involving "structure, schedules, closure on decisions, planning, follow through and a 'cut-to-the-chase' approach" (judging).[110] As noted before, most daily lawyering tasks fit extremely well with the typical lawyer traits of thinking and judging.

Third, a 1994 study on lawyers' moral orientation associated the rights or justice orientation with overall career satisfaction. Specifically, lawyers with an ethic of care were more likely to be dissatisfied with law in general (but not with their current position).[111] This relationship between an ethic of care and dissatisfaction was dramatically true for female lawyers and less so for male lawyers; care-oriented men were more satisfied in the law than were care-oriented women.[112]

This study also related "masculine" traits to satisfaction with the law. Lawyers of both sexes with more "feminine" traits reported less job satisfaction than did male or female lawyers with more masculine or androgynous traits. Masculine traits were defined as being aggressive, dominant, independent, active, competitive, decisive, persistent, and self-confident, feeling superior, and standing up well under pressure. Feminine traits were defined as being " 'communal' or were expressive characteristics, such as valuing interpersonal connectedness" and being emotional, devoted to others, gentle, kind, helpful, aware of others' feelings, understanding of others, and interpersonally warm.[113]

Finally, this study linked satisfaction in the law with lawyers who saw their fathers as encouraging their independence or who idealized their fathers. Although this was true for both male and female lawyers, it was particularly true for women.[114]

Thinking and a rights orientation both rely on logic, analysis, rights, and obligations, which are paramount in the law, so these two findings make sense. Attorneys with these traits are likely to be well-suited for the law and also may not experience too many conflicts between their professional and personal lives—and such conflicts have been linked to dissatisfaction.

Finally, a recent study by one of the primary researchers on lawyer distress found a correlation between attorney job satisfaction and social support. Lawyers who perceived their colleagues as unsupportive and who perceived general social support to be unavailable to them were more likely to be dissatisfied.[115] The more general social support the attorney believed he or she had, and the more collegial it felt, the more satisfied he or she was with his or her job. Interestingly, however, of the four subscales making up the social support scale, self-esteem was the variable most associated with attorney job satisfaction. This odd finding suggests that, despite the link between satisfaction and social support, attorney job satisfaction might have more to do with internal self-esteem than with external factors.[116]

In summary, demographic correlates of attorney job dissatisfaction have not consistently emerged in the studies to date, except for age and income level, which are already associated with job satisfaction generally (for lawyers and nonlawyers alike). Some researchers have found relationships with gender, race, practice setting, and years of practice, but these findings are not consistent. More persuasive relationships are found between dissatisfaction and one's lack of autonomy; role conflicts; the Myers–Briggs traits of introversion, feeling, and perceiving; the moral decision-making style known as an "ethic of care"; "feminine" traits; and perceived lack of social support. Because of the close correlation between attorney job dissatisfaction and attorney distress, it is logical to conclude that these factors are also linked with attorney distress.

Correlates of Lawyer Success

Finally, one fascinating and rare longitudinal study of lawyers investigated early childhood traits associated with lawyer success, including satisfaction. The Terman Study of the Gifted, begun at Stanford University by psychology professor Lewis M. Terman in 1921, studied 11 male lawyers in their 70s, all of whom were life-long participants in the study.[117] It linked certain personality characteristics to occupational, marital, and family success and overall self-fulfillment.[118]

First, the lawyers (all men) were separated into a highly successful group and a least successful group on the basis of both professional and personal success.[119] Then the study reviewed assessments of each attorney that had been made years before by his mother when he was 7 to 12 years old, and by himself at ages 12–17 and 24–30.

The successful lawyers scored higher on leadership, popularity, sociability, mood stability, and musical appreciation as children and higher on leadership, popularity, and sociability as teenagers. They reported being less moody and having fewer feelings of inferiority, less interest in religion, more interest in art and music, and more close friends than the less successful group as young adults.[120] The successful lawyers were more often characterized by others as "contented, fair-minded, sincere, ambitious, competitive, confident, outgoing, sophisticated, intelligent, capable, reasonable, and self controlled."[121] The less successful lawyers were more often seen as "cautious, dissatisfied, vulnerable, defensive, depressed, frustrated and lonely."[122] The less successful group, overall, simply appeared more neurotic, hostile, and perhaps inhibited. They were also less creative, less imaginative, and less interested in sentimental, "softer" interests.[123]

The researcher concluded that leadership, social skills, emotional stability, and diversified cultural interests are important for life-long success, contrary to some popular ideas that love and work are mutually exclusive or that bright, successful people were neurotic as children.[124] This suggests that a balanced life, with broad interests outside of work, is related to being a successful, satisfied attorney (assuming that success is defined as these researchers defined it).

Second, feelings of inferiority, social isolation, and moodiness existed in less successful, less satisfied attorneys even as children, long before law school or the practice of law. This suggests that lawyer distress and dysfunction may not be entirely caused by the problems in the legal profession but rather could reflect some long-standing internal characteristics of certain individuals in the profession that predate law school.

Finally, there was no comparison to nonlawyers, so the results of this study may simply reflect what is true of people in general. Having a more balanced life, and being less neurotic from childhood on, may relate to greater life success for everyone.

Strong empirical evidence exists to show that lawyers experience depression, alcoholism, and other forms of psychological problems at a rate that is about twice as frequent as in the general population. About 20% of lawyers, or one in five, are "walking wounded," meaning functioning and practicing law while attempting to cover up, hide, or camouflage his or her psychological distress. Probably every lawyer reading this book knows someone in the profession who fits this description. Because lawyers tend to cope with tension by becoming more aggressive and ambitious, lawyer distress may create problems reaching beyond simply the affected lawyers.

The data indicate that lawyer distress is not necessarily associated with feeling out of control of one's work, long hours, or large law firms, suggesting that it is less environmentally caused than we might think. Other professionals do not necessarily experience the same amount of distress as lawyers.

What we do know is that distressed lawyers are more likely to feel angry, hostile, and unhappy with their primary (marital) relationships. They are likely to feel isolated, alone, and lacking in social support. Distress is linked to being oriented toward valuing extrinsic rewards (such as outward success, public approbation, and approval). It is also linked to dissatisfaction with one's job. Attorney job dissatisfaction, in turn, is linked to a lack of autonomy, conflicts between personal and career demands, a lack of social support, and certain feminine or humanistic traits, such as feeling, an ethic of care, valuing interpersonal relationships, and being interpersonally warm. Finally, there is a bit of evidence that lawyer distress may be rooted in long-standing personality characteristics that are found even in early childhood. Therefore, the research hints at certain personality traits that might predispose one to develop distress in the law.

The next chapter examines possible links between lawyer distress and the lawyer personality developed in chapters 2 and 3. It explores in more detail possible causes of lawyer distress and asks to what extent the internal world of lawyers is responsible for lawyers' inordinate levels of discomfort, before exploring possible solutions.

NOTES

1. Stephen Reich, *California Psychological Inventory: Profile of a Sample of First-Year Law Students*, 39 PSYCHOL. REP. 871 (1976).
2. *Id.* at 872. See table 1 of Reich's study for a list of these scales.
3. *Id.*
4. Norman Solkoff & Joan Markowitz, *Personality Characteristics of First-Year Medical and Law Students*, 42 J. MED. EDUC. 195, 197 (1967).
5. James L. Hafner & M. E. Fakouri, *Early Recollections of Individuals Preparing for Careers in Clinical Psychology, Dentistry, and Law*, 24 J. VOCATIONAL BEHAV. 236 (1984).
6. The Sense of Well-Being Scale is one of the class I subscales of the California Psychological Inventory (H. G. GOUGH, MANUAL FOR THE CALIFORNIA PSYCHOLOGICAL INVENTORY (Consulting Psychologists Press, 1957), used by Reich, *supra* note 1, at 872–873.
7. Reich, *supra* note 1, at 873.

8. These were class II subscales, which are Responsibility, Socialization, Self-Control, Tolerance, Good Impression, and Communality; Reich, *supra* note 1, at 872–873.

9. *Id.*

10. *Id.* at 873.

11. *Id.* at 873.

12. *Id.* at 873–874. This theory echoes Alfred Adler's idea that people choose careers to master or overcome early feelings of inadequacy and discomfort, perhaps felt in childhood. See discussion of Adler's ideas in JAMES O. PROCHASKA, SYSTEMS OF PSYCHOTHERAPY: A TRANSTHEORETICAL ANALYSIS, 174–179 (Dorsey Press, 1979).

13. Reich, *supra* note 1, at 874.

14. Two early (1967 and 1968) studies found that law students scored lower on a scale measuring depression than did medical students. Norman Solkoff, *The Use of Personality and Attitude Tests in Predicting the Academic Success of Medical and Law Students*, 43 J. MED. EDUC. 1250 (1968), and Solkoff & Markowitz, *supra* note 4. In a 1957 study with a very high (73%–84%) response rate, law students' anxiety was no greater than medical students' overall. However, law students did report significantly higher levels of academic stress, meaning stress associated with the academic demands, and fear-of-failing stress, meaning stress "related to personal reactions to the academic environment," than medical students. Leonard D. Eron & Robert S. Redmount, *The Effect of Legal Education on Attitudes*, 9 J. LEGAL EDUC. 431, 520–521 (1957).

15. Stephen B. Shanfield & G. Andrew Benjamin, *Psychiatric Distress in Law Students*, 35 J. LEGAL EDUC. 65, 69 (1985). Law students had a higher rate of psychiatric distress than either a contrasting normal population or a medical student population. These authors reviewed earlier studies and noted low response rates, nonsystematic approaches, little empirical data, inordinate focus on the first year, failure to compare law students to other professional students, and use of personality tests that do not measure psychiatric symptoms. *Id.* at 65–66.

16. In this 1985 study by Shanfield and Benjamin, groups of first-, second-, and third-year law students were tested in October, and first-year students were tested again in February. The tests included a wide variety of measures designed to assess psychiatric distress, such as anxiety, depression, hostility, obsessive–compulsivity, interpersonal sensitivity, phobic anxiety, paranoid ideation, psychoticism, overall distress, intensity of symptoms, and total number of symptoms. *Id.* at 67, 74.

17. *Id.* at 72. The only area in which law students were not worse than others was "somatization," which refers to one's tendency to turn psychological problems into physical complaints. Also, in this study, women law students' distress was more severe than the men's. *Id.* at 74.

18. *Id.* at 68. These authors used the Beck Depression Inventory, a well-respected, validated self-report instrument measuring depression, Aaron Beck, C. H. Ward, M. Mendelson, J. Mock, & J. Erbaugh, *An Inventory for Measuring Depression*, 4 ARCH. GEN. PSYCHIATRY 561 (1961); the Brief Symptom Inventory, which

measures 12 items, LEONARD R. DEROGATIS & PHILLIP M. SPENCER, BRIEF SYMP- TOM INVENTORY NORMS (Clinical Psychometric Research, 1982); and the Multi- ple Affect Adjective Checklist, which is a "validated survey of feeling states," and is scored for anxiety, depression, and hostility, MARVIN ZUCKERMAN & BERNARD LUBIN, MANUAL FOR THE MULTIPLE AFFECT ADJECTIVE CHECK LIST (Education and Industrial Testing Service, 1965). *Id.* at 67–68.

19. Shanfield & Benjamin, *supra* note 15.

20. *Id.* at 73.

21. G. Andrew H. Benjamin, Alfred Kazniak, Bruce Sales, & Stephen B. Shanfield, *The Role of Legal Education in Producing Psychological Distress Among Law Stu- dents*, AM. B. FOUND. RES. J. 225 (1986).

22. *Id.*

23. These authors used a short form of the Brief Symptom Inventory known as the SCL–90 (Hopkins Symptom Checklist; L. R. Derogatis & N. Melisaratos, *The Brief Symptom Inventory: An Introductory Report*, 13 PSYCHOL. MEDICINE 595 (1983)), which measures nine dimensions; the Beck Depression Inventory (Beck et al., *supra* note 18), a well-validated, reliable measure of depression and anxiety; the Multiple Affect Adjective Checklist, ZUCKERMAN & LUBIN, *supra* note 18, which measures anxiety, depression, and hostility; and the Hassles Scale (A. D. Kanner, J. Goyne, C. Schaefer, & R. S. Lazarus, *Comparison of Two Modes of Stress Management: Daily Hassles and Uplifts vs. Major Life Events*, 4 J. OF BEHAVIORAL MED. 1 (1981)), which identifies "the irritating, frustrating, distressing demands and troubled relationships that plague us day-in and day- out." Benjamin et al., *supra* note 21, at 229–230, *citing* R. S. Lazarus & A. DeLongis, *Psychological Stress and Coping in Aging*, 3 AM. PSYCHOL. 245, 246 (date not cited). They found a consistent pattern among all symptoms of psychiatric distress in which prelaw students had the least, alumni the next highest, first year students the next, and third year students the highest level of symptoms.

24. This is what researchers call a longitudinal instead of cross-sectional design. This type of design allows the researchers to determine the effects of law school with greater specificity by studying the same individuals at different times in their law school careers.

25. Benjamin et al., *supra* note 21, at 236. The criteria for cutoff was two standard deviations above the mean.

26. More specifically, these percentages represent the number of law students or lawyers whose score for a particular symptom was more than two standard deviations above the mean on the test. This demonstrates how dramatic the results were regarding law student and lawyer distress. *See id.* at 236.

27. *Id.* at 236.

28. *Id.* at 247, *citing* J. H. Boyd & M. M. Weisman, *Epidemiology of Affective Disorders*, 38 ARCHIVES GEN. PSYCHIATRY 1039 (1981).

29. Richard Gater, Michele Tansella, Alisa Korten, et al., *Sex Differences in the Prevalence and Detection of Depression and Anxiety Disorders in General Health Care Settings*, 55 ARCHIVES GEN. PSYCHIATRY 405 (May 1998).

30. Lawrence S. Krieger & Kannon M. Sheldon, Does Law School Change Law Students? Values, Motives, and Well-Being in a First Year Class (unpublished manuscript, 2001). The study compared entering Florida State University law students to advanced undergraduate students at the University of Missouri. The law students' mental health was better than the undergraduates' at the beginning of law school but significantly declined thereafter. *See id.* The decline was related to several values and motivational changes the law students underwent, which are described in this chapter.

31. Benjamin et al., *supra* note 21, at 251.

32. Jason M. Satterfield, John Monahan, & Martin P. Seligman, *Law School Performance Predicted by Explanatory Style*, 15 BEHAV. SCI. & L. 95 (1997). This study is discussed in greater depth in chapter 3.

33. *See generally* Benjamin et al., *supra* note 21, and Shanfield & Benjamin, *supra* note 15.

34. Leonard D. Eron & Robert S. Redmount, *The Effect of Legal Education on Attitudes*, 9 J. LEGAL EDUC. 431, 520–521 (1957) (a study of law students and medical students); Karin F. Helmers, Deborah Danoff, Yvonne Steinart, Marco Leyton, & Simon N. Young, *Stress and Depressed Mood in Medical Students, Law Students, and Graduate Students at McGill University*, 72 ACAD. MED. 708, 708–714, 710–711 (August 1997) (a study of Canadian medical students, undergraduate law students, and graduate science students).

35. Leonard D. Eron & Robert S. Redmount, *The Effect of Legal Education on Attitudes*, 9 J. LEGAL EDUC. 431, 520–521 (1957).

36. M. Heins, S. N. Fahey, & L. I. Leiden, *Perceived Stress in Medical, Law, and Graduate Students*, 59 J. MED. EDUC. 169 (1984).

37. Helmers et al., *supra* note 34, at 708–714, 710–711 (this study surveyed Canadian undergraduate law students, medical graduate students, and other graduate students).

38. Roseanna McCleary & Evan L. Zucker, *Higher Trait- and State-Anxiety in Female Law Students Than Male Law Students*, 68 PSYCHOL. REPORTS 1075, 1077 (1991). This was true for state anxiety only; trait anxiety was only higher than undergraduates in female law students. *Id.*

39. Leonard D. Eron & Robert S. Redmount, *The Effect of Legal Education on Attitudes*, 9 J. LEGAL EDUC. 431, 512 (1957). This is generally referred to as the Yerkes–Dodson Law and has been demonstrated to exist in a variety of situations.

40. *Id.* at 512.

41. Lawrence Silver, *Anxiety and the First Semester of Law School*, 4 WIS. L. REV. 1201 (1968).

42. *Id.* at 1216–1217. However, the number of law students studied was too small for statistical analysis. *Id.*

43. Robert Stevens, *Law Schools and Law Students*, 59 VA. L. REV. 551, 652–663 (1973). Stevens also found that the best predictor of tension during the second semester of law school was not grades, as might be expected, but tension during the first semester. *Id.* at 656. He theorized that tension causes low grades in

the first semester, as well as more tension in the second semester, not that the low grades cause the tension. High grades appeared to foster relaxation, whereas low grades appeared to retard it. One might conclude from this that tension in law school is an inner personality trait rather than the result of the law school environment. A 1991 study suggests that this might be more true for women law students than for men. McCleary & Zucker, *supra* note 38, at 1075–1078. This study found that anxiety as a personality trait was only more frequent among women law students as compared to undergraduates, not men. Law students in general had more situation-specific anxiety than undergraduates, but only women law students had more trait-type anxiety than the undergraduates. *See id.*

44. Stevens, *supra* note 43, at 653–654.

45. For example, the law students' decline in interest is consistent with a pattern found among medical and undergraduate students. Earlier studies had found that as they neared graduation, they withdrew their involvement in school perhaps because of a growing interest in the "real world" instead of school. Stevens, *supra* note 43, at 658–659 and nn.180–181, citing H. BECKER, B. GEER, & E. HUGHES, MAKING THE GRADE (1968) and H. BECKER, BOYS IN WHITE (1961).

46. Paul D. Carrington & James J. Conley, *The Alienation of Law Students*, 75 MICH. L. REV. 887 (1977).

47. *Id.* The researchers were motivated to perform this study by the large number (up to 20%) of law students at the University of Michigan Law School who left after their first year, and they wanted to discover possible causes of dropouts as well as what they call dropping out "emotionally and intellectually" while remaining in school. *Id.* at 887.

48. Carrington & Conley, *supra* note 46, at 891.

49. Students also experienced devaluation of association with peers. *Id.* at 890–891.

50. *Id.* at 891–892.

51. *Id.* at 892.

52. *Id.* at 891.

53. *Id.*

54. *Id.* at 893.

55. *Id.* at 893–894.

56. *Id.* at 894.

57. *Id.* at 895.

58. *Id.* at 895.

59. *Id.* at 898–899.

60. There is no empirical evidence for this, but conceptually, alienation may be similar to depression and paranoid thinking, whereas dissatisfaction may be similar to the hostility and anxiety measured by the 1985 and 1986 studies on distress performed by Benjamin and his colleagues. *See* Benjamin et al., *supra* note 21, and Shanfield & Benjamin, *supra* note 15.

61. Leonard D. Eron & Robert S. Redmount, *The Effect of Legal Education on Attitudes*, 9 J. LEGAL EDUC. 431, 520–521 (1957). Medical students more often indicated that they received help or support from family or friends. *See id.*

62. Stevens, *supra* note 43, at 678–679.

63. M. J. Hamilton et al., *Thirty-Five Law Student Suicides*, J. PSYCHIATRY & L. (Fall 1983), at 335–344, 342 (1983).

64. *Id.* at 342.

65. *Id.* This is also true for medical student suicides, thus it may be a phenomenon common to professional school. The authors admit that the study may have underreported suicides, because the data were collected from law school deans, yet the same methodology was used to collect data on medical student suicides, which were more frequent. They then theorize that law school serves as a stabilizing, socially integrating influence that inhibits suicide. *Id.* at 343.

66. Leonard D. Eron & Robert S. Redmount, *The Effect of Legal Education on Attitudes*, 9 J. LEGAL EDUC. 431, 521 (1957).

67. AALS Committee Report, *Report of the AALS Special Committee on Problems of Substance Abuse in the Law Schools*, 44 J. LEGAL EDUC. 35, 42 (1994). In this study, the "vast majority" of law students reported that they started using alcohol or drugs before they entered law school. Most important, however, third-year law students' usage was significantly higher than first- or second-year students', suggesting that substance abuse increases during law school.

68. *Id.* at 41. In addition, law students appear to use barbiturates, LSD, other psychedelics, marijuana, and cocaine more often than do medical students. *Id.* at 42. Past-month usage of law students in 1994 was as follows: 81.7% of law students had consumed alcohol in the last month, 8.2% admitted to using marijuana, 1.3% admitted to cocaine use, and 8.8% admitted to using "some illicit drug." Although the percentage of law students using cocaine was low, it still translates into almost 1,700 law students. *Id.* at 40.

69. *Id.* at 44.

70. John M. Burman, *Alcohol Abuse and Legal Education*, 47 J. LEGAL EDUC. 39, 41–43 (March 1997).

71. *Id.* A 1992 study of Spanish undergraduate students found that law students underestimated the risks of alcohol use as compared to medical students. However, this attitude was unrelated to how frequently the students drank alcohol; other variables, such as the importance of religion, were more important in predicting alcohol use; A. Luna, E. Osuna, L. Zurera, M. V. Garcia Pastor, & L. Castillo del Toro, *The Relationship Between the Perception of Alcohol and Drug Harmfulness and Alcohol Consumption by University Students*, 11 MED. LAW 3 (1992).

72. G. Andrew Benjamin, Elaine J. Darling & Bruce Sales, *The Prevalence of Depression, Alcohol Abuse, and Cocaine Abuse Among United States Lawyers*, 13 INT'L J. LAW & PSYCHIATRY 233, 240 (1990).

73. Two studies, the comprehensive 1986 study and one in 1988, both found that women experienced more stress during law school than did men. Benjamin et

al., *supra* note 21, and Janet Taber et al., *Project, Gender, Legal Education &*
the Legal Profession: An Empirical Study of Stanford Law Students & Graduates,
40 STAN. L. REV. 1209 (1988). This was particularly true of women alumni
(less true of women law students). A 1997 Canadian study similarly found
female undergraduate law students to be more stressed than males. Helmers,
supra note 34, at 711 ("In all cases the women had higher [stress] scores"). A
1991 study found that women law students had consistently and significantly
higher anxiety than men. McCleary & Zucker, *supra* note 8, at 1075–1078.
In 1988, women graduates reported more stress as practicing attorneys than
did men, even though their levels of job satisfaction did not differ; Taber et al.

74. Connie J. A. Beck, Bruce D. Sales, & G. Andrew H. Benjamin, *Lawyer Distress:*
Alcohol Related Concerns Among a Sample of Practicing Lawyers, 10 J. L. & HEALTH
1, 18 (1995–1996).

75. This refers to therapist John Gray's excellent popular series of books on relationships and gender differences, beginning with MEN ARE FROM MARS, WOMEN
ARE FROM VENUS (June 1992).

76. Beck et al., *supra* note 23, at 18. None of the law student distress studies
adjusted its data to take account of this phenomenon, unlike this 1996 study.

77. Daniel N. McIntosh, Julie Keywell, Alan Reifman, & Phoebe C. Ellsworth,
Stress and Health in First-Year Law Students: Women Fare Worse, 24 J. APPLIED
SOCIAL PSYCHOL. 1474 (1994). This study tested law students at the University
of Michigan in 1989 twice, once before law school and again in the first year.

78. *Id.* at 1485–1486.

79. Benjamin et al., *supra* note 18, at 246.

80. *Id.* at 252. These researchers blamed law school's overemphasis on thinking
and underemphasis on the development of interpersonal skills.

81. *Id.* at 250, *citing* F. K. ZEMANS & V. G. ROSENBLUM, THE MAKING OF A PUBLIC
PROFESSION 1, 137 (American Bar Foundation, 1981).

82. Carrington & Conley, *supra* note 46, at 896–898. They state, tellingly, that
it is "unlikely that the sociable student's desire for more emotionally satisfying
relationships in the law school can be gratified." Yet, they concluded that
sociability was a less harmful state than alienation or dissatisfaction. *Id.* at 898.
One wonders whether Carrington and Conley's sociable students correlate with
Richard's, Miller's, and Natter's feelers, as found in Lawrence R. Richard,
Psychological Type and Job Satisfaction Among Practicing Lawyers in the
United States (1994) (unpublished PhD dissertation, Temple University); Paul
Van R. Miller, *Personality Differences and Student Survival in Law School,* 19
J. LEGAL EDUC. 460 (1967); and Frank L. Natter, *The Human Factor: Psychological*
Type in Legal Education, 3 RES. PSYCHOL. TYPE 55 (1981), respectively.

83. It distinguished different groups of law students within the school based on
their stated career interests, with respect to personality characteristics and
attitudes. Students appeared to group into clusters, with different career interests
and different characteristics, personality traits, and attitudes. James M.
Hedegard, *The Impact of Legal Education: An In-Depth Examination of Career-*

Relevant Interests, Attitudes, and Personality Traits Among First-Year Law Students, 4 AM. B. FOUND. RES. J. 791 (1979).

84. *Id.* at 866.

85. *Id.* at 865.

86. Krieger & Sheldon, *supra* note 30.

87. *Id.*

88. Krieger & Sheldon, *supra* note 30.

89. *See id.* They noted that,

> the law students also evidenced stronger valuation of money/luxuries ($t = 2.4$) and were more acquisitive in the social dilemma measure ($t = 7.0$), compared to Missouri students. Given that the latter two variables have both been associated with reduced mental health, it appears that the law students may be predisposed toward reduced well-being in certain circumstances. However these conclusions must be tempered, both because of the limited nature of this initial research, the lack of confirmation of these results among the other data at time 1, and because there are many demographic differences between the comparison sample and the law school sample (i.e., average age, graduation status, region of the country). *Id.*

90. *See* RAND JACK & DANA CROWLEY JACK, MORAL VISION AND PROFESSIONAL DECISIONS (Cambridge University Press, 1989) for a description of the conflicts inherent in changing one's values.

91. Linda M. Rio, *Time for an Ideality Check: If You Had Your Ideal Job, Would You Be Satisfied?*, BARRISTER MAG. (Spring 1995).

92. This was a 0.70 correlation; Susan Daicoff, unpublished manuscript (Stalking the Walking Wounded: An Empirical Study of Lawyer Distress, Career Satisfaction, and Personality Attributes) reporting on May, 2000 study, on file with the author.

93. *Id.* (reporting results of empirical study of lawyer distress, job satisfaction, and personality).

94. Many thanks to my former professor and mentor, Dr. Clint A. Bowers of the University of Central Florida, Department of Psychology, for this insight.

95. Beck et al., *supra* note 74.

96. *Id.* at 30–31.

97. Benjamin et al., *supra* note 21, at 246.

98. Beck et al., *supra* note 74, at 24.

99. William W. Eaton, James C. Anthony, Wallace Mandel, & Roberta Garrison, *Occupations and the Prevalence of Major Depressive Disorder*, 32 J. OCCUPATIONAL MED. 1079, 1081 (1990).

100. John P. Heinz, Kathleen E. Hull, & Ava A. Harter, *Researching Law: An ABF Update, "Content With Their Calling?" Job Satisfaction in the Chicago Bar*, 9 AM. B. FOUND. PUB. 1, at 6, 8, & 9 (1998). Lawyer/psychologist Lawrence Richard also found greater job satisfaction reported by older attorneys, Richard, *supra* note 82, at 209.

101. ABA Young Lawyers Division Survey, *The State of the Legal Profession: 1990* (1991), at 55 [hereinafter ABA/YLD 1990].

102. However, it is important to remember that job satisfaction tends to increase with age, thus this finding may also reflect an effect of young age as well as lower income. *See* Heinz, Hull, & Harter, *supra* note 100, at 6.

103. ABA/YLD 1990, *supra* note 101, at 53–54.

104. Richard, *supra* note 82, at 174–75 & 119.

105. Heinz et al., *supra* note 100, at 9. Note that African American race may be associated with lower job satisfaction in general (not just in attorneys). *Id.* at 6.

106. Richard, *supra* note 82, at 121–124.

107. Jill Chanen, *Class of '87: Big Money, Less Satisfaction*, 16 Chicago Lawyer 1 (1993).

108. Stephen L. Wasby & Susan S. Daly, *In My Father's Footsteps: Career Patterns of Lawyers*, 27 Akron L. Rev. 355, 358, and 391–393 (1994).

109. Heinz et al., *supra* note 100, at 8. Similarly, the ABA surveys also found,

> There is also a significant relationship between the length of one's legal career and the level of satisfaction expressed with regard to expectations as to financial remuneration. Those respondents who are new to the profession are less likely to indicate that their expectations have been met. For example, 48.5% of the respondents admitted before 1989 report that their expectations as to compensation have meshed very well with their experience. On the other hand, only 19.5% of those admitted in 1994 and 1995 indicate that this is the case.

> ABA Young Lawyers Division Survey, *Career Satisfaction* 12 (1995), at 12. "With regard to the concern about the balance between available time for personal life . . . [a]bout 70% of the respondents express some level of satisfaction and . . . about a fifth are very satisfied with the balance between work and their personal life. Seventy-one percent of those who experience at least some dissatisfaction indicate that they do not feel that this situation will improve in the near future." *Id.* at 15.

110. Richard, *supra* note 82, at 233–234.

111. Erica Weissman, unpublished PhD dissertation, Yeshiva University, 1991. Care-oriented lawyers were more dissatisfied with their choice of law as a career and the prospect of continuing in legal practice throughout their working lives, yet they were not more dissatisfied with their current position than justice-oriented lawyers, maybe because they had found a particular job that fit their care orientation well. *Id.*

112. *Id.* at 60.

113. *Id.* at 61–63. Specifically, women lawyers with more masculine traits were more likely to be satisfied with law as a career and law as a lifetime career. However, as a group, women lawyers were not generally more dissatisfied than men lawyers, so satisfaction was not simply a gender issue; rather it was related to gendered traits. Both masculine and feminine traits were viewed as socially

desirable in both sexes but were commonly believed to be more frequent in men or women, respectively.

114. *Id.* at 98.

115. Barbara S. McCann, Joan Russo, & G. Andrew H. Benjamin, *Hostility, Social Support, and Perceptions of Work*, 2 J. OCCUP. HEALTH PSYCHOL. 175, 175, 178, and 180 (1997) (finding that attorneys' job dissatisfaction was related to "low perceived availability of social support" and low perceived supportiveness of colleagues, meaning that the more attorneys perceived social support and collegiality to be inaccessible to them, the higher their job dissatisfaction scores were).

116. The social support measure contained four subscales: tangible support (e.g., help moving); appraisal (e.g., trusting advice of others); belonging (e.g., having people one enjoys spending time with); and self-esteem; *id.* at 178; of these, self-esteem was the most highly correlated with attorney job satisfaction; *id.* at 180.

117. Edwin S. Shneidman, *Personality and "Success" Among a Selected Group of Lawyers*, 48 J. PERSONALITY ASSESSMENT 609 (1984). The Terman study's basic finding was that gifted children are, contrary to popular opinion, generally more physically and mentally healthy than their less-than-gifted counterparts. *Id.* at 609–610.

118. *Id.* Success was defined by third-party raters who listened to taped interviews with the attorneys and then rated them on occupational life, marital life, family life, and overall self-fulfillment. Third-party ratings are deemed to be more reliable than self-report ratings from the attorneys themselves. First, this study found that lack of professional success was matched with marital difficulty, contrary perhaps to common beliefs that love and work are mutually exclusive or that professional success as a lawyer comes at the cost of marital bliss. *Id.* at 611.

119. In other words, contrary to some writers' assertions, professional success and marital difficulty do not go hand in hand. *Id.* at 611.

120. *Id.* at 614.

121. *Id.* at 613.

122. *Id.* at 614. Both groups were rated as conscientious and responsible, indicating that these traits may be unrelated to success, as defined in this study.

123. *Id.* at 615. In other words, neurotic lawyers were less successful, which simply makes common sense.

124. *Id.* at 615–616.

6

THE RELATIONSHIP BETWEEN LAWYER PERSONALITY AND LAWYER DISTRESS

Practically one in five attorneys is impaired enough to require clinical intervention. The amount of mental, psychological, and emotional distress within the legal profession is alarming. Not only is it uncomfortable for distressed lawyers and those who must work with them, but it is potentially devastating to the clients and society served by our profession. We are not likely to render entirely effective assistance of counsel when we ourselves are impaired.

An assessment of the current state of the legal profession, therefore, is incomplete without an assessment of the rampant phenomenon of lawyer distress. The previous chapter established the severity and scope of lawyer distress as a discrete problem. However, it may contribute to the other problems making up the tripartite crisis. Lawyer distress probably also fosters deprofessionalism and low public opinion of lawyers. Lawyers' excessive feelings of anger and hostility may affect their interactions with other lawyers, legal personnel, judges, and clients. These feelings may explain some of the Rambo-like behavior complained of in the profession. Law students often cope with uncomfortable feelings by becoming more aggressive and ambitious and by abusing substances rather than by relying on social support, committing suicide, or dropping out of law school; we can expect impaired attorneys

Portions of this chapter were adapted from an article by the author titled *Asking Leopards to Change Their Spots: Should Lawyers Change? A Critique of Solutions to Problems With Professionalism by Reference to Empirically-Derived Attorney Personality Attributes*, XI GEO. J. L. ETHICS 3 (1998). The author reserved the right to adapt and publish the material.

to do the same. They are likely to "hang in there," work harder, and drink more, instead of quitting, leaving the law, or asking others for help. Unfortunately, these particular coping strategies are likely to produce over-zealous representation of clients and overreaching conduct, through increased aggression and ambition. Finally, lawyer malfeasance often results from depression and substance abuse among lawyers.

What, then, causes lawyer distress? The previous chapter established links between lawyer distress and job dissatisfaction, marital dissatisfaction, lack of social support, a failure to use social systems as support when stressed, conflicts between the demands of one's personal life and one's career, and a lack of professional autonomy. It is also linked, though, to various internal factors, such as an externally based value system; the Myers–Briggs dimensions of feeling and perceiving; a moral decision-making style known as the ethic of care; an emphasis on interpersonal connectedness and on humanistic and social policy concerns; and "feminine," "communal," or "expressive" traits such as being emotional, devoted to others, gentle, kind, helpful, aware of others' feelings, understanding of others, and interpersonally warm. Finally, it may even be linked to long-standing traits (such as feelings of inferiority, moodiness, and a lack of varied, balanced interests) that are present as early as childhood.

Is lawyer distress a product of the environmental pressures of law school and law practice, or is it related in some way to the characteristics identified in chapters 2 and 3 that differentiate lawyers from "normal people"? Is there some link between the eight traits of the lawyer personality and the high levels of distress in the profession? Is there some connection between the fact that we as a profession differ, personality-wise, from the general population and at the same time suffer twice the frequency of distress? For example, does being a lawyer require one to have a set of certain personality characteristics, so that individuals in the law who are not suited for it become distressed? Or is it that the precise characteristics that fit one to be a lawyer also predispose one to develop psychological distress? To summarize, is it the lawyer personality, the nonlawyer personality, the difficult environment of modern law practice, or some combination thereof that explains lawyer distress? This chapter explores these questions.

Lawyer distress is used to refer collectively to mental distress and dysfunction, alcoholism and substance abuse, and career and job dissatisfaction. The relationship between the lawyer attributes outlined in chapters 2 and 3 and lawyer distress is unclear and probably quite complex. First, this chapter explores the interplay between external, environmental factors and internal, personality traits affecting the legal profession. Then the chapter explores four possible explanations of how lawyer personality might contribute to the inordinate levels of distress plaguing the legal profession. Each of these theories is examined in turn. Empirical data exist to support each possibility. Unfortunately, the research in this area is inconclusive and conflicting. Clearly, additional research is needed, and the reader is left to form his or her own conclusions.

EXTERNAL, ENVIRONMENTAL PRESSURES VERSUS INTERNAL, PSYCHOLOGICAL FACTORS

Many commentators have blamed lawyer distress and deprofessionalism on the intense pressures of today's practice of law. However, long before law practice, law school itself has been called an inhospitable environment.

Law School Pressures

The competition in law school and the process of learning to "think like a lawyer" are stressful. The traditional causes of law student stress are those listed in a 1979 article: the Socratic method of teaching, heavy work load, competition, isolation, loneliness, emphasis on professionalism rather than humanism or philosophy, and the lack of feedback.[1] More than 10 years earlier, in 1968, one author listed these causes of the undue anxiety of first-term law students:[2] the uncertainty involved in studying all semester without receiving any feedback (in the form of grades) on one's performance, the intimidating nature of the Socratic method used by many law professors, the unfamiliarity of the subject matter, and the ambiguity of the law. He noted that many students became used to black and white, right and wrong answers in undergraduate education. They are distressed to find few in law school. General empirical psychology has associated uncertainty and ambiguity with increased levels of stress; therefore the resulting uncertainty and ambiguity must create stress.[3]

Law students have complained that the following uncontrollable factors cause a sort of "learned helplessness" that is stressful: lack of feedback, particularly positive feedback; time and performance pressure; lack of free time; difficulty and novelty of studying the law; competitive, demanding nature of the law school environment; and lack of opportunity to socialize or engage in recreation.[4]

Empirical studies support the concept that law school fosters certain stressful conditions. First, there is pressure or a tendency in law school to keep interpersonal relationships on a professional and competitive basis rather than a cooperative basis,[5] which fosters a competitive environment. This competitive environment promotes isolation. Because social isolation or lack of social support is linked to lawyer distress,[6] this environment likely contributes to emotional distress among law students.

The fact that the higher achieving law students tend to exhibit a more pessimistic outlook on life suggests that success in law school is associated with personality traits that predispose one to develop depression.[7] It also suggests that pessimism may be inadvertently encouraged by the law school grading process. In this way, law school might foster the development of depressive, pessimistic attitudes.

Law school also appears to intensify law students' tendencies to ignore emotions, interpersonal concerns, and warm interpersonal relations. For example, the law student is trained to analyze legal rights and duties without considering the interpersonal relationships involved or greater context of the legal problem. One example used by Dean Emeritus Edward Dauer involves a family-owned business where the sole shareholder wants to issue stock in the family-run corporation to his son-in-law.[8] Law students typically begin analyzing whether more stock can be issued, what type of stock to issue, and what corporate procedures are needed. However, on gentle questioning, the client reveals that the relationship between the rest of the family and the son-in-law has been troubled for years, the son-in-law has a severe drug problem, and the family secretly hopes to straighten him out by giving him a job and some stock in the company. Certainly, in this situation, despite the family's idealistic hopes, issuing the stock is probably a terrible idea. The family relationships and the family's misguided motives are more important than the strict legal rights and duties of the parties involved. Yet law school focuses more on analysis of the legal issues and tends to ignore the interpersonal, moral, or psychological issues involved.[9]

Law school's exclusive emphasis on "objective thought, rational deduction, and empirical proof"[10] may intensify a tendency to rely on analytical, rational thought to make decisions, rather than focusing on emotions or the humanistic consequences of the decision.[11] An exclusive reliance on thinking may cause emotional distress to law students during law school and for years thereafter because it gets used in situations where consideration of extralegal matters is more appropriate. For example, lawyers' spouses often complain that the lawyers cannot turn off their "lawyer mode" at home, at times when they need to be more nonrational, subjective, or compassionate. In addition, an overreliance on thinking might contribute to an unbalanced approach to life and interpersonal difficulties with one's family and friends, which in turn leads to additional social isolation and thus more distress.[12]

In addition, law school encourages individuals to value extrinsic rewards, such as grades and the approval of others, instead of intrinsic values such as one's interests, desire for community and intimacy with others, personal growth, and inherent satisfaction. This shift has been empirically associated with a decline in satisfaction and emotional well-being, thus likely causing law student distress.

Law school fosters other shifts as well. To the extent that law school pressures individuals to change, it creates distress in the form of inner conflict between one's prelaw school values and one's newly emerging lawyer persona. For example, those who come to law school with an ethic of care, with a feeling or perceiving preference, with strong altruistic or public interest desires, or with strong intrinsic motivations may be atypical. Such people experience pressure in law school to adopt a rights orientation[13] and a personal style consistent with thinking and judging.[14] They are faced with the choice of either changing to fit the rest of the law students or becoming isolated, alienated, and even ostracized in law school. Whether they conform to the norm or resist conformity, they are likely to feel anxiety and other discomfort. This factor would explain why lawyer dissatisfaction and dysfunction have increased in recent years, because women may be more likely to be in this category and the percentage of women in the law has steadily increased since 1970.

If we change during law school, some argue that our prelaw school persona does not submerge quietly, but continues to create an inner values conflict inside us, thus contributing to distress. Although one can medicate, anesthetize, bury, or deny this conflict for awhile (through workaholism, a drive for outward success, or substance abuse), eventually it surfaces and demands to be resolved. Anecdotally, I have spoken with a number of experienced lawyers (mostly men in their 50s), who have accomplished everything externally that they ever wanted to in the practice of law but say they feel unfulfilled. They begin seeking something more and begin a process of recreating their professional selves. What they often revert to in this process is a set of values they abandoned in law school (perhaps those intrinsic values noted in the 2001 study), submerged for 20 years or so, and now rediscovered and integrated into their law practice.

John McShane of Dallas is a perfect example of this phenomenon. Having achieved everything professionally that a trial and family lawyer could want but feeling unfulfilled, he then recreated and redefined his law practice to incorporate his person-centered values, spiritual beliefs, and psychological sophistication into his work. John was profiled in the *American Bar Association Journal* in June 2000 as the "passionate practitioner."[15] He is an example of a lawyer who loves the practice of law, sees his work as an opportunity to promote healing in his clients, and who accomplishes his personal value of "doing good" in his daily work. I do not know if John's values shifted during law school, or if his humanistic, intrinsic values developed later in his life, but I do know that rather than continue to deny those parts of his personality, he has beautifully integrated them into a busy, successful, and satisfying law practice. I also know that, for many years before this, John was an example of a terribly distressed and depressed lawyer who turned to alcohol to solve his internal distress. Once sober, he began identifying his internal values and integrating them into his work.

Law school, therefore, does appear to exert some empirically demonstrable pressures on law students that may, at least in part, explain law student distress. A common myth is that law student distress is a temporary situation caused by the challenging and unrewarding law school environment. The myth goes: Once the stress is over, the student graduates and starts a job that will cover his or her escalating student debt, the distress will abate and all will be well.

Law Practice Pressures

The myth, unfortunately, is debunked by the fact that lawyer depression never returns to prelaw school levels after graduation, nor does it abate no matter how long one has practiced law. Myth #2 is that the intense pressures of law practice are solely responsible for the continued distress among law school graduates.

Clearly, it is true that practice is stressful; anyone who has practiced law lately has encountered the severe pressures of modern law practice. The pace has become frenetic, hastened by technological advances such as faxes, e-mails, voice mails, cell phones, online research databases, the Internet, and overnight mail. Overnight delivery of printed material is the norm; "snail" mail is obsolete. Clients and other legal personnel expect and demand instant responses to their requests and messages. Competition has stiffened because of the increasing numbers of new lawyers, increased mobility of lawyers within firms, increased competition for clients, greater client expectations, and decreased loyalty of clients to specific law firms.[16] Law firms have become bigger, more corporate, more impersonal, and more demanding of their employees, expecting longer hours and more bottom-line financial productivity.[17] Additional pressure comes from the profession's metamorphosis into a trade, resulting in a business-like preoccupation with income maximization.[18]

Nasty, discourteous, and even unethical behavior by other attorneys is frequently complained of; attorneys are widely scorned and criticized; and commentators cite "a startling growth in legal malpractice litigation . . . an equally shocking incidence of fraud, theft and abuse of the fiduciary relationship with clients by lawyers."[19] Commentators charge that mechanisms to discipline lawyers have failed, so that lawyer misbehavior is rampant and unchecked, legal education fails to instill or even preserve moral sensibilities in law students, and lawyer advertising has either increased or become more offensive, contributing to competition among lawyers as well as a negative attitude toward lawyers.[20]

There is no doubt that the environment is a harsh one. Some have said "it is no longer fun"[21] to practice law. The stresses of modern law practice seems sufficient to create high levels of psychiatric distress among lawyers. Yet the data in chapter 5 did not establish links between lawyer distress and these environmental, external stressors.

A DIATHESIS STRESS HYPOTHESIS

However, if the pressures of law school and law practice alone were responsible for the distress, one would expect distressed law students and lawyers to quit, drop out, and thereby relieve the pain. Some leave, but many more stay. What is it about lawyers that makes them suffer in silence, continuing despite inordinate levels of psychiatric distress, working harder and harder, and carrying those burdens until and unless they collapse?

When people are placed in an untenable, intolerable environment, they have at least three choices: (a) quit, exit the environment, and move on to some other place or situation; (b) attempt to change the environment to make it more hospitable and endurable; or (c) change nothing in the external world and simply change their internal attitudes toward the environment to accept it and make it more palatable.[22]

For example, almost everyone has been in a job he or she does not like. We can change jobs, change the working conditions (e.g., ask the employer to make certain changes in the job or surroundings to improve one's lot), or get a new attitude (e.g., this job is only temporary; I can endure it for awhile; I am learning valuable skills here and am willing to put up with difficult working conditions in order to do so; I find fulfillment through golfing, etc.).

Not all of these three solutions are equally available. Sometimes it is impossible to get another job readily (option #1). Frequently, one's attempts to change the employer or coworkers are fruitless; they heartily resist change (option #2). And sometimes one cannot simply adjust to and accept a difficult situation (e.g., sexual harassment on the job; option #3). Therefore, at times we have fewer than three options, but basically these three exist. I think of them as: change the situation, change you, or change me.

What we find with lawyers, however, is that they endure the enormous stresses of law school and law practice without exercising options 1 or 2. They might change jobs within the profession, but they do not often exit the profession, once admitted to the bar. Instead, I believe that too many lawyers simply default into a silent state of mental distress and job dissatisfaction, evidenced only by a few external clues, such as workaholism, staying too busy, substance abuse, and avoidance of clients (i.e., not returning phone calls).

The question becomes, why? What is it about lawyers that makes them choose this particular response to stress? One could call it option #4: Get depressed, feel awful inside, and then drink too much, abuse prescription drugs, work too much, and stay too busy to feel, and maybe no one including yourself will notice.

It seems inconceivable that this something is instilled by legal education or the legal profession alone and is not preexisting in the individuals who come to law school. It is more likely that a *combination* of prelaw school characteristics of *some* individuals and the stresses of law school and law practice causes the inordinate levels of depression and other forms of distress. This is known in psychology as the diathesis stress model of causation, meaning that the problem is not traceable to one factor but is caused by the interaction of two or more factors.[23] Lawyer distress is not caused by either the harsh environment of law school and law practice or the internal psychological characteristics of lawyers alone but by the combined effect of both.

For example, with respect to law student distress, a 1979 article argued,

> All law students are exposed to these same potentially stressful forces, but only some students develop adverse reactions. This suggests that there must be some internal factors which resulted in sub-optimal coping with law school in certain individuals.[24] . . .
>
> This conceptual model proposes that it is not the organization of legal education per se that creates anxiety or depression in the law students. Rather, it is the interaction of the potential stresses of the law school experience with certain individuals' specific dysfunctional attitudes that results in adverse emotional reactions.[25]

Psychiatrist and expert on lawyers Dr. Amiram Elwork presented a diathesis stress model of causation for lawyer stress.[26] He acknowledged the external stressors of law practice (e.g., time pressures, workload, competition, economy, office politics, role conflicts, and adversary system), but he also asserted that there are individual differences (with respect to flexibility, self-control, hostility, self-esteem, values, race, and gender) that make some lawyers more vulnerable to these external stressors than others.[27]

A dual-causation model also may explain why lawyers have been hated for centuries (because of the internal personality factors unique to lawyers that create misunderstandings and negative feelings between lawyers and laypeople), but only more recently have lawyers' public images dipped so low and distress levels are so high (because the external stressors present in the practice of law, such as increased competition and overcrowded dockets, have increased in intensity).

THE LAWYER ATTRIBUTES' CONTRIBUTION

Accepting that lawyer distress is multiply caused—a product of the environment of today's legal profession *and* certain internal attributes of attorneys—is easy; what is more difficult is identifying *which* internal attributes of attorneys are contributing to the problem. There are at least four possibilities of how the lawyer attributes contribute to lawyer distress.

Scenario #1: The Lawyer Attributes Themselves Lead to Distress

In chapter 4, I argued that the first two parts of the tripartite crisis were caused at least in part by the very attributes associated with the lawyer personality. Likewise, the third part, lawyer distress, may also be linked to these lawyer traits. Being competitive, aggressive, argumentative, bottom-line oriented, pessimistic, achievement-oriented, and not well-attuned to interpersonal relationships and emotions may well lead one to develop psychological distress, even if those characteristics suit the adversarial practice of law.

For example, being a predominantly rational, objective, competitive, and argumentative sort of person may allow one to function well as an advocate during the workday but be quite destructive to one's interpersonal relationships. It may bleed over into being hostile, argumentative, and aggressive in all situations, which could hamper one's ability to relate well with others and thus impair one's ability to garner social and collegial support. We know that a lack of social support and unsatisfying personal relationships are linked with lawyer distress. Thus, the very qualities that allow one to be an objective, effective, and appropriately detached but persuasive advocate and gladiator in court (such as thinking, a rights orientation, competitiveness, argumentativeness, aggression, and ambition) may simultaneously be causing problems for lawyers in the personal and social realms.

The studies showing that lawyer distress goes hand-in-hand with feeling hostile and angry support these ideas. These studies also showed that distressed lawyers felt less supported by their peers and colleagues and less satisfied with their primary relationships. The studies showing that the distress develops in law school also support this concept, in that law students may learn how to "think like a lawyer" and argue like a lawyer in law school, and not be able to "turn it off at home." Not being able to turn off the lawyerlike focus on rights, duties, responsibilities, relevant facts only (e.g., unemotional factors) and not being able to turn off one's competitive, argumentative, aggressive manner may well lead to interpersonal difficulties, social problems, and thus decreased well-being. This is probably why so many students' marriages and engagements break up in the first year of law school, with the non–law-student partner complaining, "I hardly know you anymore. You've turned into this 'lawyer' person I don't like and can't relate to. You argue about *everything,* now!"

Second, being highly achievement-oriented may be admired as "drive" and "ambition" at work but may propel one into a state of continual disappointment if a steady stream of successes and external rewards is not received. Such an achievement orientation might impair one's ability to feel good about oneself unless one is continually "winning" or excelling and thus negatively affect one's general mental well-being. In addition, the fact that our achievement orientation appears to be focused on external, extrinsic rewards and the economic bottom line suggests that we may not be satisfied with more intangible successes such as feeling satisfied with one's advocacy efforts or feeling satisfied that one has thoroughly researched, prepared, and represented the client well. We are more likely to value negotiating a large cash settlement, a portion of which will be ours as legal fees. For example, I recall the story of two lawyers in my city who reportedly had represented a client in a personal injury lawsuit that culminated in a multimillion dollar settlement. Their one third of the settlement was several million dollars. Regardless of the quality of their personal character, integrity, or competence as lawyers, they were revered in the local bar simply for having "hit the jackpot" with this case. Their experience was held up as a goal toward which others lawyers strove; other lawyers sounded jealous and disappointed that the same thing was not happening to them.

Third, the pessimism and competitiveness fostered by law school can clearly lead to depressive (via pessimism or frustrated competitiveness) thoughts. We know that an overly pessimistic outlook is associated with clinical depression. Yet pessimism may be helpful when it motivates one to work harder. Pessimists, who think that good things happen by chance and bad things are their fault, are likely to believe success is not assured and that they must continually strive to avoid failure. This kind of outlook can be adaptive in law school and law practice, to the extent that it drives one to thoroughly prepare, to study, and to take personal responsibility for the outcome of each endeavor, which may explain why pessimists had higher law school grades than optimists. However, if the desired outcome does not materialize, then this pessimistic outlook can lead to crushing disappointment and self-blame. Our competitiveness adds to it, by telling us we have "lost." Therefore, these approaches to life, which may be adaptive in law school, may unwittingly become liabilities in practice to the extent that they contribute to lawyer distress.

The competitiveness fostered by the competitive law school climate and the competitiveness of the top students in law school may also lead to hostile and angry feelings. It may encourage lawyers to see every situation as a competition in which he or she must "win," excel, or at least place well. Peers and colleagues may be perceived not as friends but as competitors or even enemies, thus adding to our social isolation. Perceived failures to win each "round" of battle may lead to frustration, disappointment, dissatisfaction, anger, and a decreased sense of personal well-being and competence. Although simply viewing the situation differently (e.g., not as a competition but collaboratively or from a "win/win" standpoint[28]) might alleviate this frustration, we as lawyers may not be disposed to view situations noncompetitively.

Other commentators have noted that having certain lawyer attributes might lead one to develop psychological distress. The research reviewed in chapter 5 also supports these commentators' ideas. For example, Beck and Burns (a law dean and a psychiatrist, respectively) asserted in 1979 that cognitive distortions among law students are one of the primary causes of anxiety and depression.[29] One such cognitive distortion is the tendency to interpret "stimuli that are neutral or mildly negative in an unrealistically bleak fashion."[30] Other suboptimal cognitive distortions they pointed to are irrational, negative thoughts *about* the themes of achievement and self-worth, perfectionism, all-or-nothing thinking (if I'm not the best, then I'm a total failure), need for approval, and need for certainty, correctness, and control of one's environment.[31]

These ideas are supported by the lawyer research. The existence of such irrational, negative beliefs is bolstered by the finding that good grades in law school were related to pessimistic attitudes.[32] In addition, lawyers do feel a lot of hostility and anger and experience more paranoia than most people,[33] which might be consistent with the unrealistically negative attitudes these authors mention. In addition, if they exist, such negative attitudes are likely to cause distress, because hostility and anger are empirically associated with psychological distress among lawyers.[34]

Achievement[35] and success are important to law students and lawyers, suggesting that perfectionism and all-or-nothing thinking about one's performance are characteristic of lawyers. Law school further promotes our need for achievement by its emphasis on extrinsic rewards such as grades, money, prestige, material success, Martindale–Hubbell ratings, and the like. And this emphasis has been empirically associated with a decline in well-being.[36]

Elwork asserted in 1995 that, based on existing empirical research on attorney personality, there are several personality traits that intensify lawyers' stress levels. According to him these are lack of flexibility, intolerance for change, an unbalanced commitment to work and personal life, a belief that destiny cannot be controlled, hostility, cynicism, aggression, fear, low self-esteem, person-centered values, and altruistic social concerns.[37] To the extent that lawyers have these traits, he argued, they will experience more disappointment and stress in practicing law.

Except for the latter two traits, most of these traits are obviously destructive—lawyers with troublesome attitudes are likely to experience trouble. However, it does pinpoint the precise attitudes among lawyers that are troublesome. It also echoes the empirical findings of the Terman study[38] of successful versus less successful lawyers that found a higher level of general neuroses among the less successful attorneys. And empirical data support some of these ideas. Of the traits discussed by Elwork, several are demonstrably characteristic of or higher-than-average among lawyers. These are aggression;[39] hostility;[40] low self-esteem;[41] awkwardness, paranoia, and insecurity;[42] and perhaps inflexibility and intolerance for change.[43]

Whether lawyers need control is questionable, however. Both lawyers and doctors reported that they felt "out of control" of their work, yet only the lawyers were depressed. However, maybe this is because lawyers *do* seek control; finding none, they become depressed; perhaps doctors have a greater ability to tolerate feeling "out of control."

Lawyers' overweening need for achievement, their preference for dominance, and their competitiveness can cause workaholism and perfectionism. In law school, if law students equate self-worth with achievement, then self-esteem depends entirely on continual external successes. Less than average academic performance equates with personal worthlessness. Therefore, law school itself frustrates individuals' need for achievement, because formerly top students in college will be average students in law school. At the same time, law school encourages law students to become more focused on external rewards such as grades, so the combination of rarer external rewards with an increased focus on external rewards is probably lethal to students' well-being. Add to this the typical law students' preexisting high needs for achievement and dominance and the combination likely has devastating effects on their self-esteem and self-worth.[44]

In law practice, these traits may easily become maladaptive. They can lead to workaholism and perfectionism, which are at first rewarded by professional and financial success, thus satisfying lawyers' drives for achievement, dominance, money, and prestige.[45] However, these behaviors can, over time and in the extreme, exact a greater toll on the individual than the benefits they provide, resulting in stress, interpersonal difficulties, and substance abuse. Also, Elwork's[46] idea that lawyers are overly committed to their work is supported by the research showing that lawyer distress is highly correlated with job dissatisfaction, which suggests that, for lawyers, work *is* life. Perhaps we overidentify ourselves with what we do for a living; if we are not entirely satisfied with our work, then we are miserable in general.

Elwork asserted that workaholism contributes greatly to lawyer stress. He said that lawyers have three personality traits that cause them to become workaholics: "justifiable paranoia," perfectionism, and an "insatiable desire for success."[47] He believed that the paranoia is caused by the adversarial legal system in which lawyers work, which causes us to suspect everyone of ulterior motives and encourages secretiveness, manipulativeness, and selfishness.[48] Empirical data about lawyers does show high levels of paranoia among lawyers as compared to the general population.[49]

Elwork also noted that perfectionism is encouraged by a profession and a personality that emphasize rules, order, organization, logical thought, and objective analysis. Mistakes are very costly, and perfectionism is rewarded both professionally and financially, thus fueling attorneys' needs to achieve.[50] Empirically, lawyers' preference for thinking, rule-based conventional morality, and the rights orientation explains our emphasis on rules, order, logical thought, and objective analysis. In addition, our preference for the dimension of judging, which focuses on closure, clear answers to problems, and task accomplishment, could also propel us into perfectionism.[51]

Lawyers' empirically demonstrated achievement orientation[52] may lead to a never-satisfied drive for success. Elwork pointed out that not only is this drive insatiable, but it is also fundamentally, on a deeper level, a need for "security, love, esteem, power, or autonomy," which is a psychological need rather than a professional goal. This is consistent with research finding that law students and lawyers, respectively, are internally insecure, awkward, and anxious.[53] They may seek security, esteem, and power to counteract this inner insecurity.[54] If insecurity indeed is one of the driving forces behind lawyers' need for achievement, then our quest for success could be unconsciously driven and easily become extreme.

Elwork asserted that this psychological need can be met more effectively by directly addressing it, rather than by the indirect means of workaholism and driving for "success."[55] Not only does workaholism *not* efficiently meet the needs driving it, but it also creates additional stress for the lawyer through increased workload, time pressures, and less available personal and relaxation time. In addition, this kind of drive for success sets lawyers up for psychological malaise, based on the finding that being motivated to achieve external, extrinsic rewards is associated with distress, whereas being motivated by intrinsic rewards is more likely to lead to satisfaction and happiness.[56]

Lawyers' coping strategies are also likely to create more stress. Instead of expressing conflicting feelings or working through them with other people, lawyers may resolve uncomfortable feelings of anger and anxiety[57] by working harder. Data suggest that law students cope with uncomfortable feelings not by using other people for social support but instead by becoming more aggressive and ambitious, turning to workaholism and substance abuse or becoming depressed.[58] In the case of increased ambition and work ethic, the initial results are more career achievement,[59] which initially makes lawyers feel more secure and confident. Yet this coping strategy can eventually lead to workaholism and complete burnout.

In summary, typical lawyer traits such as aggression, hostility, competitiveness, achievement-orientation, organization, and a preference for getting things done (judging) and for following rules and maintaining order can lead to workaholism and perfectionism. Typical lawyer traits such as a preference for objective, rational analysis (thinking) and argumentativeness may lead to interpersonal difficulties, relationship dissatisfaction, and social isolation, and thus distress. Negative thinking patterns, evidenced by hostility, anger, depressive pessimism, stress, paranoia, low self-esteem, and insecurity add to the problem. Lawyers are the kind of people who are likely not to address internal feelings of insecurity, isolation, anger, and fear directly but instead mask them with an outward appearance of confidence, competence, and an "I've got it all together" attitude. We also tend not to rely on each other for support, instead preferring relationships with other lawyers that are professional, not personal, in tone. When we feel stress, we are likely to work harder, isolate, or abuse substances to cope. All of these "typical" lawyer traits can easily lead us into psychological trouble.

Should lawyers change? Changing some of these lawyer attributes may neither be desirable nor possible. Some lawyer attributes may actually be necessary for some forms of lawyer well-being. For example, the typical lawyer traits of thinking and judging are associated with attorney job satisfaction. If lawyers became more feeling-oriented, more compassionate, more subjective, more focused on their own personal values, and more willing to leave possibilities open (i.e., more perceiving-oriented), their job satisfaction might actually decrease. As argued in chapter 4, thinking and judging fit well with the work of the legal profession. We are better able to handle absolute deadlines and strict rules, regulations, and procedures because of these two traits. We are better able to analyze clients' claims objectively and render rational, logical advice because of these preferences.

Law school also encourages law students to adopt a thinking decision-making style and a rights orientation. Perhaps legal educators correctly assume that this will adequately prepare law students to be effective and satisfied advocates. A common rationale for the emphasis on rights (which is sometimes experienced as sheer brutality) in the first year of law school runs something like, "It's a sharkfest out there in the real world of law practice. We have to toughen them up to prepare them to deal with it. Thinking like a lawyer means you have to be cold, impersonal, analytical, objective, and rational. If they are anything other than that, they will get eaten alive or be miserable." We might need strong armor if we were to become more feeling-oriented or care-oriented to withstand the inevitable slings and arrows of the current legal profession.

Other qualities, such as being argumentative, competitive, aggressive, and driven to win, are qualities that clients may want—even insist on—in their advocates. Although they are not necessarily the qualities that clients wish for in their personal relationships with their attorneys (e.g., that "bedside manner"), they do appear to be adaptive to the practice of law. In legal disputes, clients are likely to prefer a lawyer who is argumentative and aggressive, based on research finding that people in general find such lawyers more effective and more persuasive. Clients are likely to perceive such lawyers as "better lawyers." Clients are also likely to prefer lawyers who are extremely conscientious and highly motivated to win cases, even if those traits are so extreme as to lead to workaholism and perfectionism, because they will perceive such lawyers as being as committed to prevailing as they are.

To the extent that typical lawyer attributes contribute to lawyer distress, they may be maladaptive and should be changed. However, many of these attributes are likely to be quite helpful, if not necessary, in the practice of law. Clients may actually seek out lawyers who have the typical traits identified earlier as potentially troublesome. Therefore, these traits will be quite resistant to change. Finally, it is unclear whether lawyer distress is solely caused by these typical lawyer attributes. There is evidence linking lawyer distress to several traits *atypical* of lawyers.

Scenario #2: Atypical Attributes Lead to Distress

Some studies find that lawyers with more atypical traits are the ones experiencing the most distress. Two unpublished doctoral dissertations in the early 1990s linked the following two traits with attorney job dissatisfaction: a preference for feeling on the Myers–Briggs Type Indicator and an orientation toward the ethic of care. The first study linked feeling to job dissatisfaction;[60] the second linked the ethic of care to dissatisfaction with one's choice of law as a career or lifetime choice but not with one's current position.[61] In addition, feeling individuals were the most likely to drop out of law school.[62] Finally, the first year of law school tends to "beat" an ethic of care out of many law students.[63] Because of the strong link between mental and physical distress among lawyers and job dissatisfaction,[64] it is possible that being feeling- or care-oriented could lead to career dissatisfaction and thus psychological distress. This evidence supports Elwork's idea that person-centered values and altruistic social concerns contribute to lawyer distress.[65]

This makes some sense. Individuals who value humanistic concerns, interpersonal harmony, and interpersonal relationships and who seek to do "right" for others could easily feel disappointed or distressed by a career in the law.[66] So why not simply leave the law or, better yet, drop out of law school? Many students have confided to me that they know they do not "fit in" in law school because of such humanistic-type traits but feel compelled to graduate. Why? Because of other traits more typical of lawyers. To the extent that these humanistically oriented individuals are also competitive and achievement-oriented, they recoil from "quitting" law practice because it would feel like (or be perceived as) failing.

Individuals with traits atypical for law, such as humanistic values, feeling, an ethic of care, a desire for affiliation with others, and altruistic or public interest goals may develop distress as a byproduct of feeling isolated, different, or inferior and even being ostracized in the legal profession. These individuals likely felt alienated early on in law school. However, if they also had a few typical traits, for example, if they were also achievement-oriented or competitive, they were unlikely to quit. In practice, if they were also materialistically inclined, they may have felt unable to leave the law because of the lucrative nature of many law jobs. For example, one of my colleagues in the mid-1980s called his job the "golden handcuffs."

Yet conflicts between the demands of their work (or their colleagues' values) and their own atypical values may continue to cause such individuals personal angst, social isolation, and internal dissonance. Their values either cause them to gravitate toward less lucrative, less sought-after positions such as legal aid or government work, thus perhaps causing them to feel less respected within the profession or cause internal conflict as they try to be satisfied working in highly competitive private practice firms. At the least, lawyers with these atypical, humanistic traits are likely to feel alienated from, different from, and perhaps even inferior to their more typical peers. Their colleagues are likely to misunderstand them or even ridicule their values when discussing ongoing cases or clients.

Atypical lawyers, meaning those with humanistic, people-oriented, or altruistic values are thus likely to feel isolated, alienated, and devalued in the profession. They are likely to find the traditional practice of law unresponsive to their values and thus may feel dissatisfied. If they change their values to conform to the lawyer norm, they can lose themselves in the process and develop an inner dissonance that ultimately erupts in depression, substance abuse, or another form of mental distress.

Note, however, that no empirical studies to date have established a clear connection between feeling or an ethic of care and lawyer distress. My own pilot study in 2000 did not support such a connection.[67] I concluded that perhaps the lawyers I surveyed were different than those in the earlier studies in that they had self-selected into specialized niches in the profession that matched their atypical traits. For example, when I have presented the lawyer personality research to practicing attorneys and then allowed them to identify whether they are thinkers or feelers, often the feelers indicate great job satisfaction. On additional questioning, anecdotally I have found that invariably they are practicing law in a niche specialty that is perfectly suited for a feeler. They are family law judges, guardians ad litem, government attorneys responsible for broad social policy relating to families, full-time mediators, and the like.

Additional research is clearly necessary to determine why the research is inconclusive. Perhaps atypical, humanistic traits lead to lawyer dissatisfaction or distress only in typical, traditional private practice settings or primarily among women attorneys. Perhaps feeling or care-oriented lawyers are quite happy and well-adjusted when they are placed in various, highly specialized niches in the profession.

Scenario #3: Having an Extreme Version of Any Attribute Leads to Distress

It is possible that the distressed lawyers are those whose traits are extreme, whether they are typical or atypical of lawyers. It is possible that having "too much" of any trait, whether it is hard-driving competitiveness or warm-hearted humanism, leads to the rigidity and inflexibility Elwork mentioned. In turn, rigidity and inflexibility may lead to frustration and angst when those traits are not satisfied. For example, if a lawyer is so competitive, aggressive, achievement-oriented, ruthless, and interpersonally cold that he or she embodies the caricature of the Rambo lawyer, then he or she might be at risk to develop psychological distress, as Scenario #1 observes. When the real world does not fulfill his or her excessive demands to win, then he or she is likely to be frustrated and dissatisfied. On the other hand, if a lawyer is excessively conciliatory, altruistic, philosophically inclined, and interpersonally sensitive, then he or she may be distressed or even wounded by the legal system. The unofficial code of the profession that "this is war" may negatively affect such an individual deeply, on many levels.

This idea—that having any traits in the extreme predisposes one to develop lawyer distress—would explain why the empirical studies on the causes of lawyer distress are conflicting and inconclusive. It may explain why some studies find that atypical traits are associated with lawyer distress, why others find that hostility and anger are associated with lawyer distress, and why some studies find no link between personality traits and lawyer distress. No one appears to have yet investigated whether extreme traits are the culprits. However, we do know that having a trait in the extreme can lead to rigidity and inflexibility, and we do know that flexibility and adaptability are important to maintaining one's mental health.[68] Therefore, it is reasonable to think that extreme traits might result in impaired well-being for lawyers as well as others.

Research in this area might investigate whether the strength of one's preference for a particular trait, whether typical or atypical of lawyers, is associated with lawyer distress. It is possible that more balanced individuals—for example, those whose preferences are less marked—are more balanced emotionally as well. This fits with the Terman study's finding that the most globally successful lawyers were those with the most varied and diverse interests and social skills.[69]

Scenario #4: Lawyer Distress Is Unrelated to Personality Traits (And Is Instead Related to Shifting Values)

Recent empirical work on lawyer distress, however, suggests that it is not related to lawyer personality traits, as the earlier studies on thinking/feeling and the care/justice orientation found, but that it is instead more dependent on what the lawyer values as important. A 2001 study of law students established that law student distress was actually related to a shift in values that occurred during law school. The more the students' values shifted from an intrinsic motivation to an extrinsic motivation, the more likely their well-being was to decline during law school. This shift appears to have been caused by the experience of law school, because it occurred within the first year of legal education. People interested in lawyer distress have hailed this study informally as "the missing link" for which researchers have been searching, because it finally empirically links law student distress to a specific effect of law school.[70]

This missing link study explains why the lawyer distress studies found that the distress developed only in law school and did not abate after graduation. If indeed law school inexorably and permanently changes people's value systems in a direction that predisposes them to develop psychological distress, then it explains why lawyers (and law students but not prelaw students) exhibit alarming rates of mental and emotional distress.

It also hints at another, possible lawyer trait: the susceptibility to having one's values changed by external pressures. Research indicates that law school tends to shift the students' values away from an ethic of care and intrinsic values toward a rights orientation and extrinsic values, respectively, as early as the end of the first year of legal training. Either law school exerts enormous psychological pressure on these atypical individuals or they are readily willing to have these values changed. If the latter is the case, then perhaps these students' values are not so firmly entrenched that they resist being changed. The uncertainty displayed in research finding that some law students had "uncertain" career goals may extend to some students' value systems, as well.

The researchers of the missing link study concluded that, to reduce law student distress, law schools should,

1) . . . promote the regular experience of authenticity, relatedness, competence, self-esteem, and security in our students . . . 2) . . . support intrinsic motivation in law students—inherently enjoyable or personally meaningful work—while we teach the fundamentals of legal analysis and professional technique . . . [and] 3) . . . promote optimal human values in students (towards personal growth, intimacy, community enhancement, altruism), rather than the desire for money, power, status, and image.[71]

To reduce lawyer distress, then, perhaps we must encourage law students and lawyers to find and maintain a value system that depends on internal rewards (instead of external ones such as fame, success, money, number of wins, number of clients, Martindale–Hubbell ratings, size of law firm, number of billable hours worked, number of billed hours collected, size of legal fees, size of jury awards, number of luxury foreign cars owned, size of bank account, value of one's home, and so on—is it not ironic how easy it is to create a long list of external rewards?). Internal rewards might be adherence to one's own personal standards of integrity and excellence, or feeling satisfied with how one handled a particular case, client, judge, jury, or opposing counsel.

This possibility, though, points to an even more difficult task: the task of changing the legal profession's collective values. To the extent that the entire profession tends to focus on external rewards, it actually may foster psychological distress among its members. If the entire profession, meaning the legal system, the lawyers, judges, law professors, law students, and law schools, all inordinately value external rewards, the task of changing this value system is likely to be monumental. For example, simply changing law schools' almost exclusive focus on grades would be difficult. Imagine law school admissions that did not rely completely on LSAT scores and undergraduate grade point averages in their admissions policies. Imagine law schools that do not assign grades (there is at least one; Northeastern is the often cited example). Imagine law firms that do not select interviewees for on-campus interviewing by law school grade point average. Imagine a world in which the U.S. News & World Report did not rank law schools by hierarchical numbers and tiers and in which prospective law students did not select law schools on the basis of reputation and rankings. I imagine we as lawyers might feel a bit lost, or at sea, in this world with fewer external reward systems.

However, as implausible as it might seem, the value system of the world has been changing over the past decade or so. A growing dissatisfaction with the results of our current legal system and, perhaps, our society's current value system, has emerged. Alternatives to our current legal system have begun to develop. Chapter 7 examines the evidence that this global shift is being reflected within the legal profession.

A MULTIFACETED PROPOSAL

The lawyer personality research boils down to several groups of traits that distinguish lawyers from the general population:[72] (a) need for achievement (as opposed to a need for power or affiliation with others) and ambition;[73] (b) preference for dominance and leadership (as opposed to subordination or deference to others);[74] (c) competitiveness (and perhaps even aggressiveness);[75] (d) materialism (as opposed to altruism, humanitarianism, or a desire to help others);[76] (e) low interest in emotional concerns; (f) emphasis on rational analysis, based on a preference for thinking as a decision-making style as measured by the Myers–Briggs Type Indicator (as opposed to feeling);[77] and (g) an emphasis on rights, based on a preference for a "rights orientation" in making moral decisions (as opposed to an "ethic of care" or "care orientation").[78]

Typical Lawyers

For the majority of lawyers, the listed traits are adaptive to the practice of law as it has traditionally been structured. Achievement motivation is necessary to have the fortitude to get through law school and the rigorous bar exam. Dominance, leadership, competitiveness, aggressiveness, and ambition are helpful in winning legal battles. Dominance and leadership skills allow the lawyer to function as a professional on whom others depend or look to for guidance and reassurance. Realistic, pragmatic goals, such as material success, are associated with satisfaction with a legal career. Altruism and a sensitivity to emotions are liabilities in law practice when they hinder objectivity and prevent the emotional detachment necessary to effectively problem-solve. Thinking and a rights orientation allow the lawyer to adopt a neutral professional role and act instrumentally in representing clients with minimal psychological anguish over the morality of the clients' purposes. People with a preference for thinking or a rights orientation are more likely to be satisfied with legal careers or with the law, are less likely to drop out of law school, and are more plentiful in the legal profession. Thinkers represent the overwhelming majority, about three fourths, of lawyers. Thinking and a rights orientation are encouraged by law school. An emphasis on logic; objectivity; rational analysis; and rights, duties, and obligations is consistent with current legal thought and how law is taught in law school. It may also be helpful in analyzing legal problems in practice.

However, to the extent that these typical lawyer attributes have become extreme, leading to depressive pessimism, workaholism, perfectionism, and insatiable drives for achievement and external rewards, they may need to be modified. Also, because of the interpersonal and social difficulties resulting when lawyers use the lawyer personality in all settings, lawyers may need to develop more diverse traits. With family, friends, and even colleagues, we may need to put Rambo on the back burner and develop a more conciliatory, interpersonally sensitive approach.

Atypical Lawyers

What about atypical lawyers? To deal effectively with lawyer distress, they may also need to change. Anyone who has become a lawyer is likely to have some measure of achievement orientation and ambition, or he or she would have dropped out of the rigorous preparation long before being admitted to the bar. However, there is probably a substantial number of attorneys who do not share the other lawyer traits. For example, at least 20% or more of attorneys do not prefer thinking and a rights orientation. For them, the traditional approach to lawyering is demonstrably unsatisfactory and probably agonizing. Several commentators have agreed that the practice of law as it is traditionally done is difficult for individuals with an ethic of care[79] or a preference for feeling.[80] It may be unfulfilling, it may present the lawyer with a constant conflict between his or her personal values and the demands of value-neutral representation and zealous advocacy, or it may simply fail to use the individual's inherent personal strengths. Noncompetitive, altruistic, nonaggressive individuals are likely to have the same experience. At the least, they will feel alienated and different from the majority of lawyers. They may also feel somewhat insecure about their competence as lawyers, simply because they do not fit the current "mold" and not necessarily because they actually are less competent than more typical lawyers.

So what to do? Does this mean that atypical prelaw students should bail out now, or that atypical law students should give up on a legal career, or that atypical lawyers should find a new career (and pay back student loans for education they will never use)? One could advise atypical individuals simply to leave the law. For lawyers who have none of the "lawyer" traits, leaving the law may be a good option, because of the poor fit between their personalities and the law. However, for lawyers with mixed traits, such as those who prefer feeling or an ethic of care but are still competitive, aggressive, dominant, and materialistic, leaving the practice of law is an unsatisfactory solution. Leaving will be perceived as a personal failure, which is unacceptable for achievement-oriented individuals. In some cases, this explains why such individuals did not drop out of law school in the first place, even if they felt some dissonance early in law school. Not making as much money will be perceived as failure also. There are other options, both for lawyers with mixed traits and those with few typical lawyer traits. These other options are gaining in popularity and general acceptance.

Several commentators on the professionalism crisis in recent years have advocated approaches to lawyering that explicitly infuse the lawyer's personal values and morals into his or her work or adopt an ethic of care in representing clients.[81] Although these proposals for "moral lawyering" and "caring lawyering" might be inappropriate for typical lawyers, given their conflict with the typical ethical decision-making preferences associated with the lawyer personality, these commonly proposed solutions are entirely appropriate for atypical lawyers, who otherwise can feel alienated, isolated, and as if they are "swimming upstream" in the practice of law.

From a practical standpoint, there are a number of nontraditional approaches to lawyering and justice that are consistent with moral lawyering and caring lawyering. Because of their emphasis on solving problems and on maintaining or restoring interpersonal relationships, they offer hope for the atypical lawyer to finally experience his or her atypical traits as assets rather than liabilities. To the extent that those atypical traits are related to lawyer distress and dissatisfaction, these approaches also bear hope for improving lawyers' well-being. In addition, these approaches are also relevant to enhanced lawyer well-being as they are particularly appropriate for lawyers seeking intrinsic rewards and satisfactions, in lieu of more external, extrinsic values. Many of these approaches have been known for many decades, whereas others are fairly new. Currently, as we begin the next millennium and take stock of the legal profession, these approaches are gaining momentum, which may reflect a response to the many calls for more practical wisdom, moral lawyering, and caring lawyering in the profession.

To conclude, the solution to the tripartite crisis appears to reside in lawyers identifying their strengths, values, and preferences and then pursuing the most appropriate way of practicing law based on those traits. "Lawyer, know thyself" is the first step. Attorneys—indeed, law students—can identify which of the attorney attributes they possess by referring to the empirical research on the lawyer personality. Then they can choose a way of practicing law that best fits with their personal strengths, values, preferences, and skills. Clients can then exercise an informed choice between different types of lawyers[82]—ranging from full-bore, Rambo-style, gladiatorial litigators to more collaborative, empathetic, conflict-averse, interpersonally skilled types. Legal education would have to become more diverse and more explicit in offering different tracks to students, based on their preferences and personalities. Alternatively, law schools could require all students to learn various ways of practicing law before choosing their own personal style. The legal profession could come to embrace diverse approaches to practicing law as different but equally valuable. (It is important that nontraditional approaches to law that fit with feeling, an ethic of care, altruism, humanism, or other atypical traits do not become subordinate to or viewed as less desirable than traditional lawyering.) The well-being of lawyers and the legal profession and the satisfaction of clients could increase as a result of having choices between diverse styles of legal representation. Finally, this diversity might allow the legal profession to offer better representation to clients and be more responsive to client concerns, needs, and feelings.

How is this solution different from simply advocating moral lawyering and caring lawyering—in other words, has not the argument come full circle? No. It differs in that no single monolithic standard is held up to lawyers as the ideal to which they must conform, be it a traditional model or a more alternative model. A diversity of approaches to lawyering is advocated. It does not simply echo some commentators' arguments for diversity in the legal profession,[83] however, because it uses psychology to craft a solution. Specifically, it relies on the data about the lawyer personality to fit the lawyer's style of practice to his or her personality.

After a short side trip into an analogy, the various alternatives to traditional law practice are explored in the final chapter of this book.

NOTES

1. Phyllis W. Beck & David Burns, *Anxiety and Depression in Law Students: Cognitive Intervention*, 30 J. LEGAL EDUC. 270, 285–286 (1979), *citing* James B. Taylor, *Law School Stress and the "Deformation Professionelle,"* 27 J. LEGAL EDUC. 251 (1975). Beck and Burns generally discuss the benefits of cognitive–behavioral intervention, a therapy technique focused on negative, irrational thinking and typically used to treat anxiety and depression in treating law student stress.

2. Lawrence Silver, *Anxiety and the First Semester of Law School*, 4 WIS. L. REV. 1201, 1202–1216 (1968).

3. Psychological research consistently finds that uncertainty and ambiguity produce or increase stress. *Id.*

4. Suzanne C. Segerstrom, *Perceptions of Stress and Control in the First Semester of Law School*, 32 WILLAMETTE L. REV. 593, 600–602 (Summer 1996).

5. Michael J. Patton, *The Student, the Situation, and Performance During the First Year of Law School*, 21 J. LEGAL EDUC. 10, 43–45 (1968).

6. Barbara S. McCann, Joan Russo, & G. Andrew H. Benjamin, *Hostility, Social Support, and Perceptions of Work*, 2 J. OCCUP. HEALTH PSYCHOL. 175, 175, 178, and 180 (1997).

7. Jason M. Satterfield, John Monahan, & Martin P. Seligman, *Law School Performance Predicted by Explanatory Style*, 15 BEHAV. SCI. & L. 95 (1997).

8. DENNIS P. STOLLE, DAVID B. WEXLER, & BRUCE J. WINICK, PRACTICING THERAPEUTIC JURISPRUDENCE: LAW AS A HELPING PROFESSION 26–27 (Carolina Academic Press, 2000).

9. Vernellia R. Randall, *A Reply to Professor Ward*, 26 CUMB. L. REV. 121 (1995–1996); and Vernellia R. Randall, *The Myers–Briggs Type Indicator, First Year Law Studies and Performance*, 26 CUMB. L. REV. 63, 80–81, 86–87, 91–92, 96–97 (1995–1996). G. Andrew H. Benjamin, Alfred Kazniak, Bruce Sales, & Stephen B. Shanfield, *The Role of Legal Education in Producing Psychological Distress Among Law Students*, AM. B. FOUND. RES. J. 225, 250 (1986).

10. G. Andrew H. Benjamin, Alfred Kazniak, Bruce Sales, & Stephen B. Shanfield, *The Role of Legal Education in Producing Psychological Distress Among Law Students*, AM. B. FOUND. RES. J. 225, 250 (1986), *quoting* M. Meltsner, *Feeling Like a Lawyer*, 33 J. LEGAL EDUC. 624, 633 (1983).

11. Lawrence R. Richard, Psychological Type and Job Satisfaction Among Practicing Lawyers in the United States (1994) (unpublished PhD dissertation, Temple University); Paul Van R. Miller, *Personality Differences and Student Survival in Law School*, 19 J. LEGAL EDUC. 460 (1967).

12. *See* Amiram Elwork & G. Andrew H. Benjamin, *Lawyers in Distress*, J. PSYCHIATRY & L. 205 (Summer 1995).

13. Sandra Janoff, *The Influence of Legal Education on Moral Reasoning*, 76 MINN. L. REV. 193 (1991).

14. *See generally* Richard, *supra* note 11.

15. Steven Keeva, *Passionate Practitioner*, 86 A.B.A. J. 56 (June, 2000).

16. Seth Rosner, *A Decade of Professionalism*, 4 PROF. LAW. 2 (August 1995) (Rosner, who was chair of the American Bar Association Standing Committee on Professionalism at the time, cited a "continuation of the explosion in the number of lawyers at the same time that the demand for lawyers has shrunk dramatically"); and Roger C. Cramton, *Delivery of Legal Services to Ordinary Americans*, 44 CASE W. RES. L. REV. 531, 610 (1994) (asserting that "competition in legal services markets is a fact of life" and shall continue to be so).

17. William H. Rehnquist, *The State of the Legal Profession*, LEGAL ECON., March 1988, at 46 (describing larger, more corporate law firms, heavier lawyer workloads, and less firm loyalty); and Cramton, *supra* note 16, at 610 (noting negative effects of increased lawyer specialization, including greater demands by clients for lawyer accountability).

18. Paula A. Franzese, *Back to the Future: Reclaiming Our Noble Profession*, 25 SETON HALL L. REV. 488, 493 n.33 (1994) (citing SOL LINOWITZ & MARTIN MAYER, THE BETRAYED PROFESSION: LAWYERING AT THE END OF THE TWENTIETH CENTURY 245 (1994)). *See also* Louise A. LaMothe, *Opening Statement, Where Are We Going Anyway?*, 19 LITIG. 1, 2 (1992) (discussing the negative influences of an overemphasis on profit in the legal profession).

19. Rosner, *supra* note 16, at 2.

20. Harvard Law Review Association, *Lawyer's Responsibilities to the Profession: Decoding the Ethics Code*, 107 HARV. L. REV. 1581, 1604 (1994) (asserting that traditional lawyer discipline systems, such as bar associations, have failed and the judiciary, clients, and federal agencies have had to step into the gap); Edward D. Re, *The Causes of Popular Dissatisfaction With the Legal Profession*, 68 ST. JOHN'S L. REV. 85, 124–130 (1994) (asserting that the judiciary is responsible for failing to enforce rules in court and that legal education fails to concentrate on professional ideals); Elliott M. Abramson, *Puncturing the Myth of the Moral Intractability of Law Students: The Suggestiveness of the Work of Psychologist Lawrence Kohlberg for Ethical Training in Legal Education*, 7 NOTRE DAME J. L., ETHICS & PUB. POL'Y 223, 225 (1993) (asserting that law schools fail to encourage law students to become moral individuals); and John C. Buchanan, *The Demise of Legal Professionalism: Accepting Responsibility and Implementing Change*,

28 VAL. U. L. REV. 563, 567 (1994) (criticizing lawyer advertising as "unintelligent, inflammatory, and often outright misleading").

21. Rosner, *supra* note 16, at 2.

22. Thomas D. Barton, *Therapeutic Jurisprudence, Preventive Law, and Creative Problem Solving: An Essay on Harnessing Emotion and Human Connection*, 5 PSYCHOL. PUB. POL'Y & L. 921, 923 (Dec. 1999).

23. Scott M. Monroe & Anne D. Simons, *Diathesis—Stress Theories in the Context of Life Stress Research Implications for the Depressive Disorders*, 3 PSYCHOL. BULLETIN 406, 406 (1991).

24. Beck & Burns, *supra* note 1, at 286.

25. *Id.* at 287. Amiram Elwork and Andrew Benjamin appear to wholeheartedly agree with a "dual causation" model in explaining *lawyer* stress; *see* Elwork & Benjamin, *supra* note 12, at 207–208.

26. AMIRAM ELWORK, STRESS MANAGEMENT FOR LAWYERS (Vorkell Group, 1995) [hereinafter Elwork]; Elwork & Benjamin, *supra* note 12, at 207–208.

27. Elwork, *supra* note 26, at 13.

28. ROGER FISCHER, WILLIAM URY, & BRUCE PATTON, GETTING TO YES: NEGOTIATING AGREEMENT WITHOUT GIVING IN (Penguin, 1991) (discussing the concept of win–win outcomes).

29. Beck & Burns, *supra* note 1, at 285–286. At the time, Beck was the vice dean of the University of Pennsylvania Law School and Burns was an assistant clinical professor of psychiatry at the University of Pennsylvania Medical School.

30. *Id.* at 273. This erroneous interpretation of external stimuli causes the individual to feel hopeless, anxious, inadequate, and like a failure. The internal thoughts appear to continue to misinterpret the external stimuli and cause a downward, emotional spiral from which the individual finds it difficult to emerge.

31. *Id.* at 286–287.

32. Jason M. Satterfield, John Monahan, & Martin P. Seligman, *Law School Performance Predicted by Explanatory Style*, 15 BEHAV. SCI. & L. 95 (1997).

33. Connie J. A. Beck, Bruce D. Sales, & G. Andrew H. Benjamin, *Lawyer Distress: Alcohol Related Concerns Among a Sample of Practicing Lawyers*, 10 J. L. & HEALTH 1, 18 (1995–1996).

34. *Id.*

35. Leonard H. Chusmir, *Law and Jurisprudence Occupations: A Look at Motivational Need Patterns*, COM. L. J., May 1984, at 231–235 (finding high needs for achievement among lawyers).

36. Lawrence S. Krieger & Kannon M. Sheldon, Does Law School Change Law Students? Values, Motives, and Well-Being in a First Year Class (unpublished manuscript, 2001).

37. Elwork, *supra* note 26, at 15. *See also* Elwork & Benjamin, *supra* note 12, at 212–215.

38. Edwin S. Shneidman, *Personality and "Success" Among a Selected Group of Lawyers*, 48 J. OF PERSONALITY ASSESSMENT 609, 613–615 (1984).

39. Patton, *supra* note 5, at 43–45.

40. Beck et al., *supra* note 33, at 18.

41. Stephen Reich, *California Psychological Inventory: Profile of a Sample of First-Year Law Students*, 39 PSYCHOL. REP. 871 (1976).

42. Reich, *supra* note 41; G. Andrew H. Benjamin, Elaine J. Darling, & Bruce Sales, *The Prevalence of Depression, Alcohol Abuse, and Cocaine Abuse Among United States Lawyers*, 13 INT'L J. LAW & PSYCHIATRY 233, 240 (1990); and Beck et al., *supra* note 33.

43. James M. Hedegard, *The Impact of Legal Education: An In-Depth Examination of Career-Relevant Interests, Attitudes, and Personality Traits Among First-Year Law Students*, 4 AM. B. FOUND. RES. J. 791, 804–805 n.34, 814, 825, and 835 (1979) (finding authoritarianism to be characteristic of law students).

44. Chusmir, *supra* note 35 (re: achievement); Richard, *supra* note 11 (re: thinking and judging); Heather M. McLean & Rudolf Kalin, *Congruence Between Self-Image and Occupational Stereotypes in Students Entering Gender-Dominated Occupations*, 26 J. BEHAV. SCI. 142, 153–154 (1994) (re: competitiveness); Krieger & Sheldon, *supra* note 36 (re: focus on extrinsic rewards); Patton, *supra* note 59; John M. Houston, Danielle M. Farese, & Terence J. La Du, *Assessing Competitiveness: A Validation Study of the Competitiveness Index*, 13 PERSONALITY & INDIVIDUAL DIFFERENCES 1153 (1992), and Sue Winkle Williams & John C. McCullers, *Personal Factors Related to Typicalness of Career and Success in Active Professional Women*, 7 PSYCHOL. WOMEN Q. 343, 350–351 (1983) (the latter three studies relate to dominance among law students).

45. Chusmir, *supra* note 35 (achievement orientation among lawyers); Jane W. Coplin & John E. Williams, *Women Law Students' Description of Self and the Ideal Lawyer*, 2 PSYCHOL. WOMENS' Q. 323 (1978), Martin J. Bohn, *Psychological Needs of Engineering, Pre-Law, Pre-Medical, and Undecided College Freshmen*, 12 J. C. STUDENT PERSONNEL 359 (1971), and McLean & Kalin, *supra* note 44, at 153–154 (re: dominance among law students); Russell Korobkin & Chris Guthrie, *Psychology, Economics, and Settlement: A New Look at the Role of the Lawyer*, 76 TEX. L. REV. 77 (Nov. 1997); Jeff Dionise, *Lawyers at Work (Chart)*, A.B.A. J., March 1995, at 61; and Jeff Dionise, *Striving for Happiness (Chart)*, A.B.A. J., July 1995, at 41.

46. Elwork, *supra* note 26, at 16–20.

47. *Id.*

48. *Id.* at 17.

49. Beck et al., *supra* note 33.

50. Elwork, *supra* note 26, at 18–19.

51. *See* Richard, *supra* note 11 (re: thinking and judging); Lawrence J. Landwehr, *Lawyers as Social Progressives or Reactionaries: The Law and Order Cognitive Orientation of Lawyers*, 7 LAW & PSYCHOL. REV. 39 (1982) (re: conventional, stage 4 morality); Erica Weissman, Gender-Role Issues in Attorney Career Satisfaction, unpublished PhD Dissertation, Yeshiva University, New York (1994); Janet Taber, Marquerite T. Grant, et. al. *Project, Gender, Legal Education & the Legal Profession: An Empirical Study of Stanford Law Students & Graduates*, 40 STAN. L. REV. 1209 (1988), and Janoff, *supra* note 13 (these three re: the rights orientation).

52. Chusmir, *supra* note 35.

53. *See* Reich, *supra* note 41 (re: law students) and Beck et al., *supra* note 33 (re: lawyers).

54. Whether or not Reich's (*see* Reich, *supra* note 41) conflict between the outer image and inner feelings of law students exists before or develops in law school, if it continues into practice it is likely to drive attorneys to compensate for the inner insecurity in some fashion, such as an increased drive to succeed, to achieve, and to make money, or increased aggression (based on Stevens' findings; see Robert Stevens, *Law Schools and Law Students*, 59 VA. L. REV. 551, 678 (1973)), or workaholism and perfectionism, or substance abuse.

55. Elwork, *supra* note 26, at 20.

56. Krieger & Sheldon, *supra* note 36.

57. *See* Beck et al., *supra* note 33.

58. Stephen B. Shanfield & G. Andrew H. Benjamin, *Psychiatric Distress in Law Students*, 35 J. LEGAL EDUC. 65, 68–69 (1985); *see also* Benjamin et al., *supra* note 10.

59. *See, e.g.*, Chusmir, *supra* note 35, at 231–235.

60. Richard, *supra* note 11.

61. Weissman, *supra* note 51.

62. Miller, *supra* note 11.

63. Janoff, *supra* note 13.

64. Linda M. Rio, *Time for an Ideality Check: If You Had Your Ideal Job, Would You Be Satisfied?*, BARRISTER MAG., Spring 1995, at 13, 15 (discussing ABA/YLD National Survey of Career Satisfaction/Dissatisfaction (1984 and 1990)).

65. Elwork, *supra* note 26, at 15.

66. Note the dissatisfaction and malaise found among "sociable" law students, who found law school lonely and too doctrinal; *see generally* Paul D. Carrington & James J. Conley, *The Alienation of Law Students*, 75 MICH. L. REV. 887 (1977).

67. Susan Daicoff's unpublished empirical study of attorneys in Columbus, Ohio, conducted in May 2000.

68. *See* Elwork, *supra* note 26.

69. Edwin S. Shneidman, *Personality and "Success" Among a Selected Group of Lawyers*, 48(6) J. PERSONALITY ASSESSMENT 609, 613–615 (1984).

70. Quote coined by lawyer/coach and former West Publishing representative William Lindbergh of Ash Grove Consulting Group, St. Paul, MN, in personal communication with author, September 2001.

71. Krieger & Sheldon, *supra* note 36.

72. I identified others—*see* Susan Daicoff, *Lawyer, Know Thyself: A Review of Empirical Research on Attorney Personality Bearing on Professionalism*, 46 AM. U. L. REV. 1337, 1403–1410 (1997)—but these are the most relevant and in most cases, are the most empirically supported and consistently found. Others include authoritarianism, leadership and social skills, low interest in people, emotions, and interpersonal concerns. *Id.*

73. Chusmir, *supra* note 35 (attorneys' need for achievement more than needs for power or affiliation with others).

74. Jane W. Coplin & John E. Williams, *Women Law Students' Description of Self and the Ideal Lawyer*, 2 PSYCHOL. WOMENS Q. 323–333 (1978); Martin J. Bohn, *Psychological Needs of Engineering, Pre-Law, Pre-Medical, and Undecided College Freshmen*, 12 J. C. STUDENT PERSONNEL 359 (1971); Heather M. McLean & Rudolf Kalin, *Congruence Between Self-Image and Occupational Stereotypes in Students Entering Gender-Dominated Occupations*, 26 J. BEHAV. SCI. 142, 153–154 (1994).

75. Stevens, *supra* note 54 (aggression in law students); Patton, *supra* note 5 (competitiveness in law students); Houston et al., *supra* note 44 (attorneys compared to nurses); Williams & McCullers, *supra* note 44, at 350–351 (female lawyers compared to female doctors, secretaries, and medical assistants).

76. Dionese, *supra* note 45 (reporting a 1995 American Bar Association poll of attorneys' goals).

77. Miller, *supra* note 11; Frank L. Natter, *The Human Factor: Psychological Type in Legal Education*, 3 RES. PSYCHOL. TYPE 55 (1981); Richard, *supra* note 11; Vernellia R. Randall, *The Myers–Briggs Type Indicator, First Year Law Studies and Performance*, 26 CUMB. L. REV. 63, 80–81, 86–87, 91–92, 96–97 (1995–1996). This overwhelming preference for thinking over feeling is probably the most consistent finding regarding lawyer personality in the past 31 years, and has not changed even with the influx of women and minorities into the legal profession.

78. Taber et al., *supra* note 51 (female law students found contextual factors more important while male law students focused on abstract factors); Janoff, *supra* note 13 (law school tends to silence an ethic of care; women law students more often demonstrated an ethic of care whereas men law students demonstrated a rights orientation); and RAND JACK & DANA C. JACK, MORAL VISIONS AND PROFESSIONAL DECISIONS: THE CHANGING VALUES OF WOMEN AND MEN LAWYERS (Cambridge University Press, 1989).

79. JACK & JACK, *supra* note 78.

80. Richard, *supra* note 11.

81. *See, e.g.,* Robert M. Bastress, *Client Centered Counseling and Moral Accountability for Lawyers*, 10 J. LEGAL PROF. 97 (1985) (arguing that lawyers need to become more client-centered in the Rogerian sense as well as morally accountable in their representation of clients and arguing for lawyering that requires the lawyer to discuss his or her personal morals and beliefs with the client and to refuse to take actions that are inconsistent with these morals and beliefs—"moral accountability"); Carrie Menkel-Meadow, *Is Altruism Possible in Lawyering?* 8 GA. ST. U. L. REV. 385 (1992) (arguing that lawyers should become more altruistic); and Carrie Menkel-Meadow, *Review Essay: Moral Boundaries: A Political Argument for an Ethic of Care by Joan C. Tronto*, 22 N.Y.U. REV. L. & SOC. CHANGE 265 (1996) (also advocating lawyering with an ethic of care).

82. This menu is drawn from Rob Atkinson's three types of lawyers: types 1, 2, and 3. Atkinson, *A Dissenter's Commentary on the Professionalism Crusade*, 74 TEX. L. REV. 259 (1995).

83. *See, e.g.,* Atkinson, *supra* note 82, for this argument.

7

THE COMPREHENSIVE LAW
MOVEMENT

Most undergraduate psychology students are aware that the field of psychology has undergone several "revolutions," from the primacy of psychodynamic theory associated with Sigmund Freud and Carl Jung, through the ascendancy of behaviorism associated with B. F. Skinner, through the rise of humanistic psychology associated with Carl Rogers, to the present-day general acceptance of eclecticism, which embraces all of these theories plus many newer schools of thought as well. Each school of thought in psychology has had its day. Each is substantially different from the others and each perhaps developed out of dissatisfaction with the prevailing theories at the time. However, current psychological practice usually adopts an eclectic approach, meaning that all of the various schools of thought are taught, followed, and borrowed from in the education and practice of psychology. Practitioners often use many different approaches in their practices, depending on the strengths and weaknesses of the particular therapist and on the needs of the particular client at the time. Law appears to be undergoing a parallel developmental process.

PARALLEL EVOLUTION IN LAW AND PSYCHOLOGY

Law was generally regarded as a somewhat undisciplined liberal "art" (arguably parallel to the Freudian and Jungian eras in psychology) until

Christopher Langdell of Harvard convinced others that law could be scientific, through the use of the case method. As a result, for the past 100 years or so,[1] law has been seen as a scientific or at least logical and rational field of study. Legal education and the practice of law have focused on rationality; intellectual analysis; and rights, duties, and obligations over other concerns. Not surprisingly, empirical research indicates that lawyers over the past 30 years have overwhelmingly emphasized rights, duties, obligations, rationality, and logical analysis in their moral decision-making style.[2] Legal education fosters an almost blind focus on these concerns as early as the first year of law school.[3]

If the scientific, rational, logical nature of current legal analysis is analogous to the B. F. Skinner–behaviorism stage of psychology, then one would expect a Rogerian, humanistic form of legal analysis and practice to emerge next. In fact, a form of humanistic law is indeed developing. Its roots are in preventive law emerging in the 1950s, a smaller, more academic humanism-in-law movement in the 1960s and 1970s, and the alternative dispute resolution movement of the late 1960s and early 1970s, followed by the increased popularity of alternative dispute resolution (ADR) and mediation thereafter, which were in part motivated by a desire for a more humanistic, less contentious method of resolving legal conflicts. These developments may have been the first evidence of a movement toward humanism in the theory and practice of law. This early start at humanism in the law has greatly strengthened and expanded in the past 10 years by the simultaneous, synchronistic appearance of multiple, alternative approaches to law that use psychologically beneficial and humanistic ways to resolve legal issues.

These newer developments include procedural justice, therapeutic jurisprudence, therapeutically oriented preventive law, problem-solving courts, restorative justice, collaborative law, transformative mediation, holistic lawyering, and creative problem solving. Most of these newer, post-1990 developments are growing in acceptance, visibility, and popularity with lawyers and clients, although they are yet to become completely established in legal practice or education. Although these developments may at first glance appear unrelated, they share a desire to resolve legal disputes and matters in ways that are psychologically optimal for the people involved, both in procedure and substantive outcome. They seek to preserve interpersonal relationships and the relationships between people and their communities. They avoid doing harm to people and seek to maximize the emotional well-being of all involved. In doing so, they explicitly go beyond simple legal rights, duties, and obligations to focus on a broad array of concerns embedded in the particular legal matter presented.

Before this humanistic movement, legal education primarily reflected and promoted a rule-oriented, legal positivist perspective, fostered by the case method and black letter law. In the past 30 years, it has begun to incorporate and teach ways of lawyering that may be broader, more humanistic, more care-oriented,[4] interdisciplinary, and focused on concerns other than legal rights, through courses in lawyering skills, interviewing, counseling and negotiation, alternative dispute resolution, mediation, and so forth. The emergence of this humanistic movement in law may also reflect a response to legal realism and the rise of many newer diverse jurisprudential schools in reaction to the black-and-white, dichotomous, win–lose nature of legal positivism.[5]

To continue the analogy to psychology, perhaps lawyers of the future will adopt an eclectic approach, selecting from an array of approaches to resolving legal matters and disputes rather than exclusively relying on the adversarial, gladiatorial litigation model of client representation. Rather than using litigation as the ultimate fall-back method of dispute resolution, or filing lawsuits and then using the procedural mechanisms involved in formal discovery as methods of promoting settlement, perhaps lawyers will feel free to offer their clients other ways of resolving legal matters that are far removed from the specter of litigation, which inevitably and immediately pits one party against the other and forces each into emotionally adversarial, noncooperative stances. By encouraging lawyers to consider the entire situation and social context of the client, lawyers may be able to craft more creative and psychologically optimal solutions to legal dilemmas.

PHILOSOPHICAL FOUNDATIONS OF A PARADIGM SHIFT

Philosophical developments moving us as a culture away from individuality and toward greater respect for relationships and community also parallel law's evolution toward a more humanistic form. California Western Law School professor Thomas Barton brilliantly described the philosophical underpinnings of the current U.S. legal system and then asserted that a structural change is occurring. He explained that the current American legal system embodies the values of personal freedom, independence, individuation, separateness, detachment, will, and individual liberty, the values of which are typically associated with the Enlightenment period of the past 300 years or so (usually linked to 18th-century writers such as Voltaire, Kant, Montesquieu, and Bentham). The period preceding the Enlightenment was the Renaissance, which is typically associated with humanism and humanistic values. Barton argued that we are now moving into a Post-Enlightenment period, in which "the concepts of separation—both intellectual and social—are eroding in favor of the long-subordinated notions of connection."[6] This "emerging culture of connectedness" values relationships, belongingness, and loyalty. It respects community, cultural identity, cultural differences, diversity, and people's relationships to each other, to their communities, and to institutions, instead of simply individuality. Barton pointed to a number of developments as evidence that the Post-Enlightenment phase has arrived.[7]

For example, Barton identified a growing concern in the law for issues of inequality of power in human relationships (e.g., domestic violence law) and stronger recognition and protection of one's cultural identity or membership in a particular ethnic group (e.g., Native American law, recognition of specific cultural beliefs as exonerating or mitigating factors, and legal respect for cultural differences). He explained that Enlightenment law functions well when deciding right and wrong or rendering other black-and-white decisions. It does not easily accommodate or honor the fact that the parties may have an ongoing relationship with each other or with their communities. In response to these shortcomings, various alternative structures have developed, including certain forms of alternative dispute resolution and mediation, victim–offender mediation in criminal law, community-based sentencing of criminals, teen court, and collaborative approaches to divorce and child custody issues. These all explicitly focus on people's relationships with each other instead of solely on individual rights. They seek to maintain and preserve those connected relationships instead of sacrificing or destroying them in the name of individuality and separateness, which is consistent with Post-Enlightenment values of connectedness between people. Barton wrote,

> In a given case the law may oscillate between either separationist functions or connectedness values. This is because the desired outcomes often involve both protection and the building of a stronger relationship. In many instances of domestic violence, for example, the victim certainly wants and needs protection. The victim, however, may not want or may not be able to afford for the underlying relationship to be terminated. Instead, the victim desires the underlying relationship to be made more healthy and respectful. Yet this is precisely the sort of solution for which the Enlightenment legal process is poorly equipped. . . . Cases involving communities which are hostile to racial, ethnic, or sexual orientation minorities, cases involving unruly children, and even cases involving noisy neighbors may present the same challenges—to build stronger relationships among the parties while simultaneously stopping whatever immediately threatening behaviors escalated the problem to the legal domain. The fundamental need is for an integrative solution that works with, rather than ignores, the given social context.[8]

Post-Enlightenment values are also surfacing in the field of psychology. In recent years, some psychologists and forms of psychotherapy have gone overboard in overemphasizing individual freedom and underemphasizing relationships, to the ultimate detriment of the clients.[9] In the name of self-actualization, for example, therapists have sometimes encouraged people, explicitly or implicitly, to end relationships, to focus on themselves rather than on others in their decision making, and to place individual happiness above all other concerns such as their roles in their families, communities, and cultures. As a result, clients of psychology may self-actualize themselves right out of marital, employment, and family situations, with their therapist's support and encouragement, only to find themselves, after therapy concludes, ultimately alone. Psychology is thus evaluating whether it has unwittingly elevated individuality over one's connectedness with others, cultural and community identity, and relationships. It is asking whether this has been helpful to people or actually caused additional problems. In doing so, psychology parallels Barton's Post-Enlightenment values.

If the Post-Enlightenment phase indeed will be characterized by respect and honor for people's relationships to each other and to their communities, then these emerging, humanistic disciplines within the law can be seen as more evidence of a Post-Enlightenment movement. These newer forms of law and lawyering recognize the psychological and emotional destruction that litigation and rights-oriented legal positions wreak on clients, lawyers, and interpersonal relationships. To the extent that they offer ways of resolving legal matters that instead enhance and optimize interpersonal relationships and harmony, they also fall right in line with the Post-Enlightenment age.

SYNTHESIS INTO A MOVEMENT

The time has come to explicitly synthesize these emerging, humanistic Post-Enlightenment developments in philosophy, law, and legal practice and recognize that a unified new approach to teaching and practicing law is coalescing—one that is more consistent with humanistic values and an ethic of care. This movement[10] has already occurred in many legal communities and law schools across the United States; it simply has not yet been synthesized, united, named, labeled, and explicitly recognized as a widespread cultural phenomenon. Its beginnings have been present for many decades, as evidenced by long-standing areas of the law such as preventive law and alternative dispute resolution, yet the rapid, post-Cold War development of newer forms of humanistic law illustrate that the movement is gaining momentum.

Why make this movement more explicit? First, there is strength in numbers. Synthesizing the movement makes it more visible, accessible, and powerful. Second, this movement may change the face of the legal profession—as it becomes more explicit, widespread, and mainstream, it will change the types of people who are attracted to the law. Lawyers will more often function as peacemakers and healers of conflict, thus the skills and traits needed to be an effective lawyer will change. Clients and society will more often experience lawyers and the legal processes of dispute resolution as healing, transformative, regenerative, optimizing, and therapeutic. The benefits lie in improved conflict resolution process, enhanced lawyers' satisfaction with the outcomes of their work, and (ultimately) enhanced satisfaction among clients and society as a whole with the law's methods for resolving legal disputes and conflicts. Given the current tripartite crisis of deprofessionalism in law, low public opinion of lawyers, and lawyer dissatisfaction and distress, these benefits are probably long overdue.

Third, if lawyers can teach and guide clients to resolve conflicts more humanistically, society as a whole may learn more optimal ways of resolving conflict, without resorting to lawyers and the legal process. One well-seasoned, board-certified trial lawyer listening to a recent talk I gave on this topic, jokingly remarked, "And why not add to your modest goals: Simply changing the entire country, since if we change law and lawyers, society will also change?" His point is well-taken; the broader implications of this movement are far-reaching.

Several unifying themes characterize this new approach to law. First, it focuses on optimizing results or outcome (broadly and holistically defined) for the people involved in the particular legal matter or dispute, including optimizing the emotional and psychological well-being of the parties throughout the resolution process. Second, it encourages parties and lawyers to treat each other in their interactions with respect and dignity. Third, it solves problems and makes decisions by considering things other than the strict legal rights of the parties, instead exploring their needs, emotions, resources, goals, values, morals, and interpersonal relationships. In optimizing results and process, it often maximizes psychological well-being and preserves interpersonal harmony and relationships. As a result, it is frequently therapeutic to the individuals involved. To achieve its goals, it often uses explicitly interdisciplinary or holistic means. It often resolves disputes not through the raw exercise of power or aggression, interpersonal battle, rigid posturing, or contentious or aggressive interpersonal interactions but through collaboration, compromise, communication, creativity, and excellent interpersonal skills. Because it seeks to achieve positive, sometimes healing results, it is likely to be fulfilling for lawyers who want their work to have a positive impact on others or on a situation or who believe that fulfilling certain moral duties or obligations is more important than carrying out the clients' stated wishes in a more detached professional role.

What is of particular interest to me is that this new movement consists of a variety of theories, disciplines, and approaches to lawyering that are entirely consistent with many traits atypical of lawyers. Although Barton and others might argue that all lawyers need to become more attuned to human relationships, needs, emotions, connections with each other, and other nonlegal rights concerns, the lawyer personality outlined earlier in this book would suggest that such a focus would be difficult, if not impossible, for most lawyers. The majority of lawyers probably have had little interest in these matters since early childhood. However, there is an extraordinary fit between this movement and several atypical lawyer traits. Clearly, Post-Enlightenment law practice focusing on connectedness is well-suited for attorneys who are altruistic, noncompetitive, collaborative, nondominant, nonaggressive, and interpersonally attuned. But there is an even better fit between this movement and a preference for feeling and an ethic of care—two traits which have been empirically linked to dissatisfaction among lawyers.

How could these developments be fully integrated into the legal profession? Atypical lawyers could opt out of traditional practices entirely and choose to practice law in these other ways. Typical lawyers could continue to practice traditional, adversarial, or rights-focused law using an amoral professional role. Or lawyers could train themselves in all forms of practice and choose among them depending on the demands and needs of the particular client or legal matter, in a more eclectic approach.

A note on labels and nomenclature is appropriate. Currently there is no accepted label for this movement. Several of the individual approaches may be broad enough to encompass many of the other approaches, such as therapeutic jurisprudence and creative problem solving. Yet none has emerged as the overarching field. Eventually, one of these names will emerge to describe the movement or another catchy phrase will be coined that will unify these disparate approaches. There is currently a struggle to find an appealing and descriptive term; labels that have been considered and rejected for various reasons include *alternative, nontraditional, nonadversarial, conflict-averse, therapeutic, healing, holistic, creative, collaborative, cooperative, integrative, transformational, optimal, humanistic, human relations, restorative, peace-making, interdisciplinary*, and even *third force law* (a reference to Rogerian, humanistic psychology). One commentator aptly noted that "we are working at the precise place where law and psychology meet."[11] Until a term emerges that is more generally accepted, for ease of discussion, these approaches will be called collectively the *comprehensive law movement* because of their broad approach to legal matters.

VECTORS OF THE COMPREHENSIVE LAW MOVEMENT

University of California, Santa Barbara, sociology professor emeritus Thomas Scheff observed[12] in 1998 that "in recent years, an alternative approach to law, a worldwide movement, has been building momentum. This movement has two vectors, restorative justice and therapeutic jurisprudence. . . . "[13] Building on Professor Scheff's insight as to the pervasiveness and growth of the phenomenon, I believe there are at least 10 primary vectors of the movement. These are preventive law, procedural justice, therapeutic jurisprudence, therapeutically oriented preventive law, transformative mediation, restorative justice, holistic justice or holistic lawyering, collaborative law, creative problem solving, and the problem-solving court movement.[14] Other, related vectors are developments in law and spirituality, mindfulness meditation in law, and humanizing legal education.

One subset of vectors includes the growth of alternatives to litigation such as alternative dispute resolution, arbitration, mediation, and the long-standing discipline of preventive law. Legal education responded to these developments by adding elective courses in alternative dispute resolution; mediation; and interviewing, counseling, and negotiation. Lawyers now often seek continuing legal education programs to train them as mediators. To the extent that these forms of practice adopt values such as treating people with dignity, honesty, and respect in interpersonal interactions, optimizing people's well-being, and acknowledging and meeting needs other than vindication of rights, they are part of the movement. The movement is also consistent with and reflected in widespread pleas for more professionalism, civility, courtesy, and morality in the practice of law during the past 18 or so years. Finally, the past decade saw an explosion of newer vectors such as restorative justice, therapeutic jurisprudence, therapeutically oriented preventive law, procedural justice, holistic law, creative problem solving, transformative mediation, and collaborative law. Others are likely emerging. The following briefly describes each of these subdisciplines or vectors in rough chronological order.

Preventive Law

Preventive law[15] seeks to avoid litigation and intervene in situations before disputes actually arise.[16] It emphasizes a proactive approach by the lawyer, client-centeredness, and planning by the lawyer to avoid costly litigation and reach desired outcomes.[17] Its founder, Louis Brown, began practicing law this way in the 1930s in California, but did not write about preventive law until he became a law professor in the 1950s. His basic text was first published in the mid-1970s and updated in 1997; the movement has its own reporter: *Preventive Law Reporter*. It has generated a considerable following, but has never been explicitly endorsed by the majority of lawyers. One fear is that most clients will not be willing to pay for legal services if they do not currently have a legal problem.[18] Other reasons may be that it is not taught in law schools nor does it hold the potential for large legal fees that can be generated by lawsuits.[19]

Preventive law is mostly a set of techniques or strategies designed to reach its goals. For example, the preventive lawyer and the client work collaboratively to identify potential legal difficulties, develop ways to achieve the client's long-term goals, and minimize the risk of legal problems in the future. Decisions are made jointly by the lawyer and client. The preventive lawyer meets with the client regularly to receive updates on life events, not just when disputes arise. These "legal check-ups" allow the lawyer to "assist the client to improve decisionmaking and planning to prevent problems, reduce conflict, and increase life opportunities."[20] The analogy is often drawn between preventive law and preventive medicine.[21]

Some critics of preventive law argue that it is too paternalistic and invasive of the client's autonomy. Others claim that it is not a novel idea in that many good, competent lawyers already practice this type of law.[22] Also, there is a fear that clients will reject it because they resist paying for legal services to solve problems that currently do not exist.[23] Where it is most successful is in environments where legal counsel is prepaid and always at the disposal of the client, such as in the corporate setting[24] and, to a lesser degree, in local governments.[25] In addition, some lawyers are probably better at it than others—one advocate of preventive law has explicitly acknowledged that a preventive lawyer must have the "highest . . . client relations skills,"[26] must have a sensitivity to human nature and human relationships,[27] and must value "caring" over "cleverness," unlike the legal profession in general.[28]

Preventive law explicitly seeks to avoid or prevent litigation, problems, and disputes between parties. It indirectly fosters interpersonal harmony in preventing disputes. Strict legal rights may not be as important as preventing future problems or litigation. Finally, it emphasizes collaboration between lawyer and client. It is not, however, explicitly therapeutic or healing in its goals.

Certain Forms of Alternative Dispute Resolution and Mediation

Of all the vectors, ADR and mediation have probably gained the most public recognition and general acceptance. This is most likely because of their economic efficiency and their resultant value to overcrowded court dockets, overworked judges, and impatient lawyers and clients. They are quicker and cheaper than litigation. They are substantial, well-established subdisciplines used by practicing attorneys, taught by law professors, and studied by legal scholars.

ADR in general attempts to resolve disputes between parties by means other than litigation, including but not limited to, arbitration and mediation.

Because ADR seeks to avoid litigation, it may or may not result in outcomes equal to those that would result from litigation. Needs and concerns other than the strict legal rights of the parties are important in ADR (such as time, efficiency, and the need to resolve the dispute and move on with one's life).

ADR gained in acceptance in the 1970s as part of a movement to take power "back to the people" and out of the hands of government—specifically, courts. It was motivated by desires to reduce governmental involvement in people's lives, speed up the process of resolving disputes, avoid the inefficiency of litigation, and avoid the psychological brutality of litigation. Although the impetus for ADR has been multifaceted, ADR sometimes works to provide disputants with a less psychologically damaging process for conflict resolution. This can result from making the resolution process itself more harmonious, less conflict-ridden, and more collaborative, or by making the process quicker, cheaper, and less burdensome on the individual disputant than traditional litigation.

The earlier days of the ADR movement witnessed a struggle between the lawyers and the psychologists to determine who would ultimately control the movement. After about 1970, when the attorneys won that battle, ADR began to take on the flavor and feel of litigation and may have become less psychologically healing for its participants as a result. Today, not all forms of ADR, arbitration, or mediation fit within the movement. Some may be as brutal, conflictual, and rights-based as traditional litigation, although they may be cheaper and faster than using the court system.

Mediation has evolved into at least two forms of practice: evaluative and facilitative. Evaluative mediation focuses on what the parties would likely receive if the dispute were litigated. It sees the mediator's role as an evaluator of the positions of the parties and places the mediator in the position of an authority figure. It encourages the mediator to evaluate and inform the parties about the relative merits of each side's claim. In this environment, the parties can be influenced in their settlement decisions by outside information dispensed by one in authority (regarding what they would get if they litigated). In contrast, facilitative mediation focuses on the broadly defined needs of the parties, sees the mediator as a facilitator who assists the parties to come to an agreement they generate and select, and may or may not result in an outcome that resembles what they would have received via litigation. Parties in this setting compromise and reach agreement arguably free of coercive influences of the mediator or outside information. Facilitative mediation has been criticized as placing too much emphasis on the parties' needs and ignoring the parties' rights, and thereby compromising justice for some. Yet its methods are consistent with the movement.

Transformative mediation is a third form of mediation that fits squarely within the movement. Rather than focusing on achieving settlement of the legal dispute, transformative mediation explicitly seeks to foster the moral development of the parties involved in the dispute via the process of the mediation itself. Specifically, the mediator works with the disputing parties to encourage them to develop empathy for and understanding of the other's position, feelings, needs, and so forth, and encourages the parties to strengthen their own problem-solving capabilities. These two goals are known as recognition (of the other) and empowerment (of oneself). This approach to mediation explicitly focuses on improving the interaction and relationship between the parties and seeks improvement in the moral development of the individuals involved. This approach emerged in the 1990s and has since grown in popularity and usage in the United States.[29]

Proponents of ADR hope to resolve disputes other than by litigation. Depending on how ADR is practiced, it can be more collaborative and less adversarial than litigation. It may focus less on the parties' legal rights than on resolving the conflict without litigation. In its more facilitative and transformative forms, there may be no authority figure influencing the parties' agreement. Instead, the participants share equal power and reach a solution together. Finally, in transformative mediation, the focus is explicitly on improving the interpersonal relationships and fostering the personal growth of the individuals involved.

Procedural Justice

Procedural justice is associated with Lind and Tyler's research findings that people's satisfaction and compliance with judicial process depends not so much on the outcome (e.g., winning or losing) but on whether they perceive that the procedure was fair and the outcome was fair.[30] Tyler identified three elements that are important determinants of people's perceptions of procedural fairness: (a) participation, meaning the extent to which people are allowed to participate, present evidence and opinions, or share decision-making power; (b) dignity, meaning whether they are treated by legal authorities with respect, politeness, and dignity; and (c) trustworthiness of the authorities, meaning "evidence that the authorities with whom they are dealing are concerned about their welfare and want to treat them fairly."[31] Tyler empirically found that "each of these three factors has more influence on [people's] judgments of procedural justice than do either evaluations of neutrality or evaluations of the favorableness of the outcome of the hearing."[32] Studies supporting these findings have included both civil and criminal litigation.[33]

For example, if a sexual harassment plaintiff brings a lawsuit against her former employer and ultimately receives back pay and a fair damage award but is poorly treated by the judge, the attorneys, and the employer's representatives throughout the proceeding, the glow of the "win" is likely to fade substantially. If she feels as if she was not given an opportunity to tell her story because of the restrictions placed on witness' testimony or if her credibility and character are impugned during cross-examination in a way that leaves her feeling decimated afterward, and if she gets the impression that the judge does not want her to speak freely, then she is likely to feel violated by the process rather than vindicated. Tyler's work would suggest that she will feel less satisfied, or even be unhappy, with the outcome under these circumstances. Dissatisfied litigants may be less likely to comply with judgments also.

Procedural justice focuses on the emotions and needs of the participants in legal proceedings, rather than on their rights under the law. It asks people to treat others with dignity and respect. In this way, it may indirectly foster interpersonal harmony, even though harmony is not its explicit goal.

Therapeutic Jurisprudence

Therapeutic jurisprudence explores the therapeutic or countertherapeutic consequences of the law on the individuals involved in legal matters, including the clients, the clients' family members and other associates, the lawyers, the judges, and perhaps even the community.[34] It is interdisciplinary and explicitly seeks to make substantive legal rules and legal procedures more therapeutic to people. Its insights often suggest changes to the laws or the ways in which law is practiced. Therapeutic jurisprudence first began to appear in legal scholarship around 1990, and since then, it has been applied to a wide variety of substantive legal areas and issues.[35] The founders of therapeutic jurisprudence, University of Arizona and University of Miami law professors David Wexler and Bruce Winick, often quote University of Florida professor Christopher Slobogin's definition: "the use of social science to study the extent to which a legal rule or practice promotes the psychological or physical well-being of the people it affects."[36] They go on to explain that therapeutic jurisprudence sees the law, including substantive legal rules, legal procedures, and even legal actors such as lawyers or judges, as a therapeutic agent with specific psychological consequences for the individuals involved with the law. They ask us to consider whether "the law's antitherapeutic consequences can be reduced, and its therapeutic consequences enhanced, without subordinating due process and other justice values."[37]

Although therapeutic jurisprudence was first applied to traditional mental health law (e.g., the insanity defense, civil commitment of individuals with mental disorders, and civil and criminal incompetency),[38] it was quickly expanded to apply to many other areas, such as civil commitment of sexual offenders, outpatient civil commitment of drug abusers, sentencing and probation agreements, crime victims, workers' compensation law, fault-based tort compensation schemes, domestic violence, mandatory child abuse reporting, sexual orientation law and disability law, contract law,[39] and family law.[40] The therapeutic consequences of practicing law on lawyers have even been explored.[41]

Therapeutic jurisprudence is explicitly interdisciplinary and focuses on the mental health of individuals, their emotions, and their social relationships. It seeks to maximize people's emotional well-being rather than exclusively their legal rights, yet it does not advocate elevating well-being over rights where they conflict. It fosters interpersonal harmony if it would be psychologically beneficial; to the extent that interpersonal struggles are emotionally distressing, it avoids such struggles.

Problem-Solving Courts

The practice of therapeutic jurisprudence has been most successful in the court system, where it is known as the problem-solving court movement. These therapeutic jurisprudence courts include specialized mental health courts, drug treatment courts, domestic violence courts, and unified family courts, in which the court personnel explicitly use knowledge about the psychological dynamics involved in the legal issues (such as mental illness, drug and alcohol addiction, domestic violence, and divorce) to achieve better, more lasting and satisfactory resolutions of the legal problems presented.

Therapeutic Jurisprudence/Preventive Law

In a series of articles, several legal scholars proposed integrating therapeutic jurisprudence with preventive law.[42] The idea is that each will benefit from the synthesis: "Therapeutic jurisprudence alone lacks the practical procedures for law office application. Preventive law alone lacks an analytical framework for justifying emotional well-being as one priority in legal planning."[43]

An integrated, therapeutic jurisprudence/preventive law approach to a client's problem would start by identifying "psycholegal soft spots" in the client's affairs.[44] These are social relationships or emotional issues that may be adversely affected by legal procedures (including litigation)[45] or legal action (e.g., filing for bankruptcy or making certain testamentary dispositions). The lawyer considers whether legal actions or procedures will "produce or reduce anxiety, anger, hurt feelings, [or] . . . psychological well-being."[46] Examples are considering the emotional effect of a request to modify a child custody arrangement; considering the psychological consequences of leaving an inheritance in trust for one, irresponsible child and outright for another, responsible child;[47] and considering the emotional and relational consequences of designating a nonfamily member health care surrogate of a client diagnosed with AIDS when arranging the client's legal affairs.[48]

In addition, these effects are not simply considered but are evaluated and actually dictate what legal work should be done. They are also openly discussed with the client and thus lead to the identification of other emotional or legal issues. Also, the preventive law concept of continuing legal check-ups between client and lawyer is used, allowing the lawyer and client to respond to unanticipated life changes that have the potential of drawing the client into antitherapeutic legal situations or proceedings.[49] By relying on "not only economic and legal priorities, but also personal goals, values, and relationships,"[50] the lawyer can render superior legal representation to the client.

Although therapeutic jurisprudence/preventive law is theoretically applicable to any type of legal issue, certain matters are more likely to present psychological issues, such as family law,[51] elder law, HIV/AIDS law,[52] family-oriented business law,[53] disability law,[54] and mental health law.[55] Note that these areas fall into two categories: matters where the client is mentally disabled and matters involving human relationships, such as family law, employment law, estate planning, and small business law.

Therapeutic jurisprudence/preventive law incorporates all the characteristics of both genres. It is interdisciplinary, humanistic, focused on psychological well-being rather than strictly on rights, preventive, litigation-avoidant, and fosters interpersonal harmony if to do so would be therapeutic and preventive. Like therapeutic jurisprudence alone, it explicitly seeks to optimize the psychological and emotional well-being of all involved.

Restorative Justice

Restorative justice is a movement primarily in the criminal law field in which punishment of the offender by the state is deemphasized in favor of solutions to crime that take the relationships among the victim, offender, and community into account. Two of its leaders, Mark Umbreit and Mark Carey, explained that "restorative justice views crimes as a violation of one person by another, rather than as a violation against the state."[56] It is concerned with the broader relationship between the offender, victim, and the community. The Web site of the Center for Restorative Justice & Peacemaking at the University of Minnesota School of Social Work stated:

> Through restorative justice, victims, communities, and offenders are placed in active roles to work together to . . . empower victims in their search for closure; impress upon offenders the real human impact of their behavior; [and] promote restitution to victims and communities. Dialogue and negotiation are central to restorative justice, and problem solving for the future is seen as more important than simply establishing

blame for past behavior. Balance is sought between the legitimate needs of the victim, the community, and the offender that enhances community protection, competency development in the offender, and direct accountability of the offender to the victim and victimized community.[57]

It seeks to meet crime victims' needs and involve them in the criminal process (perhaps even sentencing), prevent reoffending, have the offender restore the community, build consensus, and have the participants express their humanity. It usually uses postconviction restorative conferences between the victim, offender, and members of the community to simply meet and talk or even to determine appropriate sentencing for the offender, but it has many forms, including victim–offender mediation, community conferences, circle sentencing, and family group conferences. Punishment involves "reintegrative shame," whereby community pressure is brought to bear on the offender to increase psychologically beneficial shame over the offense and induce law-compliant behavior. Sentencing usually consists of material reparations (payment of money) or symbolic reparations, such as an apology or other expression of remorse. It is used in and often based on indigenous tribal justice, and has been used in the United States, but most enthusiastically used in Canada, the United Kingdom, New Zealand, and Australia so far, with apparently good results. Participant satisfaction with these conferences has been impressively high.

Restorative justice focuses on community building and interpersonal harmony. It seeks to maintain interpersonal relationships. It is explicitly interpersonally collaborative. It focuses less on the right of society to punish the offender in a one-up, one-down, hierarchical, power-based relationship and more on community building and positive solutions to crime. It focuses less on exerting power over individuals than do traditional models of criminal justice, but it uses coercion in the form of social pressure designed to increase the offender's anxiety.

Collaborative Law

Collaborative law refers to a specific approach used by lawyers working in family law dealing with divorce and child custody issues. It was founded by Stewart Webb of Minnesota and shepherded by Pauline Tesler of California, two practicing lawyers who sought a better way to practice family law. It is explicitly nonadversarial. Both lawyers and both clients contractually agree to resolve the spouses' dispute by collaborative means alone and not through litigation, in a series of four-way conferences of the two clients and the two attorneys. In fact, if negotiations break down and the dispute goes to litigation, both lawyers are contractually obligated to withdraw from representation and refer the clients to other lawyers. Tesler explained that this aspect is critical, because it creates the only form of lawyering in which lawyers' goals are identical to clients' goals—all four individuals are working toward the same resolution. She argues that this feature fosters enormous creativity and collaboration in the lawyers. Collaborative law almost always results in a faster, cheaper, less adversarial resolution of a divorce.

The lawyers also often use an interdisciplinary team approach by involving psychologists and other mental health professionals to assist in the divorce process. Collaborative lawyers are committed to optimizing the clients' well-being and functioning. They acknowledge that family lawyers often see good people acting their very worst and they encourage the clients to make decisions and negotiate with their "higher selves," not with their "shadow selves" that emerge when they become angry, irrational, or vengeful. The lawyers are skilled in recognizing when the shadow selves have emerged and call a recess to the process to allow the client to regroup. They remind the client that an ongoing relationship will exist with the ex-spouse if children are involved and they encourage the client to develop good negotiating and coping skills to maintain the health of that ongoing relationship.

Collaborative law is explicitly collaborative and interdisciplinary. It respects and preserves harmonious interpersonal relationships. It is preventive in that it strenuously avoids litigation. Finally, at times it deemphasizes the parties' legal rights in favor of collaborative solutions to problems or disputes. It seeks to optimize human relationships and human functioning, during and after dispute resolution.

Holistic Law

Holistic law emerged around 1990 through the efforts of Vermont lawyer William Van Zyverden, who founded the International Alliance of Holistic Lawyers. In 2000, the Alliance boasted a membership of around 700. Holistic lawyers are explicitly interdisciplinary and incorporate their own values and morals into their representation of clients. They seek to do "the right thing" for themselves, their clients, and others involved. Holistic law seeks solutions to legal problems in a broader approach than is traditionally associated with lawyers, similar to holistic medicine. Its Web site states that holistic lawyers

> acknowledge the need for a humane legal process with the highest level of satisfaction for all participants; honor and respect the dignity and integrity of each individual; promote peaceful advocacy and holistic legal principles; value responsibility, connection and inclusion; encourage compassion, reconciliation, forgiveness and healing; practice deep listening, understand and recognize the importance of voice; contributes to peace building at all levels of society; recognize the opportunity in conflict; draw upon ancient intuitive wisdom of diverse cultures and traditions; and enjoy the practice of law.[58]

Holistic law focuses not only on the parties' legal rights but bows to higher purposes that may transcend legal rights at times. It allows the lawyer to infuse his or her own morals and beliefs into client representation, as long as this is discussed with the client and the client renders informed consent to that form of representation. It is broadly enough defined that it may encompass several of the other vectors.

Creative Problem Solving

Creative problem solving is a broadly defined discipline—so broadly defined that according to its supporters it encompasses all the other approaches, including holistic law, restorative justice, therapeutic jurisprudence, and preventive law.[59] It is associated with the McGill Center for Creative Problem-Solving at California Western School of Law. Although creative problem solving (CPS) for lawyers appeared in the literature as early as 1963,[60] it became a more formalized, explicit discipline in the late 1990s.[61]

Professor Linda Morton defined CPS by first reviewing some history: In 1992, the well-known *MacCrate Report* on legal education called for law schools to teach lawyering skills and professional values. It defined problem-solving skills as identifying and diagnosing the problem, generating alternative solutions and strategies, developing a plan of action, implementing the plan, and keeping the process open to new information or ideas. In contrast, creative problem solving is broader and more interdisciplinary, humanistic, and preventive.[62] Morton identified six facets of CPS: (a) It "focuses on underlying needs and interests, rather than positions, of individuals as well as society,"[63] so it emphasizes needs as well as rights. (b) It analyzes values of the parties and of the lawyers, societal values, and values of the relevant rules, so it is consistent with moral lawyering, as described previously. (c) It is explicitly interdisciplinary—recognizing that law alone may be inadequate, it looks to social sciences, humanities, technology, media, and the hard sciences.[64] (d) It requires creative thinking, risk-taking, thinking outside the box, using new paradigms, or pushing the envelope, to borrow a little new management jargon. (e) It is explicitly preventive. (f) It incorporates behaviors consistent with professionalism because it requires conscious self-reflection and analysis, asking "Did I solve the problem?"; "Was it the best solution?"; and "Who did it affect and how?"[65] Although it is probably close to the traditional solving of clients' legal problems that lawyers routinely do, it is more explicit about humanistic values, social justice, preventive efforts, and self-reflection than we have been in the past. Because of this, it is indirectly responsive to calls for more professionalism in the law. Morton agreed that it is a move away from the "traditional Langdellian 'law as science' model" and toward humanism.

Morton gave a number of examples in a 1998 article. One is a problem in which the client has been sued by a neighbor who is claiming adverse possession. Analysis of legal doctrine focuses on, "Was the use permissive?"; "Was there sufficient use of the premises to constitute ownership through adverse possession?" and may come up with a legal "answer" to who is right and who is wrong. However, the analysis does not end there; CPS also evaluates the needs and interests of the neighbors: "Is this just a case of neighbor hostility or land acquisition?"; "What does the client really want?"; "What can he or she afford?"; "What are the client's values or needs in competition with those of others involved?" It then asks, "What other disciplines should be consulted?"; "How could this have been prevented or how can additional problems between these neighbors be prevented?"; "Should the client sell the property, or can this be resolved through negotiation, mediation, or more informal talks?"; "What is the best solution?"; "What effects will it have and on whom?"[66]

Professor Janeen Kerper gave an excellent illustration of the difference between the case method of analyzing sterile appellate decisions, which is dominant in law schools, and a creative problem-solving, broad, interdisciplinary, free-of-traditional-constraints approach. She compared and contrasted how the two approaches view a famous judge's (Cardozo's) opinion in the *Palsgraf*[67] tort case, taught in virtually every first-year torts class in the nation. Mrs. Palsgraf ultimately lost her personal injury lawsuit against a railroad because the court essentially drew a line in the sand beyond which a defendant is not legally liable. From the first perspective, the opinion is "a piece of brilliant legal reasoning," because of its elegant line drawing; from a CPS perspective, once you know the actual situation of the plaintiff, her needs, her goals, and her resources, Kerper said it is "an example of particularly bad lawyering."[68] Kerper argued that law schools need to teach both: the traditional, rights-based, analytical approach as well as the creative problem-solving approach.

Creative problem solving may be broad enough to include all of the characteristics of the other nine vectors, such as avoidance of interpersonal conflict, importance of interpersonal harmony and relationships, nonexclusivity of reliance on strict legal rights, interdisciplinary approach, focus on therapeutic or psychological concerns, prevention of litigation, collaborative approach, focus on equal power relationships rather than the exertion of power or influence over or coercion of another, and moral lawyering (lawyers' own values infused into client representation). However, CPS would use these only if necessary to reach an optimal solution to the problem at hand—if another approach (such as hard-ball litigation involving extreme interpersonal conflict) is the best solution in a given situation, then CPS adherents would endorse that approach.

COMMON GROUND: THE INTERSECTION OF THE VECTORS

Although the vectors are individual and distinct movements, they share many similarities. Professor Scheff asserted that restorative justice and therapeutic jurisprudence are, when compared to the "traditional legal model of justice, courts, judges, lawyers . . . ," quite similar and that the differences are "mainly conceptual."[69] In fact, some of the vectors are converging, although originally they were discrete and unsynthesized. Bridges are forming between the vectors, primarily because of the efforts of therapeutic jurisprudence founders David Wexler and Bruce Winick. For example, Professors Wexler and Winick, and Dennis Stolle and Edward Dauer have advocated the integration of therapeutic jurisprudence and preventive law. Professor Barton has integrated restorative justice and therapeutic jurisprudence. Professor Ellen Waldman has integrated facilitative meditation and therapeutic jurisprudence. The director of the McGill Center, James Cooper, has asserted that creative problem solving encompasses holistic lawyering, restorative justice, therapeutic jurisprudence, and preventive law. The Center for Preventive Law moved to California Western School of Law, where the center for CPS is also located. Law review[70] articles have integrated collaborative law, restorative justice, and creative problem solving with therapeutic jurisprudence. Conferences[71] have subsumed procedural justice, restorative justice, and collaborative law under a therapeutic jurisprudence label. Holistic law practitioners are studying therapeutic jurisprudence and collaborative law. In 2003, an initiative to synthesize the vectors was formalized by former Notre Dame dean David Link, as president of the prestigious International Centre for Healing and the Law, in the form of a book and summit meeting of vector leaders. The synergy continues to build. The time has come to bring these developments together into a cohesive movement to gain strength in numbers, without losing the distinctiveness of each of the vectors.

Although the vectors are clearly different and their vitality depends on preserving those differences, it is important to point out their theoretical intersection, to ensure that they really are related. Many of them share four or more characteristics with several other approaches, but only two characteristics are common to all of the vectors and different from traditional lawyering. These are a goal of optimizing human well-being and the nonexclusivity of rights. Notably, these are consistent with post-Enlightenment values deemphasizing individual rights in favor of preserving human connectedness and relationships. Finally, these approaches are unfortunately often defined by what they are not because they are a departure from traditional lawyering. This should change as they become more mainstream. These two points of intersection, along with other points of intersection between some of the approaches, are explored more fully in the next section.

Optimizing Human Well-Being

All of the vectors seek to make things "better" for people—meaning more psychologically satisfying, therapeutic, beneficial, or healthful. Some do this by avoiding brutalizing people with the law or legal processes and by explicitly avoiding the interpersonal battle of litigation, such as collaborative law, preventive law, and some forms of ADR and mediation. Many enhance human satisfaction and well-being by fostering positive interpersonal interactions between the players—meaning lawyers, clients, judges, crime victims, offenders, and the community. Others improve the parties' lives by explicitly trying to foster interpersonal harmony, such as restorative justice, preventive law, and collaborative law. Others value interpersonal harmony when it is therapeutic (therapeutic jurisprudence/preventive law) or optimal (CPS). Procedural justice is included because adherents advocate treating people with respect and dignity and reject power plays. Many of these approaches rely on close interpersonal collaboration between lawyers, parties, and others in the community (preventive law, restorative justice, ADR, mediation, collaborative law, and CPS). Finally, many explicitly seek to maximize individuals' psychological well-being (therapeutic jurisprudence/preventive law, collaborative law, procedural justice, holistic lawyering, transformative mediation, CPS), thereby optimizing life for the people involved. No matter the route each vector takes toward optimizing human well-being, each one somehow seeks to achieve a more psychologically satisfying or healthy outcome or process than would traditional law or litigation for the individuals involved.

In their individual ways, each vector has a humanistic effect, meaning a positive cumulative effect on the individuals involved, either on the individual personally or through preserving or improving his or her relationships with others and with the community. Many of these approaches view law in the context of people's relationships with each other, including relationships between clients, plaintiffs and defendants, victims and offenders, and legal actors (such as attorneys and judges) and clients and others. Some of the vectors explicitly emphasize protecting and maintaining those relationships or healing them when needed. Some seek to prevent harm to people, to their needs, and to their interpersonal relationships. Specifically, some optimize human well-being by avoiding power struggles, aggression,[72] and violence between people.

In addition to their relationship-enhancing qualities, each vector asks what is "best" in a broad, holistic sense for the client, rather than simply seeking to win or lose or to maximize clients' finances. Traditional law seeks to obtain a judgment proclaiming, "You are right and the other side is wrong," and either obtain a monetary award for a plaintiff or avoid paying out any monetary damages for a defendant. In contrast, these approaches seek to maximize the well-being of the person, whether that means optimizing the person's financial resources, preserving the person's relationships with others, keeping the person's job, obtaining an apology from someone else, or helping the person learn better ways of negotiating with others and dealing with conflict.

The contrast was nicely illustrated by the recent film, *A Civil Action*. In this movie, the actor John Travolta plays a lawyer who loses everything in bringing a lawsuit against two large company-owned factories whose toxic waste killed eight children. He repeatedly refuses to settle the case, apparently believing he can win. He turns down a $20 million offer to settle from the larger, wealthier defendant right before a development in the trial that excused that defendant from liability completely. From a lawyer's perspective, Travolta's character was outlawyered by that defendant's counsel. After his law firm is financially decimated by the costs of proving the case, his partners eventually convince him to settle with the remaining defendant for $8 million. The clients receive a mere $375,000 per dead child. In the parlance of traditional lawyering, the plaintiffs' attorney failed miserably.[73] However, the plaintiffs in the case only wanted two things: They sought an apology and they wanted the company to clean up the toxic waste. They never wanted money and they never believed that money was the solution. After losing everything, including his law partners, Travolta's character continues to pursue the two defendants, this time via the Environmental Protection Agency. Eventually, because of his efforts, the EPA finds the companies criminally liable for their actions and they are fined $69 million to be used to clean up the toxic waste. From the traditional lawyer's perspective, it was still a loss, because the families never got more money and the lawyer only recouped his expenses. From the plaintiffs' perspective, however, it was a win. They got what they wanted, for the most part, and true community improvement occurred when the waste was cleaned up. Success was defined not by winning or losing in the civil suit, nor by money damages. It was defined by the total, overall outcome of the case and by the true needs and wants of the plaintiffs.

Because the vectors take a more holistic, broader view of success, they are likely to be satisfying to clients. They are also likely to be fulfilling for attorneys, particularly atypical attorneys who prefer feeling or have an ethic of care, seek to avoid harm to others, are compassionate, care about others' well-being, are altruistic, or are nonmaterialistic. They may be most appropriate for lawyers who value things other than materialism, monetary success, and traditional lawyer-defined "wins."

"Rights Plus": Nonexclusivity of Rights

All of the vectors explicitly acknowledge that an emphasis on legal rights, duties, and obligations sometimes overlooks other important concerns (such as psychological needs, emotions, and relations with others) and that sometimes those other concerns should be considered along with legal rights in determining the preferred course of action in a particular legal matter. Although legal rights should not be ignored, sometimes it is more important to fulfill human needs, particularly when an exclusive focus on rights would inadvertently do violence to those needs. All of these approaches acknowledge the existence, validity, and importance of nonrights concerns and factor them into the collaboration with the client regarding what to do.

These nonrights concerns include the parties' needs, emotions, resources, goals, values, morals, and relationships; efficiency; and the consequences of various courses of action on people and society. None would advocate elevating these other concerns over rights, where they conflict, and all acknowledge that the primary function of law is to safeguard individuals' rights. Comprehensive law practitioners would likely insist on the primacy of legal rights and on the client's complete autonomy to choose whatever course of action he or she desires, regardless of nonrights concerns. However, practitioners would realize that an exclusive focus on rights is often not the most efficient or optimal way to resolve disputes and thus they look to other concerns to make decisions about what course of action to take. San Francisco collaborative lawyer Pauline Tesler called this feature "rights plus."[74]

For example, therapeutic jurisprudence/preventive law and TJ explicitly consider clients' emotional needs and the therapeutic or nontherapeutic consequences of legal action or proceedings on the client's mental well-being or social relationships. Preventive law, ADR, mediation, and collaborative law acknowledge the need to achieve efficiency, dispute resolution, settlement, and avoidance of litigation. Transformative mediation explicitly emphasizes its twin goals of empowerment and recognition over strict legal rights. Collaborative law explicitly subjugates rights to the overarching goal of resolving the divorce satisfactorily. In restorative justice, the victim's and society's rights to punish the offender may be less important than the need to find a better, more community-based solution to healing the impact of the crime. Procedural justice clearly focuses more on the emotional needs of the parties than on their legal rights. Holistic justice recognizes a higher purpose to lawyer–client interactions beyond simply enforcing the client's legal rights. Finally, collaborative law and CPS may sometimes deemphasize client's legal rights in favor of finding collaborative or optimal solutions to client's problems.

Because nonrights concerns can often include psychological, sociological, economic, medical, biological, and environmental factors, the vectors often require the lawyer to be interdisciplinary. Then attorney general Janet Reno called for the legal profession to become explicitly problem solving and explicitly interdisciplinary in her remarks to law professors attending the annual meeting of the Association for American Law Schools in January 1999. Many of these approaches require that lawyers be open to the insights to be gained from professionals in other areas; evaluate the psychological impact on people of various laws, legal actions, or legal procedures; or form interdisciplinary teams to resolve the legal matters. For example, interdisciplinary lawyer–psychotherapist teams are often formed in collaborative divorce law to resolve the dissolution optimally and coordinate the professionals' efforts.

Because the vectors do not focus exclusively on rights, they require the lawyer to be sensitive to and identify nonrights concerns. Lawyers with a thinking preference, conventional morality, or a rights orientation may be more focused on rules, rights, duties, and obligations in making decisions. In contrast, lawyers with a feeling preference or an ethic of care frequently subordinate legal rights to other values, such as moral duties to prevent harm to others, others' feelings, and preserving relationships, consistent with a feeling approach to practicing law. Lawyers who prefer feeling or an ethic of care or both are therefore well-suited to practice these forms of law.

Nonglobal Similarities

Aside from these two characteristics shared by all the vectors, other characteristics are common to only certain vectors. These are listed in Table 7.1.

Thus, even though the intersection of all 10 vectors is narrower, the overlap between many of these approaches is quite extensive. The

TABLE 7.1
Features Shared by Certain Vectors

Characteristic	Shared by
Prevent/avoid litigation	PL, TJ/PL, ADR, FM, TM, CL, CPS
Collaborative approach to problem solving	ADR, FM, TM, CL, CPS, RJ
Explicitly therapeutic to parties involved	TJ, TJ/PL, RJ, TM, PJ, CPS
Interdisciplinary	TJ, PJ, HJ, CL, CPS
Does not value exerting power over others; allows parties to share equal power	RJ, PJ, CL, CPS, FM, TM
Allows infusion of lawyer's morals and beliefs	HJ, CL, CPS

Note. ADR = alternative dispute resolution; CL = collaborative law; CPS = creative problem solving; FM = facilitative mediation; HJ = holistic justice; PJ = procedural justice; PL = preventive law; RJ = restorative justice; TJ = therapeutic jurisprudence; TM = transformative mediation; TJ/PL = therapeutic jurisprudence/preventive law.

movement's Venn diagram is one of interlocking circles of varying sizes with varying degrees of overlaps.

FIT WITH ATYPICAL LAWYER TRAITS:
FEELING AND AN ETHIC OF CARE

As noted briefly earlier, the fit between the two common characteristics of the movement and these two moral decision making styles atypical of lawyers is extremely close. Working toward optimal human well-being and considering factors other than legal rights come naturally to individuals with a preference for feeling or an ethic of care.

First, most of the vectors ask the lawyer to exercise some independent judgment in client representation and not to respect the client's autonomy to the extent that the lawyer unquestioningly accepts the client's stated goals. In doing so, the vectors may allow the lawyer to consider and integrate his or her personal values, morals, and needs into his or her approach to representing the client. Recent commentators on professionalism have consistently called for the infusion of the lawyer's personal values and morals into client representation as a way to combat the amorality and perceived lawlessness resulting from the neutral, amoral professional role.[75] Thus there is already a growing sentiment in the legal field that the lawyer's total abandonment of his or her own personal moral values in his or her work is detrimental. Some argue it is detrimental to lawyers' mental health; others argue that it leads to lawyers being (or being perceived as) immoral when they adopt an amoral stance and blindly represent immoral clients. Although the amoral professional role is well-suited to lawyers with the typical traits of thinking and a rights orientation, a more involved role is better suited to lawyers with a feeling preference or an ethic of care. These atypical lawyers naturally tend to infuse their personal values and beliefs into decision making and tend not to be totally objective.

Second, many of the vectors optimize human well-being by preserving or improving human relationships. The lawyer preferring feeling or an ethic of care inherently values human relationships and interpersonal harmony. He or she will naturally tend to avoid interpersonal conflict when it is destructive of interpersonal harmony and relationships. As a result, this kind of lawyer should be best-suited to practice comprehensive lawyering. For lawyers with an ethic of care, avoiding harm to people and relationships is important. Because of the intensely collaborative nature of some of the vectors, such atypical traits should allow lawyers to excel at these ways of practicing law. Finally, these atypical traits will assist the lawyer to maintain and develop good lawyer–client relationships, which are important when practicing "comprehensively."

The need to consider people's relationships, values, goals, needs, emotions, and resources also comes as second-nature to lawyers with a preference for feeling or an ethic of care. Such lawyers are already attuned to these issues and may have had these aptitudes frustrated in the typical practice of law. They will be able to practice the movement without substantial retraining or retooling.

As a final note, lawyers with other atypical traits, such as altruism, nonmaterialism, or noncompetitiveness, may also enjoy practicing the movement, because many of the vectors promote values other than wealth maximization and winning adversarial battles, unlike traditional law. Also, such lawyers are likely to be able to evaluate various options for the client in a way that makes sense to the client, because both lawyer and client will be able to acknowledge the importance of nonmonetary factors in the decision-making process.

ISSUES RAISED IN IMPLEMENTATION

A number of concerns are raised by the emergence of the comprehensive law movement. Most of the following concerns are mentioned as areas needing to be addressed by listeners every time I speak about these emerging forms of practice.

First, the comprehensive law movement should not be second class compared to traditional law. It is important to be explicit about the fact that more women are likely to be drawn to practicing law in these humanistic ways. Individuals with a feeling preference or an ethic of care, who are likely to be drawn to these types of practice, may be more likely to be female. However, law need not split along gender lines nor should this movement become subordinate or seen as inferior to traditional forms of practice. It must be an acceptable, mainstream, equally valuable alternative to the more traditional ways of representing clients. The perception that such law is "touchy-feely"—what soft hearts do because they just cannot cut it in litigation or what one does if one flunks out of litigation or fails at traditional law—is enormously detrimental to the success of this movement, both for lawyers and for clients.

These approaches are not appropriate for all lawyers, all clients, or all legal matters. Traditional law will still be needed in many cases, thus providing an outlet for lawyers with the typical lawyer personality. Law must still be the last repository of protection for legal rights, because there will be unavoidable interpersonal conflict and there will be intractable individuals who refuse to negotiate, collaborate, or even be honest or civil in their dealings with others. Traditional law, although it might be seen as a last resort when other methods fail, must be available to deal with these situations and individuals, both in criminal and civil settings. In addition, the majority of lawyers still have the typical lawyer traits. For them, the traditional practice of law is entirely appropriate, and they should excel and thrive practicing it.

However, it is not entirely a black or white issue with regard to who should practice traditional law and who should practice these other approaches. Many good, experienced, traditional lawyers are likely to be excellent at skills consistent with these approaches, such as preventive law, therapeutic jurisprudence, collaboration, and sensitive, wise client counseling. Probably, training in these skills would be good for all lawyers, irrespective of personality. Lawyers could identify themselves as exclusively one or the other sort of lawyer or could choose to practice both traditional and comprehensive law, using one or the other, depending on the needs of the client and the abilities and skills of the lawyer. Law firms, however, might want to offer both types of services to their clients. If one approach failed, then the other might be used—for example, if attempting a collaborative settlement of an employment discrimination case failed, then perhaps full-bore litigation would begin. Or if litigation produced facts unfavorable to the client or became too expensive for the client, the lawyers could switch to collaborative settlement. Or the collaborative law model could be adopted, where the firm withdrew from the matter once collaboration failed and referred the client to another firm. The loss of income could be replaced by traditional referrals from other firms whose collaborative work had also failed.

Clients need to exercise full, informed consent about their choice of approach. They need to know their legal rights before choosing to pursue goals other than rights, and the psychological influence of the professional over the layperson client needs to be acknowledged in this process. Clients may go along with what their lawyers recommend simply because of the credibility lent by the title "attorney-at-law." Lawyers who do not know themselves well could unwittingly bias clients toward a comprehensive approach when it is not appropriate; thus there is a danger of overriding client's true needs in an attempt to be helpful. Lawyers need to be attuned to this pitfall, and good, psychologically sound procedures for obtaining clients' informed consent must be used if these approaches to law are going to be consistent with the current U.S. code of professional legal ethics.

Some believe that the "zealous advocacy" concept contained in the code of ethics conflicts with comprehensive law. Thus, the code of ethics may need to be broadened to explicitly encompass the movement's focus on rights plus and acknowledge that legal representation can value goals other than the client's stated ones. However, some commentators would argue that the ethics code already acknowledges this. In fact, they say that lawyers do not competently represent their clients unless they are acknowledging and considering factors other than strict legal rights. For example, the medical malpractice defense counsel who insists on litigation because the doctor–client is clearly owed certain legal entitlements does harm to his or her client when the physician is not emotionally prepared for the onslaught of a medical malpractice trial that will question his or her competence.

The comprehensive law movement is most appropriate in situations where the individuals involved are in some sort of ongoing relationship with others, such as family law, employment law, small business law (corporate and partnership), some transactional law, estate planning, petty neighborhood crimes such as vandalism, and domestic violence. I tend to think of these areas as "relationship law." They require that the lawyer design solutions to legal problems that are respectful of the existing or ongoing human relationships presented by the problem. The vectors work particularly well in these situations.

The comprehensive law movement also echoes Wexler's thoughts about the need to change Deborah Tannen's "argument culture" with which our country has fallen in love.[76] It also echoes others' investigation of the difference between the American adversarial legal system and the nonadversarial, inquisitorial system of other countries such as the Netherlands. As it changes the American legal system, it may result in a dual system of legal representation such as the United Kingdom's system of barristers and solicitors. However, the traditional model of lawyering should not be relegated to litigation alone. Traditional, noncollaborative, rights-based law continues to be needed in transactional, regulatory, and commercial law.

Law schools need to offer courses in the subdisciplines of the comprehensive law movement, and optimally at least one introductory course would be required. Law students need to be exposed to these alternative ways of lawyering, educated about their career options, and presented with the movement as a credible alternative. At the least, they need to develop some minimal competence in interpersonal skills, collaboration, problem solving, therapeutic jurisprudence preventive law, and so forth.

Why synthesize these approaches? There is strength in numbers, increased visibility, and the hope that the legal profession and law schools will more readily embrace the comprehensive law movement if it is seen as a broad, wide-ranging discipline. Atypical lawyers need alternatives. Clients need alternatives and better legal care. Of the three problems that make up the tripartite crisis, only lawyer distress and dysfunction has been convincingly established to exist—and the comprehensive law movement could be particularly ameliorative for lawyer distress, to the extent that distress is related to attorney job dissatisfaction, atypical lawyer traits, and a lack of focus on intrinsic rewards. The comprehensive law movement holds hope because it directly addresses personality characteristics that have been empirically associated with attorney job dissatisfaction and distress. Admittedly, these connections are somewhat tenuous and theoretical and more research is clearly needed. Yet the dawning of a new age of humanistic, connectedness-oriented, post-Enlightenment law brings hope for a broader, more encompassing, diversified, and happier legal profession and society. Change of this sort seems appropriate.

NOTES

1. *See* ROBERT M. HARDAWAY, PREVENTIVE LAW: MATERIALS ON A NON ADVERSARIAL LEGAL PROCESS xl (Anderson 1997).
2. Studies establishing lawyers' overwhelming preference for thinking are Paul Van R. Miller, *Personality Differences and Student Survival in Law School*, 19 J. LEGAL EDUC. 460 (1967); Frank L. Natter, *The Human Factor: Psychological Type in Legal Education*, 3 RES. PSYCHOL. TYPE 55 (1981); Lawrence R. Richard, *How Personality Affects Your Practice*, A.B.A. J., July 1993, at 74; Lawrence R. Richard, Psychological Type and Job Satisfaction Among Practicing Lawyers in the United States (1994) (unpublished PhD dissertation, Temple University); and Vernellia R. Randall, *The Myers–Briggs Type Indicator, First Year Law Studies and Performance*, 26 CUMB. L. REV. 63, 80–81, 86–87, 91–92, 96–97 (1995–1996).
3. Sandra Janoff, *The Influence of Legal Education on Moral Reasoning*, 76 MINN. L. REV. 193 (1991) (law school tends to silence the ethic of care; the shift to a rights orientation occurs as early as the first year); and Erica Weissman, Gender-Role Issues in Attorney Career Satisfaction (unpublished PhD dissertation, Yeshiva University, 1994) (finding that a minority of lawyers endorsed a preference for the ethic of care, as compared to the rights orientation or a balanced mix of the two styles).
4. *See* Carrie Menkel-Meadow, *Narrowing the Gap by Narrowing the Field: What's Missing From the MacCrate Report—Of Skills, Legal Science and Being a Human Being*, 69 WASH. L. REV. 593, 620 (1994); Carrie Menkel-Meadow, *Review Essay: What's Gender Got to Do With It?: The Politics and Morality of an Ethic of Care*, 22 N.Y.U. REV. L. & SOC. CHANGE 265 (1996); David B. Wexler, *Therapeutic Jurisprudence and Legal Education: Where Do We Go From Here?* 71 REV. JUR. U. P. R. 177, 184 (2002) (arguing, among other things, for the infusion of the care ethic into legal education: "lawyering with an ethic of care needs to be fully legitimated within the law school environment"); CAROL GILLIGAN, IN A DIFFERENT VOICE: PSYCHOLOGICAL THEORY AND WOMEN'S DEVELOPMENT (1982) (the seminal work establishing the concepts of the ethic of care and the rights orientation).
5. *See, e.g.*, Part III. EVA H. HANKS, MICHAEL E. HERZ, & STEVEN S. NEMERSON, ELEMENTS OF LAW (Anderson Publishing, 1994). (cataloguing and describing legal positivism, legal realism, and the many, diverse schools of jurisprudential thought following these two primary movements).
6. Thomas D. Barton, *Troublesome Connections: The Law and Post-Enlightenment Culture*, 47 EMORY LAW JOURNAL 163, 163–164 (Winter 1998).

7. *Id.*

8. *Id.* at 214–215.

9. In therapists' push for clients' self-actualization, self-esteem, and assertiveness, it is possible that they may inadvertently encourage their clients to end unfulfilling and empty relationships; however, an unintended bias toward encouraging divorces and employment resignations can result, which may not always be healthy.

10. For example, the fall 1999 newsletter of the American Bar Association's Section on Legal Education and Admissions to the Bar, Syllabus, described creative problem solving as part of a "movement in law for the coming millennium," at 15.

11. Pauline Tesler, *Collaborative Law Training*, conference paper, January 6, 2000, Dallas, Texas.

12. Thomas J. Scheff, *Community Conferences: Shame and Anger in Therapeutic Jurisprudence*, 67 REV. JUR. U. P. R. 97, 97 (1998).

13. *Id.* at 97.

14. Facilitative mediation is not included in the list of vectors and will not be explored in detail in this chapter, because of its more tangential link to the comprehensive law movement but it may be related to the movement or be a precursor to it. *See* Ellen Waldman, *The Evaluative–Facilitative Debate in Mediation: Applying the Lens of Therapeutic Jurisprudence*, 82 MARQUETTE L. REV. 155 (Fall 1998).

15. *See generally* Dennis P. Stolle, David B. Wexler, Bruce J. Winick, & Edward A. Dauer, *Integrating Preventive Law and Therapeutic Jurisprudence: A Law and Psychology Based Approach to Lawyering*, 34 CAL. W. L. REV. 15, 16 (1997); and HARDAWAY, *supra* note 1.

16. Stolle et al., *supra* note 15, at 15.

17. *Id.* at 16; *citing* HARDAWAY, *supra* note 1, at xxv. One of the first scholars to develop this concept was Louis Brown who (starting in the 1950s) promoted a client-centered approach to settling disputes; David F. Cavers, *Through Life: The Origin of Preventive Law by Louis M. Brown*, 60 S. CAL. L. REV. 1621, 1621–1622, 1624–1625 (1987). *See also* Stolle et al., *supra* note 15, at 16 (asserting that this is the process a lawyer should follow when practicing preventive lawyering).

18. Dennis Stolle and his colleagues mentioned that clients may complain if they come to a lawyer for one problem and end up paying more than they expected for legal services to deal with problems of which they were not even aware. Stolle et al., *supra* note 15, at 17.

19. Scott E. Isaacson, *Preventive Law: A Personal Essay*, 9 UTAH B. J. 14, 14–17 (1996) (making both these arguments). Isaacson later explicitly acknowledged that the preventive lawyer is caring, sensitive to human nature, involved in his or her clients' lives, and respectful of human relationships. *Id.* at 17, 34.

20. Stolle et al., *supra* note 15, at 16–17. *See also* Forrest S. Mosten, *Unbundling of Legal Services and the Family Lawyer*, 28 FAM. L. Q. 421, 440 (1994).

21. Stolle et al., *supra* note 15, at 16–17.

22. *Id.* at 17. Ironically, they also concurrently say it is "impossible." *Id.* Finally, other critics say that it may "come dangerously close to improper solicitations of legal business." *Id.* at 17.

23. *Id.* at 17.

24. John H. Roberts, *The Role of the Scientifically and Technologically Literate Attorney in the Application of Preventive Law to Low Entropy Corporate Decision Making and Long-Range Planning*, 32 IDEA: J. L. & TECH. 155 (1992) (exploring preventive law in the corporate setting). *See also* Thomas H. Gonser, *Preventive Law— The Role of Inside Counsel*, C800 ALI-ABA 203 (1992) (re: same).

25. John J. Copelan Jr. & Barbara S. Monahan, *Preventive Law: A Strategy for Local Governments in the Nineties*, 44 SYRACUSE L. REV. 957 (1993) (advocating preventive law for local governments).

26. Gonser, *supra* note 24, at 208.

27. Isaacson, *supra* note 19, at 17 & 34.

28. *Id.* at 34.

29. Transformative mediation is extensively described in ROBERT A. BARUCH BUSH & JOSEPH P. FOLGER, THE PROMISE OF MEDIATION: RESPONDING TO CONFLICT THROUGH EMPOWERMENT AND RECOGNITION (Jossey-Bass, 1994).

30. Tom R. Tyler, *The Psychological Consequences of Judicial Procedures: Implications for Civil Commitment Hearings*, in DAVID B. WEXLER & BRUCE J. WINICK, LAW IN A THERAPEUTIC KEY: DEVELOPMENTS IN THERAPEUTIC JURISPRUDENCE 6–7 (1996) [hereinafter Key].

31. Tyler in Key, *supra* note 30, at 9–11.

32. *Id.* at 12.

33. *Id.* at 6–7, *citing* E. Allan Lind et al., *In the Eye of the Beholder: Tort Litigants' Evaluations of Their Experiences in the Civil Justice System*, 24 LAW & SOC'Y REV. 953, 968–971 (1990).

34. Therapeutic jurisprudence studies the extent to which substantive rules, legal procedures, and the roles of lawyers and judges produce therapeutic or antitherapeutic consequences. Dennis P. Stolle, *Professional Responsibility in Elder Law: A Synthesis of Preventive Law and Therapeutic Jurisprudence*, 14 BEHAV. SCI. & L. 459, 462 (1996) (*quoting* David B. Wexler & Bruce J. Winick, *Therapeutic Jurisprudence as a New Approach to Mental Health Law Policy Analysis and Research*, 45 U. MIAMI L. REV. 979, 981 (1991)). Therapeutic jurisprudence recognizes that the law is a social force with negative and positive consequences that affect all the parties involved in a conflict. For example, a legal dispute or a harsh application of the law may pose serious physical or psychological risks to the individual beyond the legal consequences. The goal is to minimize the negative ramifications of the law and make existing law more therapeutic. Stolle et al., *supra* note 15, at 17.

35. These are DAVID B. WEXLER & BRUCE J. WINICK, ESSAYS IN THERAPEUTIC JURISPRUDENCE 9 (1991) [hereinafter Essays]; and Key, *supra* note 30. An earlier therapeutic jurisprudence collection is DAVID B. WEXLER, ED., THERAPEUTIC JURISPRUDENCE: THE LAW AS A THERAPEUTIC AGENT (1990) [hereinafter TJ]. This 1990 work appears to contain one of the earliest uses of the term *therapeutic*

jurisprudence, yet since 1990 the concept has been widely cited and used. A Westlaw search in July 2002 yielded more than 600 journal and law review articles citing the topic of therapeutic jurisprudence; 91 contained "therapeutic jurisprudence" in the title. There is also a Web site dedicated to the topic, which includes an exhaustive and massive bibliography of books and articles on therapeutic jurisprudence; David B. Wexler, *International Network on Therapeutic Jurisprudence* (retrieved September 8, 2003) http://www.therapeutic jurisprudence.org or http://www.law.arizona.edu/depts/upr-intj/.

36. Key, *supra* note 30, at xvii, in part quoting Christopher Slobogin, *Therapeutic Jurisprudence: Five Dilemmas to Ponder*, 1 PSYCH., PUB. POL. & L. 193 (1995) (reprinted in Key, *supra* note 30, at 775).

37. Key, *supra* note 30, at xvii.

38. *Id.* at xix.

39. *See id.* at xvii, xix, and Contents.

40. Barbara A. Babb, *An Interdisciplinary Approach to Family Law Jurisprudence: Application of an Ecological and Therapeutic Perspective*, 72 IND. L. J. 775 (1997) (proposing an interdisciplinary approach to resolving family law issues).

41. Amiram Elwork & G. Andrew H. Benjamin, *Lawyers in Distress*, 23 J. PSYCHIATRY & L. 205 (1995).

42. *See generally* Dennis P. Stolle & David B. Wexler, *Therapeutic Jurisprudence and Preventive Law: A Combined Concentration to Invigorate the Everyday Practice of Law*, 39 ARIZ. L. REV. 25 (1997); Dennis P. Stolle, *Professional Responsibility in Elder Law: A Synthesis of Preventive Law and Therapeutic Jurisprudence*, 14 BEHAV. SCI. & L. 459, 462 (1996); Dennis P. Stolle & David B. Wexler, *Preventive Law and Therapeutic Jurisprudence: A Symbiotic Relationship*, 16 PREVENTIVE L. REP. 4 (1996); and Stolle et al., *supra* note 15.

43. Stolle et al., *supra* note 15, at 19.

44. *See id.* at 42. This concept grew from Louis Brown's concept of "legal soft spots," meaning "factors in a client's affairs that may give rise to future legal trouble." *Id.*

45. *Id.* at 42 & 43.

46. David B. Wexler, *Practicing Therapeutic Jurisprudence: Psycholegal Soft Spots and Strategies*, 67 REV. JUR. U. P. R. 317, 320 (1998).

47. *See* Stolle, et al., *supra* note 15, at 42–43.

48. *Id.* at 27, 28.

49. *Id.*

50. *Id.*

51. *See* Babb, *supra* note 40 (family law decision makers need to take an interdisciplinary approach to recognize the complex factors that affect families during divorce proceedings); and Kathryn E. Maxwell, *Preventive Lawyering Strategies to Mitigate the Detrimental Effects of Clients' Divorces*, 67 REV. JUR. U. P. R. 135 (1998) (there are many negative effects that divorces have on children; lawyers can and should play a role in lessening these negative effects and take some responsibility for the children's well-being).

52. Stolle et al., *supra* note 15, at 20–29.

53. *Id.* at 29–31 (family law) and at 31–32 (corporate and business planning law). *See also* Steven H. Hobbs & Fay Wilson Hobbs, *Family Businesses and the Business of Families: A Consideration of the Role of the Lawyer*, 4 TEX. WESLEYAN L. REV. 153 (1998) (taking an interdisciplinary approach to family business law).

54. Rose Daly-Rooney, *Designing Reasonable Accommodations Through Co-Worker Participation: Therapeutic Jurisprudence and the Confidentiality Provision of the Americans With Disabilities Act*, 8 J. L. & HEALTH 89 (1994) (arguing for therapeutic ways to implement the Americans With Disabilities Act).

55. For example, there are many articles dealing with the application of therapeutic jurisprudence to mental health law in David Wexler and Bruce Winick's 1992 book, ESSAYS, *supra* note 35. *See also* TJ, *supra* note 35, and Key, *supra* note 30 (also collecting articles applying therapeutic jurisprudence in various areas of the law).

56. Mark S. Umbreit & Mark Carey, *Restorative Justice: Implications for Organizational Change*, 59 MAR. FED. PROBATION 47 (1995).

57. The Web site is: http://ssw.che.umn.edu/rjp/ (retrieved September 8, 2003). The director of the center is Professor Mark Umbreit, who has also written and researched extensively about the topic.

58. To reach the International Alliance of Holistic Lawyers or founder William Van Zyverden, visit the Web site at http://www.iahl.org/index.htm (retrieved September 8, 2003).

59. James M. Cooper, *Towards a New Architecture: Creative Problem Solving and the Evolution of Law*, 34 CAL. WEST. L. REV. 297, 314 (Spring 1998) (explicitly including these other movements in CPS). The McGill Center for Creative Problem Solving is a nonprofit think tank established in 1997 as a department of California Western School of Law. Its Web site is http://www.wic.org/orgs/mcgill.htm (retrieved September 8, 2003).

60. Gordon A. MacLeod, *Creative Problem-Solving—For Lawyers?!*, 16 J. LEGAL EDUC. 198 (1963) (describing an early course in CPS offered by Buffalo Law School in 1962).

61. *See* Phyllis C. Marion, *Problem-Solving: An Annotated Bibliography*, 34 CAL. WEST. L. REV. 537 (1998) (collecting works on problem solving in general and creative problem solving in particular; many related works appear earlier, but most CPS works date in the late 1990s).

62. Linda Morton, *Teaching Creative Problem Solving: A Paradigmatic Approach*, 34 CAL. WEST. L. REV. 375, 376–378 (1998); *see also* Cooper, *supra* note 59, at 312 (also defining the parameters of CPS).

63. Morton, *supra* note 62, at 378.

64. *Id.* at 378, and Cooper, *supra* note 59, at 301.

65. Questions from Morton, *supra* note 62, at 378.

66. Example and questions from Morton, *supra* note 62, at 386–387.

67. Palsgraf v. Long Island R.R. Co., 162 N.E. 99 (N.Y. 1928).

68. Janeen Kerper, *Creative Problem Solving vs. the Case Method: A Marvelous Adventure in Which Winnie the Pooh Meets Mrs. Palsgraf*, 2 CAL. WEST L. REV. 351, 365 (1998).

69. Thomas J. Scheff, *Community Conferences: Shame and Anger in Therapeutic Jurisprudence*, 67 Rev. Jur. U. P. R. 97, 97 (1998).

70. *See Therapeutic Jurisprudence Forum*, 67 Rev. Jur. U. P. R. 1998; *Therapeutic Jurisprudence and Preventive Law's Transformative Potential for Particular Areas of Legal Practice*, 5 Psychol. Pub. Pol'y & L; and *Conceiving the Lawyer as Creative Problem Solver*, 34 Cal. Wes. Law Rev. (Spring 1998). For individual articles, *see, e.g.*, Robert F. Schopp, *Integrating Restorative Justice and Therapeutic Jurisprudence*, 67 Rev. Jur. U. P. R. 297 (1998) (integrating holistic lawyering with RJ and TJ); and Pauline H. Tesler, *Collaborative Law: A New Paradigm for Divorce Lawyers*, 5 Psychol. Pub. Pol'y & L 967 (1999) (discussing TJ and collaborative law).

71. *E.g.*, the Second International Conference on Therapeutic Jurisprudence, Cincinnati, OH, May 2001; and the Second International Psychology and Law Conference, European Association of Psychology and Law/American Psychology–Law Society, Trinity College, Dublin, Ireland, July 1999.

72. Although aggression is clearly discouraged, appropriate assertiveness is encouraged. For example, victim's rights developments and other developments (such as facilitative mediation) encourage individuals to express themselves to others openly and honestly.

73. A Civil Action (Touchstone Pictures 1999), based on Jonathan Harr, A Civil Action (Vintage Books, 1996).

74. Personal interview with Pauline H. Tesler of Tesler, Sandmann and Fishman, Dublin, Ireland (July 8, 1999). Tesler is one of the two founders of the collaborative law movement and a collaborative divorce lawyer in the San Francisco area.

75. *See* Robert M. Bastress, *Client Centered Counseling and Moral Accountability for Lawyers*, 10 J. Legal Prof. 97 (1985) (arguing that lawyers need to become more client-centered (in the Rogerian sense) and arguing for lawyering that requires the lawyer to discuss his or her personal morals and beliefs with the client and to refuse to take actions that are inconsistent with these morals and beliefs—i.e., moral accountability); *cf.* Bruce A. Green, *The Role of Personal Values in Professional Decisionmaking*, 11 Geo. J. Legal Ethics 19 (Fall 1997) (suggesting that lawyers' personal values often must be excluded in professional decision making and, therefore, lawyers are not always able to be accountable to their consciences in all aspects of their professional lives).

76. David B. Wexler, *The Argument Culture and the Courts* (book review), Court Review 4, 4–5 (Summer 1998) (noting the love affair American society has with argumentation and critique and exploring the negative emotional consequences of focusing on conflict, including the sacrifice of compromise "in favor of polarized, rigid ideology").

AUTHOR INDEX

White, J., 45, 48, 82, 90, 92
Wilkins, M. A., 49
Willging, T. E., 90, 91, 95–96, 97
Williams, J. E., 86, 166, 168
Williams, S. W., 42, 44, 78, 79, 83, 86,
    166, 168
Winick, B. J., 43, 163, 180, 187, 197,
    198–199, 200
Winter, D. G., 43

Young, S. N., 133, 135

Zelan, J., 83
Zemans, F. K., 136
Zucker, E. L., 21, 133, 134, 136
Zuckerman, M., 132
Zurera, L., 135

SUBJECT INDEX

ABOUT THE AUTHOR

Susan Swaim Daicoff, JD, MS, LLM, has been a law professor since 1995, beginning at Capital University Law School and moving to Florida Coastal School of Law in 1998. Before becoming a professor, she practiced corporate, tax, and securities law for approximately five years and became trained and worked as a psychotherapist for approximately two years. She teaches contracts, tax, commercial law, law and psychology, and law as a healing profession. She is a fellow of the International Centre for Healing and the Law. She received her undergraduate and law degrees (with honors) from the University of Florida, earning law review and Order of the Coif, and a master's degree in tax from New York University, where she was a Wallace Scholar. She later earned a master's degree in clinical psychology from the University of Central Florida. She has been researching and writing about the lawyer personality since 1991.